YOUR CHILD
FOR LIFE

Unlike the earlier TA books, RAISING KIDS O.K. has
been developed exclusively for parents, by specialists who
have worked closely with parents, and who are themselves
parents. Using a TA framework, they get down to the
real issues of parenthood—

- Being an OK Parent
- Needs and the Family
- Child Ego
- Punishment
- Learning to Trust
- Toilet Training
- The School Years
- Sexuality
- Marriage and Remarriage
- Experimental Life Styles
- Disability and Illness (including Birth Defects)

With a special chapter on the most common crises
parents encounter in the growth of a child

Extensive exercises to help parents master the
tools of TA

"LACED THROUGHOUT WITH CARING
AND UNDERSTANDING"
Jacqui Lee Schiff, *TA pioneer*

raising
kids
O.K.

Transactional Analysis
in Human Growth & Development

Dorothy E. Babcock & Terry D. Keepers

 AVON
PUBLISHERS OF BARD, CAMELOT AND DISCUS BOOKS

AVON BOOKS
A division of
The Hearst Corporation
959 Eighth Avenue
New York, New York 10019

First Avon Printing, April, 1977

AVON TRADEMARK REG. U.S. PAT. OFF. AND IN
OTHER COUNTRIES, MARCA REGISTRADA,
HECHO EN U.S.A.

Printed in the U.S.A.

To:
Donna
Phyllis
Karen;
Michael
Sarah

Our Children
Our Teachers

CONTENTS

Table of Figures   xv

Foreword, by Jacqui Lee Schiff   xvii

Introduction and Acknowledgments   xix

PART I Parents, People and Families   1

Chapter 1: Being an O.K. Parent   2

History of Childrearing Practice   2
Sources of Useful Information   3
The Tasks of Parenthood   6
The Rewards of Parenthood   7
Summary   8
Exercises   9
Readings   10

Chapter 2: Human Needs   11

Needs and the Family   11
The Stroke Economy   15
    A Fairy Tale   15
Fact and Fiction About Strokes   20
    Fiction   20
    Fact   20
Giving and Getting Strokes Effectively   21
Different Strokes for Different Folks   21

Time Structures in Families   23
  Structure Hunger   23
Summary   25
Exercises   26
Readings   28

Chapter 3:   Grown-up Personality   29

Parent, Adult, Child   29
Child Ego State   30
  Natural Child   32
  Little Professor   32
  Primitive Parent   33
How Can We Tell Our Ego States Apart?   33
  Child Ego State   34
    Vocabulary   34
    Voice   34
    Behavior   34
    Social Response   34
    History   34
    The Function of Emotions   35
  Adult Ego State   36
    Vocabulary   37
    Voice   37
    Behavior   37
    Social Response   37
    History   38
  Parent Ego State   38
    Vocabulary   40
    Voice   40
    Behavior   40
    Social Response   41
    History   41
Transactions   41
Games   43
  Drama Triangle   43
Basic Position   44
Life Script   47

Passive Thinking and Passive Behavior   48
  Passive Thinking   48
  Passive Behavior   49
Summary   50
Exercises   51
Readings   53

Chapter 4: Programs for Raising Children   54

Marriage Scripts   54
Having Children   56
Script Foundations   59
  Conception   59
  Gestation   60
  Naming the Baby   61
New Sources of Information   63
Summary   64
Exercises   65
Readings   66

PART II Psychological Development   67

Chapter 5: Learning to Trust (Attachment) 68

Symbiosis   69
Parenting for Different Traits   72
Stroking the Baby   75
Psychological Tasks of New Parents   77
Needs of New Parents   80
Summary   82
Exercises   83
Readings   85

Chapter 6: Introduction to Physics (Exploration) 86

Stimulus Hunger   86
  A Guide List for Parenting a Young Physicist 90
Safety   91
Change in Stroke Economy   92

Energy Crisis   95
Summary   98
Exercises   99
Readings   100

Chapter 7:   Deciding to Think (Separation)   101

Toilet Training   102
"No-No" vs. Positive Commands   104
Separation = Exasperation   105
Purpose of Anger   106
Intellectual Development   108
    Parenting for Thinking   109
Psychological Tasks of Separating Parents   110
Summary   111
Exercises   113
Readings   114

Chapter 8:   Script: First Draft (Socialization)   115

Considering Future Life Scripts   116
Sexuality   121
    O.K. Messages   122
Typical Banal Script   123
    Statements That Produce Stereotypes   123
Position in the Family   126
Expanding Imagination   128
Psychological Tasks of Parents   131
Summary   131
Exercises   132
Readings   133

Chapter 9:   The Little Lawyer (Construction)   135

The Grade-School Years   135
    Teasing   138
    Testing Family Rules   141
Children and Contracts   146
Leaders and Followers   148
Parenting Construction Age Children   150

Psychological Tasks of Parents 156
Summary 158
Exercises 159
Readings 159

Chapter 10: Firming Up the Script
 (Expansion/Consolidation) 161

Script Revision 161
Recycling 165
 Attachment 165
 Exploration 167
 Separation 168
 Socialization 170
 Construction 174
Script Modification 176
Parenting Adolescents 178
Psychological Tasks of Parents 180
Becoming a Grownup 182
Summary 183
Exercises 184
Readings 185

Chapter 11: Finding the Cast (Emancipation) 187

Inventing New Modes of Living 187
 Adolescent Resolution 188
 Scripts on Growing Up 188
 Finding the Cast 189
 Careers 190
Experimental Life Styles 191
 Selecting a Mate 192
 Rules for Fighting Effectively 192
Emotional Maturity 194
Summary 195
Exercises 195
Readings 197

Chapter 12: Living Out the Script (Creation) 198

Getting Enough Strokes 198

Learning New Stroking Patterns   199
Meshing Scripts   201
Establishing New Patterns of Communication   203
Starting a Family   205
Pregnancy   206
Parenthood as a Psychological Phase   208
Living Out Our Marriage Scripts   211
Psychological Distance   212
    A Structure for Solving Stroke Hunger   213
Living Out Careers   215
Summary   216
Exercises   217
Readings   218

Chapter 13: Script Revisited (Evaluation)   219

Recycling Our Own Uncertainty   220
Climacteric   222
Retirement from Parenthood   224
Careers   226
Script Revisited   227
Aging   229
Summary   230
Exercises   231
Readings   232

Chapter 14: Epilogue (Resolution)   234

Retirement from Work   234
Recycling   235
Reviewing Our Life Script   236
Myths of Old Age   238
Making Peace with Significant Others   240
Dealing with Losses   240
Coming to Terms with Death   243
Summary   243
Exercises   244
Readings   245

PART III Troubleshooting   247

Chapter 15: Troubleshooting   248

Why Problems?   248
What's Wrong?   250
How to Analyze Problems   251
  Review of Stroke Economy   251
  Who's O.K. and Who Isn't?   252
Games and Time Structure   253
  Childhood Games   253
  Identifying Games   256
Passive Thinking and Passive Behavior   257
Ego State Inventory   258
The Think Structure   260
How To Change Behavior   261
Types of Learning   262
  Operant Learning   263
  Punishment   265
  Emotional Learning   267
  Modeling   268
Summary   269
Exercises   270
Readings   270

Chapter 16: Problems and Action Plans   272

Physical Disabilities and Illness   272
  Birth Defects   272
  Illness   274
Sick and Disabled Parents   275
Problems in Meeting the World   276
Multiple Parents   278
Remarriage   279
Children and Death   280
Grief   281
The Dying Child   282
How To Know When You Need an Expert   282
  How To Find an Expert   283

How To Get What You Need   284
Contractual Obligations   285
Summary   286
Readings   287

*The International Transactional Analysis
    Association (ITAA)*   288

Appendix I: Glossary   290

Appendix II: Ages and Stages   294

Games, Scripts and Archetypes Index   299

Subject Index   303

Authors and Therapists Index   309

FIGURES

Figure 1. Hierarchy of Human Needs   12

Figure 2. Kinds of Strokes   13

Figure 3. Stroke Graph   27

Figure 4. Time Structure Graph   28

Figure 5. Ego States   30

Figure 6. Child Ego State   32

Figure 7. Internal Dialogue   40

Figure 8. Common Parent Ego State Gesture   41

Figure 9. Complementary Transaction   42

Figure 10. Crossed Transaction   43

Figure 11. Ulterior Transaction   44

Figure 12. Drama Triangle (in Three Steps)   46

Figure 13. The Four Basic Positions   48

Figure 14. Personality Structure at Birth   69

Figure 15. Initial Symbiosis   70

Figure 16. Symbiosis with More Than One Grownup   71

Figure 17. Reversed Symbiosis   74

Figure 18: Structural Diagram of an Exploratory Infant   89

Figure 19. Structural Analysis of Trapped-Mother Syndrome   96

Figure 20. Toilet Training Out of Parent's Adapted Child   103

Figure 21. Two Child Ego States   106

Figure 22. Transmission of the Injunction "Don't Feel" (Anger)   107

Figure 23. Structural Analysis of Parent and Child Resolving Symbiosis   109

Figure 24. Portraits   120

Figure 25. Nutrition: Proper vs. Creative   120

Figure 26. Typical U.S. Banal Scripts Promote Symbiosis and Competition   125

Figure 27. Structural Diagram of Young Child (During Socialization Stage)   129

Figure 28. Drawing of a Cup with Water Tilted (by a Six-Year-Old)   139

Figure 29. Structural Diagram of Completed Construction Stage   147

Figure 30. The Suffering of Sarah Heartburn   164

Figure 31. Traditional Symbiotic Marriage   201

Figure 32. Optional Cooperative Marriage   202

Figure 33. Marital Ulterior Transaction   204

Figure 34. Chart of a Marriage Over Time   214

Figure 35. What We Do About Problems from the Four Basic Positions   252

Figure 36. Helpers   257

Figure 37. Games Are Symbiotic   257

Figure 38. Ego State Inventory   259

Figure 39. A Think Structure   260

Foreword

Jacqui Lee Schiff

Jacqui Lee Schiff, M.S.S.W., one of the pioneering creators of a theory of human development from a Transactional Analysis viewpoint, is presently Training Director of Cathexis Institute, a non-profit educational corporation training professionals in the various fields of social psychiatry. She is also "mother" of the Schiff Family, a therapeutic community composed of individuals recovering from emotional disorders who live and work together in a mutually supportive environment. A clinical teaching member as well as a member of the board of directors of the International Transactional Analysis Association (ITAA), Jacqui Lee Schiff is author of All My Children *(Evans Publishers: 1971).*

It is a special pleasure to welcome *Raising Kids O.K.*, a contribution both to the practices of childbearing and to the theory of Transactional Analysis.

In the last half-century we have entered an era of new consciousness of our roles as parents. Previously most families were concerned with issues of survival, haunted by threats of poverty or disease. Then, as social consciousness evolved, the emphasis in parenting shifted to teaching children skills and ethics in order to ensure their contributions to the tasks of civilization. It is only recently that we have put aside archaic fears sufficiently to dedicate ourselves to ensuring and protecting the individuality and happiness of our young.

Dorothy Babcock and Terry Keepers have applied themselves to this issue with remarkable sensitivity and warmth. Their practical presentation of ideas and procedures is laced throughout with caring and understanding of children and demonstrates significant respect for the basic O.K.-ness and problem-solving capacities of normal parents. Theirs is a book of new ideas and common sense, and as such will be appreciated by parents and professionals.

Introduction and Acknowledgments

This book is written for parents who are interested in learning more about themselves and their children, and who also want their children to learn to feel O.K. about themselves and others. Much of the information in the book is effectively being used in the families of the authors, their friends and colleagues, and the many parents who have attended our courses on "TA and Kids." Mental health professionals who seek Transactional Analysis (TA) viewpoints of child care and family life will find here a basis for integrating TA with their existing skills.

Using a TA framework, we examine principles of communication, behavioral change, and child development, combined with practical illustrations.

Our motivation for writing about child development arises from two sources. The first source is the expressed need of the numerous parents who have come to our child development courses for "something in writing." Their continuing requests convinced us that we have some important and useful things to say.

Our second motivational source is our fascination with the human species, which has governed our selection of professionals and activities. Both of us are interested in people and the reasons we act as we do.

After many years of teaching and psychotherapy, we have come to the conclusion that people need education far more than therapy. Unfortunately the necessary education is rarely available in schools. Many people lack tools with which to think about their own and other's behavior. We find that many parents profit greatly from learning the behavior analysis tools of TA and having organized information about human development as it occurs throughout the life span.

Throughout the book, the term "we" appears frequently. According to context, "we" will most commonly mean "us parents" or "us human beings." "We" also refers to Dorothy Babcock and Terry Keepers, which should be clear from the context. The "we" that refers to Dorothy and Terry refers to two very different people. When we disagree, or when knowledge of the specific speaker is important, we will be identified separately.

In our collaboration on the book, Terry wrote Part I, Parents, People, and Families and Part III, Troubleshooting, and Dorothy wrote Part II, Psychological Development. Both of us, however, have contributed to, reviewed, and revised all portions of the book.

Since you are entitled to know something about us as persons we are including statements about ourselves:

DOROTHY: I played "nurse" and "teacher" during my childhood, stimulated by two hospitalizations and weekly visits to an orthopedic clinic during my early school years. In nursing school I was exhilarated by what I learned from my experience in psychiatric nursing and have been doing and/or teaching some phase of it ever since.

When our first daughter was due, I retired from teaching and began a ten-year period of parenting and wifing during which I learned what twenty-four-hour parent duty is like. My husband and I have three daughters, Donna, Phyllis, and Karen. Since I did not want my children to duplicate my life script, I have depended a great deal on the new information I learned about psychology. While this psychological information was helpful, I find that the TA framework makes even more practical sense. I'm having fun sharing my children's childhood. They are giving me trampoline lessons, and have taught me five tricks that "old dogs" theoretically can't learn.

TERRY: My interest in psychology began when I was approximately fourteen months old. At that age I discovered that I could manipulate my parents by acting in certain ways (I have since learned that mine was not a unique discovery). In my grade-school years, I learned how to keep from being beaten up by "psyching out" the neighbor kids. One of my favorite lines was, "Who can you brag to if you beat me up?" My experience in making life safer for myself convinced me that I was on to something useful. High school taught me the word for what I was doing: "Psychology." So I decided to become a psychologist, and now I am one, and it's great. I have a son Michael, and a daughter Sarah. For fun, I like to fly kites, watch clouds, and sail sailboats.

The two of us learned about TA and met each other when we attended the first official introductory TA course taught in the Denver area. This course was taught by Jonathan Weiss, Ph.D., and Warden Rimel, M.D.

This book is written from a TA viewpoint because we have repeatedly experienced the effectiveness of the tools that TA provides. We have also seen many other people profit from using TA to think about and change their behavior. The tools TA teaches are readily usable and easily learned by both children and grownups. In this book we teach you these tools and give you some tips on teaching them to your children.

TERMINOLOGY

FAMILY

For our purposes we define a family as any combination of parent(s) and child(ren). We are aware that many people are living together without permanent or legally recognized commitments to each other. Many of them are concerned about good parenting, even though they are exercising nontraditional options about sexual partners and life styles.

Whatever the status of the parenting figures, young children are still faced with the psychological tasks of each developmental stage. Likewise parents themselves have to come to grips with their own developmental needs, whatever their living arrangements.

SEXUAL STEREOTYPES

In a book which examines and suggests alternatives to the usual sexual stereotypes, we regard it as inappropriate to use the term "he" as a pronoun for both sexes. To do so is to encourage women and girls to be discounted.

Revision of one of the basic building blocks of the English language is not easy, however, and we offer stopgap solutions. Some of the existing alternatives such as "she/he" or "s/he" are unwieldly and therefore interfere with readability. We use the plural pronouns "they" and "them" since they are not gender-specific and do not interfere with readability. When we use "he," we are referring to males; "she" refers to females. We have also used personal names to help solve the problems in deleting the universal "he." All of the examples in this book describe real people and real situations. We have fictionalized names and changed sexes at times to protect our friends, patients, and families from unwelcome notoriety, and to challenge sexual stereotypes.

ACKNOWLEDGMENTS

In recent years TA theorists have begun to look at human development, especially in terms of the development of the three ego states: Parent, Adult, and Child. The outstanding pioneers in this area of TA theory are Jacqui Lee Schiff, M.S.S.W., of Cathexis Institute, Alama, California; and Pamela Levin, R.N., of Grouphouse, Berkeley, California. Much of their theory developed from their work in "reparenting" in which psychologically disturbed persons repeat earlier developmental stages and get new parenting to replace the pathological parenting. This work was begun initially by Jacqui Schiff and later taken up, in a somewhat different manner, by Pamela Levin.

In addition, the theoretical contribution of Aaron Wolfe Schiff and Jacqui Schiff on "Passivity and Discounting" is also crucial to the development of responsible behavior and effective problem-solving.

The theoretical approaches of all three are, for the most part, consistent with our own clinical experience with children. While we preserve the general spirit of their work, we have revised and expanded their ideas to fit families and children. For example, we have renamed the developmental stages on the basis of function, and extended the developmental theory to cover the entire life span. We take full responsibility for the ways in which we present their ideas, while acknowledging our indebtedness to their pioneering and innovative work.

The work of Erik H. Erikson, whose theories of development include the life span, have been highly influential for us, as has been the work of Margaret Mead, who has investigated family life in numerous cultures.

Our colleagues at the Rocky Mountain Transactional Analysis Institute have been interested and willing partners in helping us to clarify our ideas. Jon Weiss, Laurie Weiss, Maggy Holmes, Aaron Schiff, and Jan Vanderburgh have been particularly helpful. Laurie read our manuscript very thoroughly and helped clarify many passages. The members of the Rocky Mountain TA Seminar were helpful in expanding the developmental theories.

The members of the Denver Area TA Seminar have provided an eager forum in discussing practical applications of TA to childbearing.

Many members of the staff of the Mental Health Center of Denver General Hospital have shared their knowledge and asked important questions. Our students and patients have taught us much and kept us on our toes. Our own families loved us and nurtured us and, in turn, helped us to nurture wisely. Dorothy's neighbors have shared much of their lives with her and contributed a greater understanding of the function of a neighborhood and friendship.

We received useful information and technical guidance in the actual writing of the book from The Ghost Ranch Writers' Institute. The typing skills of Jeanne Mathews and Edie Shank, and Edie's commentary as a fully qualified, practicing parent have been invaluable, as has been the editorial assistance of Jan Vanderburgh. Jerry Simpson made the illustrations and figures.

Dorothy E. Babcock
Terry D. Keepers

PART I

PARENTS, PEOPLE AND FAMILIES

All are needed by each one.
Ralph Waldo Emerson

1

Being an O.K. Parent

History of Childbearing Practice

Prior to this century we handed down information about raising children by word of mouth and behavioral example. The information remained virtually unchanged from generation to generation. Parenthood and the tasks of raising children were buried within the other concerns of society, and childrearing methods were unquestioned. Parents raised children to follow in their own footsteps, assuming that this path would be adequate for the child to function successfully.

In recent years we have experienced change with bewildering rapidity. Many of the old ways no longer work well. Few of our children will follow in our own footsteps, and the personality traits that were useful in a tradition-oriented society are no longer functional. Because of the rapid changes in our world, we are not in a position to predict precisely the personality traits that will be most useful to our children. Adaptability to change and comfort with unfamiliar situations will certainly have great survival value in rapidly changing societies.

The experiences of immigrant sub-cultures coming to this country demonstrate that several generations are often required to shift comfortably from one pattern of living to another. Such an extended time to accommodate to change is now a luxury; we need to find ways to speed up the process of adjustment. We all need tradition and some sense of continuity, in order to feel that we have a firm footing on which to stand. Fortunately, we Americans already encourage change to some extent, in our tradition of "pioneering spirit." Each new generation has found new ways to carry out this spirit and it serves us well as we continue to experiment with new patterns of living.

Oral traditions about raising children have given way to "science" as children have come to be considered worthy of scientific study. Alfred Binet's investigations of intelligence at the start of the century were among the earliest efforts at studying children systematically. Since then the information boom about children has reached the point where any self-respecting family magazine has several expert articles (often contradictory) on the "science" of being a parent. Many conscientious parents, when faced with so much advice, have come to doubt their own sensibilities about childrearing. The contradictory nature of such articles is often destructive rather than helpful.

Sources of Useful Information

Some of the new information about child development has been carefully researched. It is useful and sound, as in Gesell and Ilg's *The Child From Five to Ten*. In addition millions of parents have found solace in Benjamin Spock's *Baby and Child Care*. Other significant information about children has been less available to the general public because of its specialized or technical nature. For instance, Margaret Mead has emphasized that childrearing practices differ in specific cultures because each values certain traits and rejects others. From the psychoanalytic framework, Erik Erikson has defined patterns of psychological growth and demonstrated the function of certain patterns of parenting. The psychologist Jean Piaget has outlined the rich complexities of children's mental and social development.

An awareness and understanding of the traits valued in our culture allows us to assess ourselves and our patterns of childrearing. This assessment in turn can help us to determine where we wish to flow with the culture and where to disregard or oppose it. Each generation has experimented with styles of living. Bohemians, beatniks, and hippies have all conducted experiments in life patterns which have influenced many others. Some of these experimenters seem to be seeking a return to life within an extended family (e.g., communes), while others are reassessing the role of competition and the work ethic.

Many of us have more personal reasons for looking at and changing childrearing practices. Dissatisfaction with the ways in which we were raised and emotional scars from our own childhood are strong motivators to seek more effective ways of raising kids.

Some of us have made resolutions in our youth that state: "When I grow up I'm never going to spank my kids," or "When I grow up I'm always going to let my kids have their way." These resolutions are often exaggerated, as befits the rebellious spirit in which they were made. The results of such resolutions are frequently unsatisfactory because they represent another extreme. We all need ways to realistically evaluate our programs for childrearing, and any methods which clarify our thinking are welcome.

Within the last few decades, a theory of human personality has been developed which provides new tools for us to use in guiding our lives and developing greater autonomy. This new tool is called Transactional Analysis (TA) and was developed principally by Eric Berne. TA provides a system for thinking about human behavior and describes methods for changing behavior in ourselves and others. TA allows us to look at ourselves as parents, and evaluate our goals in the rearing of our children. Recently those of us who are knowledgeable about TA have been inspecting the stages of childhood development, seeking to describe the psychological purposes of the various childhood stages and define the consequences of effective and ineffective parenting.

In this book we share with you our understanding of the psychological stages in human development, and describe some of the ways in which needs at each stage can most adequately be met. We invite our readers to look at their own programming regarding childrearing.

We will provide information about problem-solving methods which can be used in the family.

We make no pretense that this is a dispassionate scientific work, since our own values about how parents should act and the children should be treated are deeply imbedded in the context. Our values and biases are as follows:

1. People who are flexible and adaptive survive more effectively.

2. Everyone is entitled to a life of dignity.

3. Effective parents feel O.K. about themselves and their children.

4. Effective parents know their own strengths and shortcomings and have a sense of self-worth which guides their actions.

Parenting can be an exciting, challenging, and self-fulfilling job. However, raising kids also has its energy-draining aspects. All parents strongly experience both anger and fear in response to their children. Often we have had no clear guidelines for dealing with these feelings. We have lacked perspective on both our role and our children's behavior.

Every culture has an ideal concept of what a family should be like. In our culture, the "ideal" family is a nuclear family: mother, father, and several children. The current ideal is that there should be two children, the older a boy and the younger a girl. This ideal of the nuclear family is relatively recent; even fifty or sixty years ago, the ideal in our country was to be part of an extended family with strong ties between aunts and uncles and other relatives. While there are a number of drawbacks to the small nuclear family, deviations from this ideal are often considered not-O.K.

Especially during the grade-school period, children are constantly confronted with the ideal of the nuclear family through television and textbooks. They are also inclined to define family patterns which differ from this ideal as not-O.K. In actual fact, numerous families do not meet this ideal because of divorce, separation, illness, or personal choice. Both children and parents in such situations need to deal with their response and the response of others to their "differentness." Many divorced parents lament their deviation from this model, instead of using their energy to construct a meaningful family life for themselves and their children.

Whatever the composition of the family, the tasks of the parent or parents remain the same. Parents are people, too. In addition to fulfilling the parental role of raising children, they are also in a particular stage of development of their own. Contrary to some views, we do not stop growing and changing just because we are grownups. Having children and rearing them can fit into our own growth needs. In the period of our lives when most of us have children, self-fulfillment is found in creating things, teaching, and guiding others. Thus the creative endeavor of childrearing fits in with our own needs during this part of our lives.

Unhappy and dissatisfied parents are discontented because the needs of the children conflict with their needs. Such conflict is exemplified with the arrival of a "menopause baby." A forty-five-year-old woman who has spent twenty years raising kids is unlikely to be pleased when faced with another round of diapers and 2 A.M. feedings.

The Tasks of Parenthood

Parents sometimes frighten themselves by defining their job as impossible. Unfortunately, much of the popular information about childrearing encourages this viewpoint. While the job of being a parent is sometimes complex, it also can be pleasurable and fulfilling. Every parent is aware of the daily necessity of providing for safety, health, cleanliness, and nurturing supervision. Some of the tasks of parenthood are less apparent. For instance, while it is not often thought of in this way, one of the crucial tasks of parents is to define reality for the new infant. In the first months of life, nearly all stimuli in the child's world have equal value. Out of this confusion, certain stimuli such as food and physical stroking quickly take on greater importance. Our child-care patterns quickly emphasize certain aspects of the child's world and de-emphasize others. Some infants are swaddled, some are kept in cribs, some are constantly around other people, and others are isolated in private rooms. Each of these patterns of infant care defines important stimuli and establishes patterns of safety. Infants reared in a quiet household, for example, may be distressed when around a noisy household.

We begin to define an infant's reality as soon as the child is born. As the child grows, we emphasize different realities at different ages. The toddler, for instance, is interested in the reality of the physical world, while the preschooler focuses on the realities of the social world.

As parents, we define reality by using the basic principles of learning, even though we are often not aware of it. As parents, we provide attention and stroking in response to some things that children do while we ignore or punish other behavior. Thus we attend selectively to our children's behavior, and provide rewards and punishments for certain actions. Consequently our children conform to our expectations and to our view of reality.

As parents our basic task is to guide and nurture a helpless creature, who could not otherwise survive, to a point of adequate self-sufficiency. In order to successfully fulfill this task we need to be aware of our children's expression of need and be willing to respond in a way that fosters growth. Our children's needs change radically as they develop, and an understanding of the needs of children at particular stages is invaluable in helping us to recognize and respond adequately to their needs.

The Rewards of Parenthood

The rewards of parenthood are greatest when the timing is right—that is to say, when the child arrives at a time that is convenient for the parents and consistent with their own needs. Most of us have children at a time in our life plan when a good deal of pleasure is derived from being productive and creative; one of the pleasures of parenthood lies in the creative aspect of raising kids. We also take satisfaction in fulfilling a part of our own life span, contributing to the survival of the species, and in doing something that clearly is of social value. The days are gone, however, when status was conferred on extremely large families. Not too long ago, television studio audiences would give a round of vigorous applause when Mrs. Jones announced that she was the mother of eleven children; now, concern for diminishing resources and increasing population has made the smaller family more fashionable.

Children are also a rich source of information for us. They provide firsthand information about how human beings grow and develop. Often, too, they stimulate us to recall problem parts of our own past. Our children sometimes help, or even compel, us to re-examine and solve our own unworked problems. Besides, kids themselves can be fun and engaging. They help us to recapture our own free, spontaneous, and creative parts, in which we are also forever young.

In the following chapters we have selected those ideas in TA that are particularly useful in understanding children and families. Since we are emphasizing a particular part of the theory, many aspects of transactional analysis have been deleted. There are many excellent general sources on transactional analysis. Two excellent resources for persons new to TA are *Introduce Yourself to TA*, by Leonard Campos and Paul McCormick, and *Born to Win*, by Muriel James and Dorothy Jongeward.

SUMMARY

Until recent years, the job of being a parent was embedded in the traditions of our culture. The role of parenthood was carried out as a matter of routine, with little pressure on our part to think about doing the job differently. However, as our pace of life continues to accelerate, traditional ways of raising kids are becoming less functional. Our traditions are no longer adequate to deal with such a rapidly changing world.

In order to meet an environment characterized by rapid change, several personality attributes are important. Those that will best serve our children are a sense of security in the face of change, and flexibility in dealing with unfamiliar situations. When we understand our parental functions and the developmental needs of our children, we are in a position to parent them in a way that will encourage these traits.

The principal task of parents is to raise kids from helpless infants to persons capable of functioning independently in society. This is a complex task, for which most parents have received a great deal of programming. To carry out this task successfully we need to be aware of our own needs and be active in meeting them. Parents who take good care of their children also need to take good care of themselves.

The rewards of parenthood are numerous: satisfaction in teaching children what they need to know in order to succeed, satisfaction in meeting some of the expectations of society, and the pleasures of sharing with others. Most parents are in a life stage where a good deal of pleasure is derived from being productive and creative. One of the important outlets in expressing this productivity and creativity is in having and rearing children. Problems in childrearing can develop if persons become parents at a time that is not congruent with their own developmental need. Parents who have children while they are still teenagers, or after ordinary childbearing ages, face this additional stress.

EXERCISES

Identify some of your own family patterns for yourself. Answer the following questions:

1. What kind of life did my grandparents live?
   a. Did they live in the city or the country?
   b. How many children were there?
   c. How was the work divided up amongst the family?
   d. What was their attitude toward change?
   e. What did they do for fun?
2. What kind of life do/did my parents live?
   a. In the country or city?
   b. How many children?
   c. How were chores divided up when you were a child?
   d. What is their attitude toward change?
   e. What do they do for fun?
3. What kind of life do I live? Is it the same as my ancestors or different? Why?

4. What kind of life do I want for my children? Why?
5. What do I think about being a parent? How do I feel about being a parent? Do I want to change either of these? If I do, what do I want the new way to be like?

READINGS*

Campos, Leonard, and McCormick, Paul. *Introduce Yourself to Transactional Analysis*. Stockton, California: San Joaquin TA Institute, 1969.

Erikson, Erik. *Childhood and Society*. New York: W.W. Norton, 1963.

Erikson, Erik. *Insight and Responsibility*. New York: W.W. Norton, 1964.

Gesell, Arnold, and Ilg, Frances. *The Child From Five to Ten*. New York: Harper and Brothers, 1946.

James, Muriel, and Jongeward, Dorothy. *Born to Win*. Reading, Massachusetts: Addison-Wesley, 1971.

Mead, Margaret, and Hayman, Ken. *Family*. New York: Collier Books, 1971.

Spock, Benjamin. *Baby and Child Care*. New York: Simon and Schuster, 1945.

Toffler, Alan. *Future Shock*. New York: Random House, 1970.

* These readings were useful in preparing this chapter and are also sources of additional information for our readers. We include such readings at the end of each chapter.

2

Human Needs

All of us need certain things in order to survive and to feel satisfied with our lives. We develop ways of getting our needs met, and strive to maintain a balance between our needs and the sources that fulfill these needs. Abraham Maslow asserts that human needs have an ascending order of urgency. Basic needs must be met before other, more complex needs can be experienced and met. Our basic need for food, air, and water takes precedence over our need for safety and security. Only when these needs are met are we aware of our need for love, self-esteem, and self-actualization.

Needs and the Family

One of the main functions of the family is to form an effective unit for meeting the needs of each of the family members. A family that is functioning effectively is meeting the needs of the members of the family much of the time.

One of our basic needs is a need for stimulation from outside ourselves. *The most effective way of meeting our need for stimulation is physical contact from another human being.* Eric Berne acknowledged this connection early in his writings and defined "strokes" as the basic unit of recognition between persons. He noted René Spitz's

11

studies in which it was demonstrated that infants who are not stimulated fail to thrive and often die. Stroke-deprived grownups may have at least temporary mental disturbances; lack of stimulation is a frequent cause of the rapid decline in elderly persons who live isolated lives.

Physical stroking is a particularly important component in the survival of all infants. Quantity of stroking is not the only factor; the ways in which babies are stroked

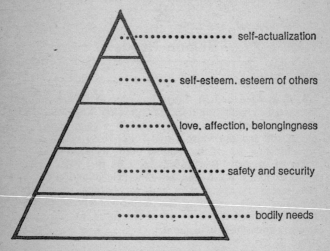

Figure 1. Hierarchy of Human Needs

help to define their world: rough, gentle, secure, indifferent. Adequate physical stroking when we were infants forms a base from which we all expanded to a more active approach to the world. As we grew we also came to accept other strokes: a smile, a frown, words of praise or punishment.

Stroking not only ensures our survival; as a primary reinforcer it is also used as a reward to help us learn things, and to maintain social patterns. We are stroked because we exist; we are also stroked for doing some things and not stroked for doing others. There are four categories of strokes: *positive* strokes, *negative* strokes, *unconditional* strokes, and *conditional* strokes (see Figure

2). These four categories allow us to look at the kind of strokes we are getting. We can also use them to help us figure out the kind of strokes we want that we are not getting.

We have all learned individual ways to give and get strokes in the families where we were raised; we also teach our children our own family stroke patterns. The kind of strokes that we learn to prefer as children are the kinds that we seek from others throughout our lives

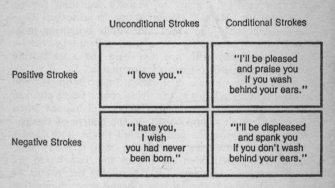

Figure 2. Kinds of Strokes

unless we make concerted efforts to change our preferences and our techniques for getting strokes.

In some families most available strokes are negative; in such families, the family members come to develop a preference for negative strokes. This raises a question: how does someone develop a preference for something that doesn't feel good?

A preference for negative strokes develops in situations when the child is ignored unless something wrong happens. *Negative strokes are better than no strokes at all.* If children are raised in families where they are disregarded unless there is trouble, they will learn to be disruptive and negativistic in order to gain the strokes that they need to survive.

Consider the following family drama and its cumulative effect when repeated thousands of times during a child's formative years: the characters are "Mama," a suburban housewife, and "Sandy," an active, inquisitive, and healthy three-year-old. Mama and Sandy are the only ones at home. Mama is in the family room ironing and watching "As the World Turns" on daytime TV. She is absorbed in these activities. Sandy, on the other hand, has exhausted the possibilities of her toys and is restless for some strokes. Since Sandy has not been "adequately civilized" yet, she will ask for and even demand some strokes (asking for strokes directly will later be forbidden) by tugging at Mama's legs and saying, "Pick me up, Mama!" Since Mama is absorbed elsewhere she replies, "Go away, kid, you're bothering me!" Clearly, Sandy's need for stimulation will not be met by Mama, and Sandy will turn elsewhere and start casting about for some other form of stimulation.

In the course of such exploration Sandy happens upon Mama's expensive lamp in the living room. Being curious, Sandy conducts an experiment: "What will happen when I pull hard on this lamp cord?" In the course of this experiment in physics the lamp crashes to the floor loudly and breaks. Mama's response to the noise is predictable. She unplugs herself from the TV set and dashes into the living room to investigate. On discovering the results of Sandy's experiment, she delivers a heavy dose of negative strokes to Sandy's behind and a number of scolding strokes to her ears.

In this drama, Sandy has learned some important psychological information: 1) "I don't get positive strokes when I ask for them, I get ignored." 2) "The way to get strokes around here is to do something that Mama doesn't like."

In the course of this drama Sandy's Mama is completely unaware of the way in which she is promoting Sandy's negative behavior. In fact, the next time she discusses childrearing with someone she will probably complain, "I really don't know what's gotten into Sandy. Every time I turn my back that little rascal is into some kind of trouble." If this drama is repeated often enough and long enough, Sandy will grow up to be an accomplished "Kick Me" player who continues to get into trouble in order to get strokes.

Behavior that is stroked will be repeated. What you stroke, is what you get. If bad behavior is punished and there are no positive strokes for good behavior, the bad behavior will persist. If we want our children to be good, one way is to follow Wesley Becker's dictum:

CATCH THEM BEING GOOD.

Each of us has been raised on a variety of strokes, though different families show preference for various types of strokes. In some families, especially those which are quite achievement-oriented, children are given a very heavy diet of conditioned strokes. Such children learn that, in order to get strokes, they must perform and produce. These children may grow up to be workaholics, who don't feel stroked unless they are striving, and who don't know how to be comfortable with leisure time. In other families, the stroking is largely unconditional (either positive or negative). A child from this kind of family does not respond energetically to the demands of school and work, and is therefore considered "unmotivated." Whatever the specifics of the family situation may be, the ways in which behavior is defined and solicited by stroking and withholding strokes is called the family *stroke economy*.

The Stroke Economy

Here is a story about a stroke economy.

A FAIRY TALE

by Claude Steiner, Ph.D.

Once upon a time, a long time ago, there lived two very happy people called Tim and Maggie with two children called John and Lucy. To understand how happy they were, you have to understand how things were in those days. You see, in those days everyone was given at birth a small, soft, Fuzzy Bag. Anytime a person reached into this bag he was able to pull out a Warm Fuzzy. Warm Fuzzies were very much in demand because whenever somebody was given a Warm Fuzzy it made him feel warm and fuzzy all over. People who didn't get Warm

Fuzzies regularly were in danger of developing a sickness in their back which caused them to shrivel up and die.

In those days it was very easy to get Warm Fuzzies. Anytime that somebody felt like it, he might walk up to you and say, "I'd like to have a Warm Fuzzy." You would then reach into your bag and pull out a Fuzzy the size of a little girl's hand. As soon as the Fuzzy saw the light of day it would smile and blossom into a large, shaggy, Warm Fuzzy. You would lay it on the person's shoulder or head or lap and it would snuggle up and melt right against their skin and make them feel good all over. People were always asking each other for Warm Fuzzies, and since they were always given freely, getting enough of them was never a problem. There were always plenty to go around and as a consequence everyone was happy and felt warm and fuzzy most of the time.

One day a bad witch became angry because everyone was so happy and no one was buying her potion and salves. This witch was very clever and she devised a very wicked plan. One beautiful morning she crept up to Tim while Maggie was playing with their daughter and whispered in his ear, "See here, Tim, look at all the Fuzzies that Maggie is giving to Lucy. You know, if she keeps it up, eventually she is going to run out and then there won't be any left for you."

Tim was astonished. He turned to the witch and said, "Do you mean to tell me there isn't a Warm Fuzzy in our bag every time we reach into it?"

And the witch said: "No, absolutely not, and once you run out, that's it. You don't have any more." With this she flew away on her broom laughing and cackling hysterically.

Tim took this to heart and began to notice every time Maggie gave a Warm Fuzzy to somebody else. Eventually he got very worried and upset because he liked Maggie's Warm Fuzzies very much and did not want to give them up. He certainly did not think it was right for Maggie to be spending all her Warm Fuzzies on the children and other people. He began to complain every time he saw Maggie giving a Warm Fuzzy to somebody else, and because Maggie liked him very much, she stopped giving Warm Fuzzies to other people as often, and reserved them for him.

The children watched this and soon began to get the idea that it was wrong to give up Warm Fuzzies any time you were asked or felt like it. They too became very careful. They would watch their parents closely and whenever they felt that one of their parents was giving too many Fuzzies to others, they also began to object. They began to feel worried whenever they gave away too many Warm Fuzzies. Even though they found a Warm Fuzzy every time they reached into their bag, they reached in less and less and became more and more stingy. Soon people began to notice the lack of Warm Fuzzies, and they began to feel less and less fuzzy. They began to shrivel up and, occasionally, people would die from lack of Warm Fuzzies. More and more people went to the witch to buy her potions and salves even though they didn't seem to work.

Well, the situation was getting very serious indeed. The bad witch who had been watching all of this didn't really want the people to die so she devised a new plan. She gave everyone a bag that was very similar to the Fuzzy Bag except that this one was cold while the Fuzzy Bag was warm. Inside the witch's bag were Cold Pricklies. These Cold Pricklies did not make people feel warm and fuzzy, but made them feel cold and prickly instead. But they did prevent people's backs from shriveling up. So, from then on, every time somebody said, "I want a Warm Fuzzy," people who were worried about depleting their supply would say, "I can't give you a Warm Fuzzy, but would you like a Cold Prickly?" Sometimes, two people would walk up to each other, thinking they could get a Warm Fuzzy, but one or the other of them would change his mind and they would wind up giving each other Cold Pricklies. So the end result was that while very few people were dying, a lot of people were still unhappy and feeling very cold and prickly.

The situation got very complicated because, since the coming of the witch, there were less and less Warm Fuzzies around, so Warm Fuzzies, which used to be thought of as free as air, became extremely valuable. This caused people to do all sorts of things in order to obtain them. Before the witch had appeared, people used to gather in groups of three or four or five, never caring too much who was giving Warm Fuzzies to whom. After the coming of the witch, people began to pair off and to reserve

*all their Warm Fuzzies for each other exclusively. If
ever one of the two persons forgot himself and gave a
Warm Fuzzy to someone else, he would immediately feel
guilty about it because he knew that his partner would
probably resent the loss of a Warm Fuzzy.*

*People who could not find a generous partner had to
buy their Warm Fuzzies and had to work long hours to
earn the money. And the thing which happened was that
some people would take Cold Pricklies—which were
limitless and freely available—coat them white and
fluffy and pass them on as Warm Fuzzies. These counter-
feit Warm Fuzzies were really Plastic Fuzzies, and they
caused additional difficulties. For instance, two people
would get together and freely exchange Plastic Fuzzies,
which presumably should have made them feel good, but
they came away feeling bad instead. Since they thought
they had been exchanging Warm Fuzzies, people grew
very confused about this, never realizing that their cold
prickly feelings were really the result of the fact they
had been given a lot of Plastic Fuzzies.*

*So the situation was very, very dismal and it all started
because of the coming of the witch who made people
believe that some day, when least expected, they might
reach into their Warm Fuzzy Bag and find no more.*

*Not long ago a young woman with big hips, born
under the sign of Aquarius, came to this unhappy land.
She had not heard about the bad witch and was not worried about running out of Warm Fuzzies. She gave them
out freely, even when not asked. They called her the Hip
Woman and disapproved of her because she was giving
the children the idea that they should not worry about
running out of Warm Fuzzies. The children liked her
very much because they felt good around her and they
too began to give out Warm Fuzzies whenever they felt
like it. The grownups became concerned and decided to
pass a law to protect the children from depleting their
supplies of Warm Fuzzies. The law made it a criminal
offense to give out Warm Fuzzies in a reckless manner.
The children, however, seemed not to care, and in spite
of the law they continued to give each other Warm Fuzzies whenever they felt like it and always when asked.
Because there were many children, almost as many as*

grownups, it began to look as if maybe they would have their way.

As of now it is hard to say what will happen. Will the grown-up forces of law and order stop the recklessness of the children? Are grownups going to join with the Hip Woman and the children in taking a chance that there will always be as many Warm Fuzzies as needed? Will they remember the days their children are trying to bring back when Warm Fuzzies were abundant because people gave them away freely?*

Tim and Maggie and the children live in a world where their welfare is dependent on giving and getting strokes —and so do all of us. We all live within a *stroke economy* that defines the rules for giving and getting strokes. Strokes are often treated as a commodity that is in limited supply, to be exchanged, traded, and monopolized. We all lose some of our capability for being spontaneous, aware, and intimate, because we have been raised in situations where the supply of strokes is limited and the price exacted for them is high. To regain this ease and freedom, we need to reject much of our basic training about exchanging strokes. Because the stroke economy is rarely identified and defined, we are often unaware of the limitations in which we exist.

According to Steiner, the restrictive stroke economy under which many of us have been raised is based on these rules:

1. Don't give strokes if you have them to give.
2. Don't ask for strokes if you need them.
3. Don't accept strokes if you want them.
4. Don't reject strokes when you don't want them.
5. Don't give yourself strokes.

As a consequence of following these rules a number of fictions have developed about stroking.

* Reproduced with the permission of Claude Steiner, Ph.D., from *Scripts People Live.*

Fact and Fiction About Strokes

FICTION

All strokes have to be earned.

It is not O.K. to ask for strokes.

Physical strokes between grownups are always sexy.

If people start asking for strokes they'll be greedy and insatiable.

It is not O.K. to brag. Bragging will give you a swelled head.

Anyone older than five years is too old to get physical strokes.

It is O.K. to be angry about having to ask for strokes.

FACT

It is O.K. to get strokes just for being you.

Asking for strokes is O.K. and does not diminish their value.

Physical strokes between grownups don't have to be sexy. We choose to make strokes sexy or not. Sexy strokes are also O.K.

Since people cannot read minds you need to ask for the kind of strokes you want.

You never outgrow your need for strokes.

You are supposed to ask for strokes from people who will give them willingly.

Strokes are like any other need. When we have enough, we stop. Similarly, people usually don't eat when they're not hungry.

Timely bragging is O.K., and is a way of letting people know you feel O.K. about yourself. Contrary to popular belief, scientific research has failed to show that anyone's head has ever swelled even as much as one millimeter as a result of bragging.

Children know innately how to seek strokes. Watch any healthy two-year-old: when they want to sit on a lap they look for a likely lap. If the first lap owner doesn't want to get sat on, they seek out someone with an accommodating lap.

Giving and Getting Strokes Effectively

Young children are very clear and insistent about the kind of strokes they need. This capacity is one of an infant's chief survival instincts. At every age, children have the capacity to ask for the kinds of strokes they need. In order really to hear what the need is, we parents need to set aside our own fictitious programming about strokes, responding openly to the child's need. Many of us need to do some reprogramming for ourselves about what kind of stroking is O.K. and what is not O.K.

Different Strokes for Different Folks

Part of the complexity and fascination of childrearing is that children need different kinds of stroking at different ages. Infants need cuddling; older kids need talking to as well as hugging, and need talking to about particular things at particular stages. Raising kids is like shooting at a moving target; adequate stroking at one age is often not appropriate at another age. (The specific stroke needs at various ages will be covered in later chapters.)

As Solon Samuels notes, we all have individual predilections, too. Sometimes we want talking strokes, sometimes roughhouse strokes, sometimes cuddly strokes. In some families positive stroking is carried out through a "secret code" that sounds superficially like negative stroking. Those who do not know the code only see the negative strokes and not the hidden positive strokes.

Helen Colton tells it like this:

Tottela was now fourteen years old. He had just made the winning touchdown in a high-school football game. The crowd in the stands roared their approval, and teammates slapped him on the back. Overflowing with happiness, Tottela ran toward his folks, grinning, "Pretty good, huh?" "By Red Grange was it good?" chopped Dad, *secretly filled with pride.*

Tottela was now eighteen years old. He was telling Momma some achievements he was planning in his future. "Yeah, I should live so long," chopped Momma, *secretly filled with pride.*

While many families stroke in this indirect way, Colton traces its frequency in Jewish culture as a protective device against letting anyone know that things were good. She states, "Such insurance gave rise to negativisms of Yiddishisms, in which many of us grew up with negative putdowns and chops, not knowing that the double level message was often warm, loving, proud, and nurturing."

Some secret code strokes:

Negative Statement	*Translation*
I should only live so long.	I would like to live to see that day and share that future joy with you.
Oi, such a momzer.	A darling child whom I love dearly.
You're too smart for your own good.	He's such a brainy one, I'm very proud of him.

Many families are secretly loving and proud while appearing to observers who do not know the secret code to be hostile, angry, and deriding. Knowing the "secret code" is important to understanding the true stroke economy in a family. Since it is based on magical thinking and has an ulterior basis, "secret code" reaps a legacy of misunderstanding and many not-O.K. feelings.

Time Structures in Families

STRUCTURE HUNGER

All of us have two important problems that have to be solved and resolved every day of our existence. The first of these is, "How am I going to get my strokes?" The second is, "How will I fill my time?" In addition to learning preferred ways of getting strokes, we also learn preferred ways of enjoying, using, wasting, marking, or frittering away time. We learn ways to fill time that are acceptable in our family and our culture. These ways of thinking about time are often very basic to our view of the world.

There are six ways to fill time (according to Berne):

1. Withdrawal
2. Ritual
3. Activity
4. Pastimes
5. Games
6. Intimacy

Each of these ways of filling time has its uses. As grownups we know how to make use of all of them.

Withdrawal does not involve any social transactions with other persons, and therefore has few risks. We control the strokes to ourselves through internal dialogue or such activities as bathing or masturbation, but these are rarely satisfying for long. When we withdraw we are also not getting strokes from other people.

Ritual is any prescribed set of social transactions. Rituals, from "Hello" to an elaborate church service, are predictable and therefore safe. They involve set patterns of stroking, and the stroking is impersonal. Stroke rituals are often learned when a child is around three to four, and young children often enjoy stroking rituals. For example, a standard bedtime ritual:

	DADDY	SUSIE
Stroke #1	Goodnight.	Goodnight.
#2	Sleep tight.	O.K.
#3	Don't let the bedbugs bite.	I won't.
#4	See you in the morning.	O.K.
#5	Do you want your door open or shut?	Open.
#6	Goodnight.	Goodnight.

If Daddy were to leave out any of the steps of the ritual he would be promptly confronted and Susie would insist that the ritual be repeated precisely.

Activity structures time around some task. The strokes received around a task are also relatively predictable and focused on the job at hand. Grade-school children often enjoy complex activities together and will spend long hours doing things such as building a fort, constructing a treehouse, or digging a big hole.

Pastimes are ways of structuring time through mutually acceptable stroking. They play a part of the social selection process. They are means of self-expression, providing a way to decide whom you wish to get to know better. Grade-school children like to pastime about things like "Boys are better than girls," "Bugs are interesting," "Ain't school awful," and "My Daddy is better than your Daddy." Teenage pastimes may center around who is seeing whom, the latest rock band, and "Ain't school awful."

Games. A psychological game is a series of transactions with a hidden intent. At the end of the series of transactions the players take a "payoff," which is usually some form of negative feeling. Games provide intense stroking; however, the stroking received is frequently unpleasant. In extremely destructive games, the payoff may even be physical injury or death. We play games when we are refusing to recognize (i.e., discounting) some need. The game is a crooked alternate way to get the need met. The most commonly discounted need underlying games is our need for strokes. It is important for us all to be in touch with our need for strokes, and active in doing something about that need. When we give up playing games, we relinquish a source of intense stroking; therefore we need to substitute some other form of stroking.

Intimacy. In intimacy we engage in unconditional stroking, without defense. Intimacy may occur briefly or it may be extended over a lifetime relationship. Happy children have a capacity for intimacy that is refreshing to grownups who have come to take a more guarded approach toward opening themselves up intimately to others. Indeed, the decision to be intimate with another person often seems risky. We risk the possibility that our vulnerability will be used by the other person as part of a game, rather than returned with intimacy (our thanks to Aaron Schiff for this point).

Early in infancy we begin to learn about these various ways to fill time. We are taught different techniques for filling time according to the patterns of our family. We also practice using different ways of filling time at different stages. A young toddler in the Exploration stage (8-10 mos. to 2-2½ yrs.) fills a great deal of time with the activity of investigating objects. Social programming for transacting is taught during the Socialization stage, which occurs during the pre-school years.

Eric Berne points out that parents in all parts of the world teach their children "manners," which means that they learn the proper greeting, eating, eliminative, courting, and mourning *rituals*. Children are also taught to carry on topical conversations tactfully and diplomatically, and thereby learn to *pastime*. Children who are not taught the appropriate rituals and pastiming techniques for their social and cultural group are considered uncivilized until they learn them. The extent to which we fill our time with withdrawal, games, and intimacy is largely programmed through the patterns of the family in which we were reared.

SUMMARY

We all strive to keep our needs satisfied and to maintain our sources of supply to meet those needs. Survival needs, like food and strokes, take precedence over security and self-actualization needs.

A principal function of the family is to maintain a unit for meeting the needs of all of its members. Stimulation from outside ourselves is a basic need, and is best satisfied by a wide variety of physical and verbal stroking from other persons. *Strokes* are defined as any unit of recognition. The term originates from the physical stroking that is requisite for the survival of infants.

Strokes can be categorized four ways: *positive, negative, unconditional, and conditional.* We all learn how to go about getting different kinds of strokes, and have preference for different kinds, sometimes including strokes which are not good for us. Each of us lives within a *stroke economy* which controls the kind and intensity of strokes available. Many such economies are built around fictions which are designed to control us in ways that are not good for us or our families.

Children know innately how to seek the kinds of strokes that they need at various ages. They are persistent at doing this even in the face of demands that they ignore their own needs. Many of us need to examine our own fictions about strokes and redesign our own ways of giving and getting strokes.

Families teach children preferred ways to fill time. Children need to fill their time differently at different developmental stages. There are six ways of filling time, ranging from withdrawal, from which few strokes are available, to intimacy, which has extremely high stroke value. People who have little intimacy need to spend more time in games, pastimes, rituals, or activities to get an equivalent amount of strokes.

EXERCISES

1. What kind of strokes do you get in your family? Draw a stroke graph like the one below to show the proportional amount of each kind of stroke you receive. Now redraw this graph to show how you would like the strokes to be in your family. What can you do to change to the stroke pattern you want?
2. Draw a stroke graph of the kind of strokes that you typically give to the other members of your family.

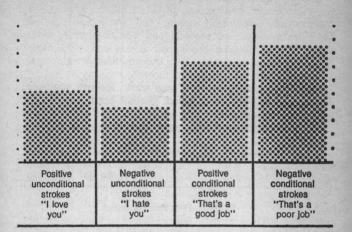

Figure 3. Stroke Graph

Now redraw this graph to show the kinds of strokes you would like to be giving to the members of your family. What can you do to change the kind of strokes you are giving?

3. Ask yourself and each member of the family, "What are your favorite kinds of strokes?" You will find that some members of the family like talking strokes, some like cuddling strokes, some like to have the undivided attention of others, and others like the kind of stroking that goes on during mutual projects.

We frequently give the kinds of strokes that we would like to get. What kind of strokes are you giving because you are not getting them?

4. Now draw a time structure graph, showing how you spend your time in the family. The way the graph is drawn here does not represent any ideal; draw the graph the way it is for you. Now redraw the graph to show the ways you would prefer to spend time with your family. What can you do to change the ways in which you fill your time with the family?

5. Draw a Warm Fuzzy and a Cold Prickly.

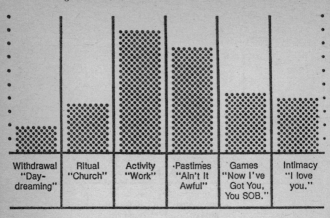

Figure 4. Time Structure Graph

READINGS

Berne, Eric. *Games People Play*. New York: Grove Press, 1964.

Colton, Helen. "You Should Only Choke on Your Stroke, Knock on Wood." *Transactional Analysis Journal* I, 3 (1971).

Ernst, Franklin H. Jr. *Who's Listening?* Vallejo, California: Addressoset, 1968 (reprinted 1973).

Maslow, Abraham. *Motivation and Personality*. New York: Harper and Row, 1970.

Maslow, Abraham. *Toward a Psychology of Being*. New York: Van Nostrand, 1962.

Samuels, Solon D. "Stroke Strategy." *Transactional Analysis Journal* I, 3 (1971).

Spitz, René. "Hospitalism, Genesis of Psychiatric Conditions in Early Childhood." *Psychoanalytic Studies of the Child*, Vol. I. New York: International Universities Press, 1945.

Steiner, Claude. *Scripts People Live*. New York: Grove Press, 1974.

Steiner, Claude. "The Stroke Economy." *Transactional Analysis Journal* I, 3 (1971).

3

Grown-up Personality

The long period of growth into adulthood, which is unique to the human species, is important to the development of the complex civilization in which we live, and our preparation for adult life within it. None of us will ever escape the fact of having been a child; the events and experiences of childhood are heavily bonded into our unique personalities. In this chapter we outline the main components of adult personality.

Parent, Adult, Child

Ego states are organized ways of defining reality, processing information and reacting to the world. *Parent, Adult,* and *Child* are terms used for *the three separate ego states* which we all have. These three ego states allow us a great deal of flexibility in dealing with the world around us. They also account for much of our apparent inconsistency, since we have at least three ways of reacting to anything that happens in our lives. The three ego states can be diagrammed by three circles.

The three circles of the diagram signify that each of the three ego states is separate and discrete and can be identified by different contents and action. At birth we have only a *Child* ego state, which is not enough for us to think effectively with or to take care of ourselves or

others. To fill this need the Child ego state creates the
Adult and the *Parent* ego states in the course of our long
childhood. The function of the Adult and Parent ego
states is to better take care of our Child ego state and
provide effective and appropriate means of getting our
Child needs met.

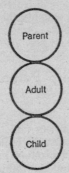

Figure 5. Ego States

Child Ego State

Eric Berne states (*Games People Play*, p. 25):
> *The Child is in many ways the most valuable part of*
> *the personality and contributes to the individual's life*
> *exactly what an actual child contributes to family life:*
> *charm, pleasure, and creativity. In the Child reside intui-*
> *tion, creativity, and spontaneous drive and enjoyment.*

The Child ego state is the repository of our emotions
and a basic sense of who we are. Since Child includes
this sense of identity each of our Childs is a him or a her.
Not an it.

We have not only a grown-up Child that is of our
chronological age; we also have a Child that has recorded
all the significant emotional events of our lives even from
infancy.

At times we respond to events in the present as if they
were identical to ones in the past. This is how this experience works:

Sam has a job. And on this job he has a boss. And this boss has a secretary. This secretary has a telephone. And every once in a while she calls Sam on the telephone and says to Sam, "Sam, the boss wants to see you at two o'clock, will you come?" Sam says, "Yes," puts down the phone and is scared. Sam thinks maybe he is in trouble with the boss and thinks about all the naughty things he has ever done at work. Just to make sure he is scared, he even thinks of some things he *might* have done. Sam is really scared now, and is sure that he is in trouble. When Sam sees his boss, he finds that he is not in trouble; all his boss wants is some information. Sam has been scared for many hours and didn't have any real reason to be scared. He had made up the things to be scared about.

Why did Sam scare himself? Well, when he was in high school every once in a while he would get a note from a boss called the Dean of Boys; the note said, "Please come to the Dean of Boys' office." When he got to the office, he found out that he was in trouble and that was scary. When Sam was a very little boy and did something naughty, his mother said to him, "Wait until your father gets home. Then you'll get it!" When Daddy came home, he and Mama went into the kitchen and whispered. When they were done whispering, Daddy said to Sam, "Come here, Sam, I want to see you." And that was scary and Sam would get paddled for what he did wrong. Finally Sam decided that he wanted to stop being scared of the boss, and decided to think about *why* he was scared. He thought about the Dean of Boys and about his Daddy and decided that the boss was not the Dean of Boys and was not his Daddy, and that he didn't have to be scared of him anymore. So he stopped. When Sam had been called in to see the boss his Child part was not 35 years old, his Child was feeling about 7 years old. Sam has now learned how to take his grown-up Parent, Adult, and Child in to see the boss instead of his scared Child.

We have our Child ego state a long time before our Adult and Parent ego states start developing. This Child ego state creates a primitive Adult and a primitive Parent to do the job of surviving until the more effective and grown-up Adult and Parent ego states are developed. These primitive ego states are diagrammed as in Figure 6.

NATURAL CHILD

When we are first born, we have learned very little. We do have, however, automatic responses to our own needs. When babies are hungry, they cry. The ego state with

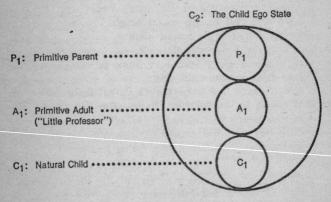

C_2: The Child Ego State

P_1: Primitive Parent .... P_1

A_1: Primitive Adult .... A_1
("Little Professor")

C_1: Natural Child .... C_1

Figure 6: Child Ego State

which we are born is called *the Natural Child* (C_1). This is the part of us that is most in touch with our internal needs. This is the part of us that, from the day we are born to the day we die, takes the stance: "I want what I want when I want it and there's no good reason I can't have it."

LITTLE PROFESSOR

The Primitive Adult in the Child (A_1) is called *the Little Professor* (of psychology). Little Professor is a creative, intuitive part of us that seeks to answer the question,

"What do I have to do to survive around here?" Little Professor is extremely curious about the workings of the world, and it is in the Primitive Adult that we have our basic ideas about how the world is constructed. These ideas develop when as infants we start conducting experiments in physics and psychology. "What will happen when I drop my milk over the side of the high chair? Does it *always* go down? What will Mama or Daddy do?"

PRIMITIVE PARENT

The Primitive Parent (P_1) is the least understood part of our personality structure. As a result, people have called it a number of names like "Electrode," "Supernatural Child," and "Pig Parent." Many people, especially those who call it the "Pig Parent," think that this part of us is only destructive and should not be used. Other TA theorists strongly suspect that the Primitive Parent has positive functions or it would not exist.

We do know that the Primitive Parent is the part of us that adapts to the demands of the grownups in our life. This adaptation, of course, ensures our survival as youngsters. It also helps us to learn to fit into society and to compromise our own needs with the demands of our culture. Sometimes fitting in is functional and sometimes it isn't. Fitting in by learning acceptable ways of passing time is functional. Fitting in by agreeing that it is O.K. to kill people is not functional. So far, we know most about the Primitive Parent when it has taken in destructive messages and wants to carry them out. Some of the destructive messages that the Primitive Parent may have are: Don't Be, Don't Grow Up, Don't Be A Child, Don't Be You.

How Can We Tell Our Ego States Apart?

We switch among Parent, Adult, and Child ego states, depending on circumstances and on our learned ways of responding to things. A number of clues can be used to determine which ego state someone is using. Here are some clues to the *Child* ego state:

CHILD EGO STATE

VOCABULARY

When people are using their Child ego state, they continue to use childlike words like "wow," "yuk," "oh geez," "shit." Child ego state sings in the shower, makes up poems, and swears.

VOICE

When we are in Child ego state we sound childlike: loud, soft, whining, singsong. When in Child ego state we often revert to the dialect of the place where we were raised as a child. Sonja lived in South Texas until she was five years old, and then moved over a thousand miles north. When she is in her Child ego state, she frequently has a Texas accent.

BEHAVIOR

When we are in our Child, we wiggle, slouch, act coy, fluster, and sit with our heads cocked listening with some angle in mind. "What's in this for me?" (See *Who's Listening?* by Frank Ernst.)

SOCIAL RESPONSE

When someone is being attractive and playful in their Child ego state, we typically respond with our own playful Child. If someone is acting helpless, we are likely to respond with our Nurturing Parent ego state; if they are being rebellious in Child ego state, we are likely to turn on our own Critical Parent ego state. We can use our responses to others to assess their ego states.

HISTORY

As the story of Sam demonstrates, our Child ego state has a lot of information stored from our past. We can use this knowledge of our emotional history to understand what's going on with us when we are not feeling the way we want to. In addition, our Child ego state has been taught to express feelings in certain ways. All of us develop favorite bad feelings in accordance with the feeling expressions allowed in our families. These feelings are called *racket* feelings and are substitutes for authentic feelings. People who end up feeling angry or sulky when most other people are sad, or people who run around with a chip on their shoulder, are expressing a racket feeling. People who use racket feelings act as if they were collecting *trading stamps*. They collect injustices and bad feelings until they think they are entitled to cash them in on some "prize," just as trading stamps at stores are cashed in. A very devoted stamp collector may even save a very large quantity to cash in on a guilt-free murder or suicide.

THE FUNCTION OF EMOTIONS

Whenever we experience emotion, we are in our Child ego state. Our emotions are signals which tell us if our needs are being met adequately. A newborn infant has only two ways of expressing feelings: quiescence, when the infant is feeling good; and arousal, when the infant is feeling bad. Fairly quickly the infant begins to express fear and anger which can be differentiated from each other. To put it colloquially, an infant of a month old or older has three basic feelings: *mad, glad,* and *scared*. Most infants also learn a fourth feeling by the time they are a year old and this feeling is *sad*. This feeling may be a combination of mad and scared. We call these four feelings—glad, mad, scared, and sad—"authentic feelings" to distinguish them from racket feelings, which are cover-ups for true feelings. It is important for us to be aware of our authentic feelings, since they are accurate signals of our inner needs. After we are aware of these feelings, we need to think and to do something about them.

Our authentic feelings give us strong indications of the action we need to take.

Mad: When I am angry it is probably because I am being restrained or manipulated in some way, and I need to think of things to do about such restraint and manipulation.

Scared: When I am scared, it is probably because I have lost support—physical support, or the psychological support of predictability. When I feel scared I need to think about and do something about getting support. Support can come from physical stroking (being held, touched, or tucked in) or from the psychological support of getting information which increases the predictability of the situation.

Sad: When I am sad, it is probably because I am lacking strokes or because I have lost some important source of stroking. In response to this feeling, I need to seek out other sources of strokes.

Glad: Glad is a signal that things are O.K., that what I am doing is working, and that I can keep it up. Glad is a temporary feeling. This is true for two reasons:

1. A number of things can go wrong to interfere with our sources of supply.

2. When we have a need for something and the need is met, we are then satiated. We no longer experience that need for a while, and may instead experience one of the higher order needs. If we are not starving, we can think about safety; if we are safe, we can think about affection and love.

People who have not allowed themselves to be in touch with their needs often feel that their particular need is insatiable. For example, people in a chronic stroke deficit may feel that they will never get enough strokes even if they ask for them. They do not recognize that, like all needs, there is a satiation point. For example, a baby who experiences the need of hunger cries, and the food need is met by nursing. Then the baby no longer experiences that need and goes on to do something else. Similarly, when people have enough strokes, they will stop seeking strokes and look for some other form of stimulation. They may even choose to withdraw from stroking and do nothing for a while.

ADULT EGO STATE

While we can think in our Child ego state, we do not think logically. We use hunches, think by analogy, and think intuitively. In Adult ego state, we follow the rules of logic to arrive at conclusions. We form premises or deal with objective information and estimate probabilities. When Nancy crosses the street on her way to school, she uses a complex set of calculations to determine such things as her walking speed, the speed of an oncoming car, the relative distance to be covered by her and by the car, and the estimated point of intersection where her path will cross the path of the car. She makes all of these calculations in less than a second of time using her Adult ego state, and she is able to make these calculations so rapidly because of the twelve billion or so nerve cells in her brain.

Our Adult ego state is first truly available somewhere around age three. At that age our Adult ego state still lacks a great deal of information, and the logic is unsophisticated. In fact, children do not possess the capacity for full use of systematic, abstract logic until about the age of fourteen. Adult ego states can vary in sophistication, but we all possess a functional Adult ego state. This ego state places at our disposal the most elaborate computer system known—the human brain.

Following are the clues we can use to determine if someone is using the *Adult* ego state.

VOCABULARY

Vocabulary used in Adult ego state includes impartial information and probability estimates: "The temperature at 2:00 today was 74 degrees Fahrenheit; the probability of measurable precipitation is 20%."

VOICE

In Adult ego state the voice is usually somewhat monotone and without much change in inflection. The voice tone of astronauts communicating with the Mission Cotrol Center is an excellent example of Adult ego state voice.

BEHAVIOR

In Adult ego state, people sit relatively still and have an attentive stance with a somewhat slow and regular eye-blink rate.

SOCIAL RESPONSE

A usual social response to someone in Adult ego state is Adult attentiveness.

The history of our education, both formally and informally, leaves our Adult ego state variously informed on various subjects. The historical content of Adult ego state can be checked by asking ourselves, "What factual information do I have on this subject?"

PARENT EGO STATE

The Parent ego state is the part of us which contains all the rules we've learned about how things should be or shouldn't be. That is, it is our morals and manners department. Our Parent ego state also defines for us what is important. For instance, in our culture we have just a few words for snow. In Eskimo culture it is important to know a great deal about snow. As a result, Eskimos have a classification system for snow that has as many as thirty categories. The Adult ego state provides the actual information about snow; the classification system comes from the Parent ego state and is handed down from generation to generation.

The Parent ego state contains a large number of *structures.* (Structures are like computer programs for doing things and thinking about things.) Thus the Parent ego state contains instructions about all the things that we should know in order to get along well in our culture. For these structures to be useful, they need to be reviewed periodically by our Adult ego state and the information that is no longer useful discarded.

In *Little House on the Prairie*, Laura Ingalls Wilder's autobiographical story of homesteading, she tells about her father's expectations about behavior. The family lived in an inhospitable environment, and the children were expected to obey their father immediately and without question. Obeying was sometimes a question of survival. When Pa told the girls to chain the dog up when the Indians came to visit, the safety of the family depended on their prompt and unquestioned action. After the Indians had gone, Laura asked about letting the dog Jack loose:

"After this," he said in a terrible voice, "you girls al-

ways remember to do what you're told. Don't you even think of disobeying me. Do you hear?"

"Yes, Pa," Laura and Mary whispered.

"Do you know what would have happened if you had turned Jack loose?" Pa asked.

"No, Pa," they whispered.

"He would have bitten those Indians," said Pa. "Then there would have been trouble. Bad trouble. Do you understand?"

"Yes, Pa," they said. But they did not understand.

"Would they have killed Jack?" Laura asked.

"Yes. And that's not all. You girls remember this: you do as you're told, no matter what happens."

"Yes, Pa," Laura said, and Mary said, "Yes, Pa." They were glad they had not turned Jack loose.

"Do as you are told,"· said Pa, "and no harm will come to you."*

On the prairie, unquestioning obedience to parents was an important survival trait. Many parents continue to treat immediate obedience with the same intensity as if family survival were somehow dependent on it. When the issues are things like taking out the trash or how to fix a meal, it is clear that instant obedience is no longer functional. In fact, blindly following the parent structure which says, "Do as you are told," interferes with flexible thinking about problems.

The Parent ego state, when activated, can be directed toward other people, in telling them what to do and how to act or in taking care of them. It can also be expressed through an internal dialogue in which our own Parent ego state tells us our Child ego state what to do or takes care of our own Child ego state. In an internal dialogue our Child ego state can choose to disregard the Parent message, or he or she can listen to the message and either comply or rebel.

---

* From *Little House on the Prairie* by Laura Ingalls Wilder. Text copyright 1935 by Laura Ingalls Wilder. Copyright renewed 1963 by Rogert L. MacBride. Reprinted by permission of Harper and Row, Publishers, Inc.

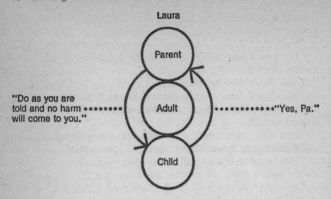

Figure 7. Internal Dialogue

Here are some ways to identify the *Parent* ego state:

VOCABULARY

Parent ego state talks about values and often talks in absolutes. In Parent ego state, things are good or bad, right or wrong; things are judged by these values. "Do as you are told and no harm will come to you." "Good little children should always eat their spinach." "It's a sin to think bad thoughts." "Always read the instructions before putting something together."

VOICE

The voice in Parent ego state may be stern and commanding or soft and nurturing.

BEHAVIOR

Parent ego states may include such things as rigid posture or a nurturing stance. A frequent cue to judgmental expression of Parent ego state is the pointing finger that is used to remind, condemn, or scold.

Figure 8. Common Parent Ego State Gesture

SOCIAL RESPONSE

When someone is in Parent ego state, a typical response is for the listeners to switch into Child ego state and look for ways to comply or rebel.

HISTORY

The history of the Parent ego state can frequently be assessed by asking, "What did my parents say, think, and feel about this subject? Am I acting as my mother or father, or second-grade teacher or preacher would in this situation? What messages am I following?"

Transactions

A *transaction* is an exchange of strokes between two people. When I stroke you, and this stimulates you to respond by stroking me, we have engaged in a transaction. Your response may then serve as a stimulus for my response and that would be another transaction. An ordinary conversation about nothing in particular may contain a hundred or so transactions, meaning that we would each give and receive a hundred strokes.

When we transact we use our ego states. The way we use our ego states in transactions results in several patterns of communication. There are three basic rules of communication.

1. If the ego state addressed is the one that responds, communication can proceed indefinitely. This type of transaction is called a *complementary transaction.*

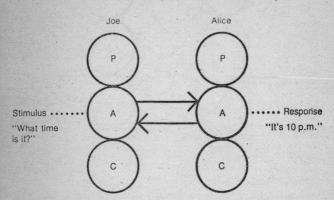

Figure 9. Complementary Transaction

People who are engaging in complementary transactions can be exchanging strokes from a number of ego states. They can be engaged in critical gossip (a Parent-to-Parent transaction), solving a problem (an Adult-to-Adult transaction), playing together (a Child-to-Child transaction), or one person reprimanding the other (a Parent-to-Child transaction).

2. If the ego state that we respond with is not the one the other person intended, communication is broken off. This is called a *crossed transaction.* In a crossed transaction, the initial subject is lost unless the transaction is successfully recrossed. Adolescents are particularly adept at crossing transactions when talking with their parents.

3. If there is a covert psychological communication along with an overt communication, the hidden message is the one that will be responded to. The opening moves of psychological games are made thus with an *ulterior transaction.* The overt message is usually carried in the content, while the covert message is carried in word connotations, voice, and gestures.

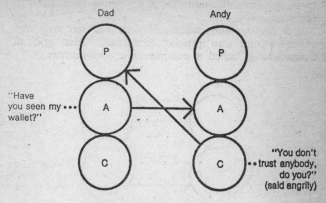

Dad

Andy

"Have you seen my ••• wallet?"

"You don't ••trust anybody, do you?" (said angrily)

Figure 10. Crossed Transaction

Games

Psychological games are series of ulterior transactions that lead to a "payoff" of intense feelings. Games are ways of getting strokes, filling time, and living out a life plan. The payoff is a way of justifying a feeling that we already have. One of the most useful ways of looking at games is with the "Drama Triangle."

DRAMA TRIANGLE

The *Drama Triangle* is a way of analyzing what is going on in families when people play games. When we get into the Drama Triangle, that means we are not engaged in effective problem-solving. In the Drama Triangle there are three positions: the Persecutor, the Rescuer, and the Victim. Each of the three players takes a prescribed role, and then in order to make things more interesting and dramatic, the players switch.

Step 1 in the Drama Triangle depicts a common family drama.

Step 2 shows a frequent second step, and Step 3 depicts

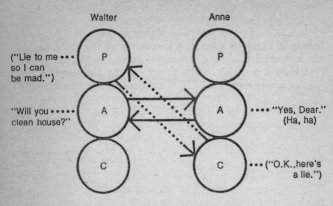

Figure 11. Ulterior Transaction

the final move where each family member has taken a turn in Persecutor, Rescuer, and Victim position. When people are in the Drama Triangle they refuse to recognize their ability to think about and solve problems; usually they collect a large number of negative strokes.

Basic Position

Early in life, after we come to tell the difference between ourselves and others, we decide upon a basic position which defines us in relationship to other people. After we have made this decision we begin to collect experiences that confirm our position. There are four basic positions: I'm O.K.—You're O.K.; I'm O.K.—You're not-O.K.; I'm not-O.K.—You're O.K.; and I'm not-O.K.—You're not-O.K.

Each of the four basic positions contains a program for what to do about solving problems. Only the I'm O.K.—You're O.K. position is effective in solving problems over a long period of time. In the I'm O.K.—You're O.K. position, the problem-solving stance is to figure out what can be done and do it. In the I'm O.K.—You're not-

O.K. position the person often thinks, "If there is any kind of a problem, then it's your fault; I don't need to change, you do. We can solve this problem by getting rid of you." In the I'm not-O.K.—You're O.K. position, the person is likely to think, "Whatever is wrong between us has happened because I am inept, dumb, stupid, and sick, so I should go away." The person in the I'm not-O.K.—You're not-O.K. position feels helpless and hopeless about the situation, and arranges to end up getting nowhere.

When two-year-old Samantha dribbles honey all over the living room rug, Papa can behave in several different ways.

I'm O.K.-You're O.K.: Be mád at her, clean up the mess, and figure out how to keep it from happening again.

I'm O.K.-You're not-O.K.: Paddle her soundly, insist that she clean up the mess (with a two-year-old this ensures an even bigger mess), send her to bed for the day and say, "You are a stupid, rotten little idiot and I feel like killing you for this."

I'm not-O.K.-You're O.K.: Clean up the honey, and don't chastise her; sit down and cry and berate himself for being a stupid inadequate father and go to his room and sulk for the rest of the day.

I'm not-O.K.-You're not-O.K.: Sit down in the mess and cry, and don't do anything about it.

Since we have decided to take a particular basic position, we can also decide to revise our basic position by behaving differently. Most of us use different basic positions for various situations. For example, George may feel "I'm O.K.—You're O.K." with the boys at the clubhouse, "I'm O.K.—You're not-O.K.' with his wife and children, "Im not-O.K.—You're O.K." with the boss and "I'm not-O.K.—You're not-O.K." with the tax auditor. We can change the not-O.K. positions by thinking about the problem and deciding what can be done to move to the I'm O.K.—You're O.K. position and get on with the solution.

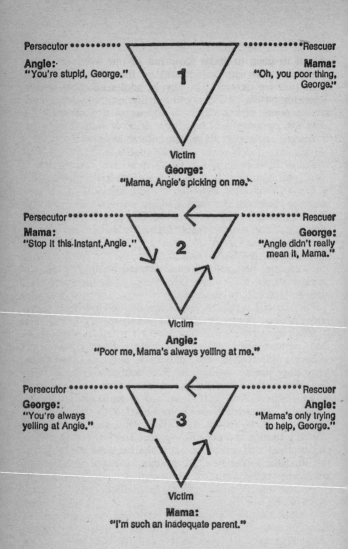

Figure 12. Drama Triangle (In Three Steps)

Life Script

All of us need to make sense out of our lives and make plans for what our future will be like. The overall life plan that we develop (usually in adolescence) is a program for how we will live out our life and how it will end. It has many of the dramatic elements of a play with a cast of characters and a direction. It is therefore called a *life script*. When we make a life script plan, we incorporate into it our previous life experience. It includes all that we have learned about strokes in our own family stroke economy, our favorite ways of structuring time, our preferred ways of transacting, the psychological games that we have learned, our chosen basic position, and the cultural and historical influences which we have experienced. Script decisions are often phrased as resolution, "Well, if this is the way things are, then from now on I'll always (or never) do. . . ." For example: Samantha's mother believes that men are no good. To support her belief she married a man she didn't like. She told Samantha, "Men are no good; look at the drunken bum of a father you have." Father supported Mother's opinion by beating Samantha periodically while in a drunken rage. At about age twelve, Samantha decided, "Well, if that's the way men are, I'll never get close to men." She confirmed her script decision by gathering information to prove she was right, by dating obnoxious boys in high school and later seeking employment within jobs where the male employers were abusive. Finally she married a drunken husband— just like Mama did—and continued to live out an unhappy script. Her script was based on a resolution which rested upon inadequate information. Her basic assumption was that all men were like her father; she set out to prove it. If she chose to do so, Samantha could change her script by collecting new information and making new decisions, based on a new understanding of what more constructive men are like.

Scripts can be categorized according to their course and outcome. Some are tragic, ending in illness, imprisonment, disgrace, or death. Some call for the person to be a winner by making great achievements and accomplishing set goals. Others call for the person to be a loser by setting goals and not making them. Some scripts are dull and humdrum, without much going on. In the developmental chapters, the life script pattern will be dealt with more extensively.

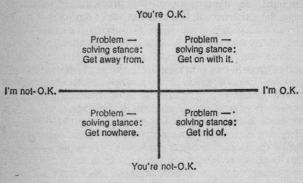

Figure 13. The Four Basic Positions

Passive Thinking and Passive Behavior

Effectively functioning grownups make flexible use of all of their ego states. At times however, we all long to return to an earlier age where other people did our thinking for us. When we disregard our own ability to think—or to feel—we will have difficulty in problem-solving. The means by which we undermine ourselves are called *passive thinking* and *passive behavior* by Aaron and Jacqui Lee Schiff.

PASSIVE THINKING

When we think passively we do not use information that is available about ourselves, other persons, or the situation. Passive thinking is called *discounting,* because we are disregarding information which we have. As a result we may:

1. *Discount the problem* as if no problem exists. For example, the family is at the Grand Canyon. Three-year-old Georgie is in front of his parents a foot-and-a-half from a thousand-foot drop. The parents continue to look up and discuss the view.

2. *Discount the significance of the problem.* When we discount the significance of the problem, we acknowledge the existence of the problem and deny that it is important. Example: Four-year-old Johnny has just hit his little sister with a stick. Father says to mother, "Boys will be boys (sigh)."

3. *Discount the solvability of the problem.* When we discount the solvability, we acknowledge that there is a problem and that the problem is significant, but we exclude any possibility of solving it. For example, in the previous hitting incident, if mother replies to father, "That child is impossible to control," she is discounting the solvability of the problem.

4. *Discount the person.* When we discount ourselves we acknowledge that there is a problem, that it is significant, and that it is solvable, but we deny that it is solvable by *us*. For example, "I can't make Joey mind, but the baby-sitter can."

These passive ways of thinking lead to several types of behavior.

PASSIVE BEHAVIOR

We use *passive behavior* to compel other persons to be more uncomfortable about our problem than we are: we attempt to get someone else to take over the problem-solving job.

There are four kinds of passive behavior.

1. *Doing nothing.* Angie, who is two years old, has just dribbled honey all over the kitchen floor. Mother's boyfriend, John, sees the mess and does nothing. Finally one of the older children takes over and cleans up Angie's mess.

2. *Overadaptation.* When we overadapt we do not identify a goal for ourselves in solving a problem, but try to achieve what we believe is someone else's goal. Example: Angie's mother asks the baby-sitter to clean up the dishes

that he and Angie used for their snack. The baby-sitter does that, and also wipes off the table, the counters, the stove, and the refrigerator, and empties the trash. He does this because he thinks it will please Angie's mother. The problem is that, while the baby-sitter is doing these chores he was not asked to do, Angie is upstairs messing around with Mom's lipstick and perfume.

3. *Agitation.* Agitated behaviors are not goal-directed. They drain off energy that could be used to solve the problem. For example, Angie has spilled honey all over the floor. Mama comes in and sees the mess. She begins to pace the floor, wringing her hands and saying over and over again, "Oh dear, what will I do?"

4. *Incapacitation or Violence.* When persons resort to incapacitation or violence, other persons are forced to take over for the time being. For example: Angie's mother sees the mess, screams, "I can't stand it!", works herself up into a migraine headache, and then goes to bed. She incapacitates herself. Or, violence: Angie's mother comes in, sees the mess, and beats Angie severely, instead of doing anything about the problem.

In the course of our evolution from helpless infancy to effective adulthood, we learn and practice the skills needed to take care of ourselves. We also conduct experiments in passive thinking and passive behavior, to see whether others will support our lack of responsibility. Grownups who support passive thinking and passive behavior in their children are doing them a disservice. In each of the chapters on development we will present ways in which parents can help their children learn to think effectively and behave responsibly.

SUMMARY

Grownups possess three fully functioning *ego states.*
Parent ego state defines the aspects of the world we consider important and contains programs for raising kids. *Adult* ego state assesses probabilities, performs logical functions, and sorts information. *Child* ego state includes feelings, intuitions, and "magical thinking." It is the part of us that is forever young.

Fully functioning persons need to be aware of both their feelings and thinking and to use both for problem-solving. Four fundamental feelings are *glad, sad, mad,* and *scared.* Each functions as a signal and needs to be listened to for problem-solving purposes. People often confuse feeling with thinking; this confusion interferes with effective functioning.

Transactions are exchanges of strokes between two or more people. We choose which ego state to transact form, and thereby enhance or interfere with our communications with others.

We all operate from a basic position that defines ourselves in relationship to others. This basic position shifts according to circumstances, but most of us maintain a persistent home base. The basic positions are I'm O.K.—You're O.K., I'm O.K.—You're not-O.K., I'm not-O.K. —You're O.K., I'm not-O.K.—You're not-O.K.

Each of us has constructed a life script for ourselves, which is a plan, partially in awareness, about how our lives should go. Some scripts are exciting, some boring, and some tragic. In addition to an overall script, we have specific script messages about how to raise kids and what it is supposed to be like as a parent.

At times we all long to return to that state when other people did our thinking for us; we may try to trick others into thinking (or feeling) for us. We do this through *passive thinking* (discount the problem, its significance, its solvability, or our ability to solve the problem). Passive thinking is observable through *passive behavior.* With passive behavior, instead of solving problems we do nothing, overadapt, agitate, or incapacitate ourselves. If we do any of these very often we soon have problems in functioning well.

EXERCISES

EGO STATES

Parent

1. List three things your parents did when you were young that you liked.

2. List three things your parents did when you were young that you did not like.
3. Do you do any of these now yourself?

Adult

1. How do you plan your day?
2. Name three skills you have and enjoy.

Child

1. What did you do for fun as a kid?
2. Do you do that now? If not, why not?
3. How did people feel in your family when things went wrong? Do you feel that way now when things go wrong?
4. What does you child voice sound like? Practice it and see.

EMOTIONS

1. What do I think and do when I am mad?
2. What do I think and do when I am scared?
3. What do I think and do when I am sad?
4. What do I think and do when I am glad?

TRANSACTION

1. Think of an example of a complementary transaction.
2. Think of an example of a crossed transaction. What did you think when this happened? What did you feel? What did you do?
3. Think of an ulterior transaction that occurred recently. What was the outcome of this transaction?

BASIC POSITION

Which basic position is implied in the following statements?
1. "Teenagers are all lazy and no good."
2. "As parents we have failed our children."
3. "The only thing we can be sure of is death and taxes."
4. "What shall we do about getting the chores done?"

LIFE SCRIPT

1. Imagine your life as a play. What kind of a play is it? Drama, tragedy, melodrama, comedy? What is the reaction of the audience watching this drama?

2. Are you satisfied with the story? If not, how would you like it to go?

PASSIVE THINKING AND PASSIVE BEHAVIOR

1. When there are chores to do in the house do I and/or others procrastinate, act helpless, get angry and blaming, get headaches or stomach aches?
2. Is there any one in my life around whom I act stupid or helpless?

READINGS

Berne, Eric. *Games People Play.* New York: Grove Press, 1964.

Berne, Eric. *What Do You Say After You Say Hello?* New York: Grove Press, 1972.

Campos, Leonard, and McCormick, Paul. *Introduce Yourself to Transactional Analysis.* Stockton: San Joaquin TA Institute, 1969.

Ernst, Franklin H. Jr. *Who's Listening?* Vallejo, California: Addressoset, 1968 (reprinted 1973).

Harris, Thomas A. *I'm O.K.—You're O.K.* New York: Harper and Row, 1969.

James, Muriel, and Jongeward, Dorothy. *Born to Win.* Reading, Massachusetts: Addison-Wesley, 1971.

Karpman, Steven B. "Fairy Tales and Script Drama Analysis." *Transactional Analysis Bulletin* 7, 26 (1968).

Piaget, Jean. *Logic and Psychology.* New York: Basic Books, 1957.

Schiff, Aaron Wolfe, and Schiff, Jacqui Lee. "Passivity." *Transactional Analysis Journal* I, 1 (1971).

Steiner, Claude. *Games Alcoholics Play.* New York: Grove Press, 1971.

4

Programs for Raising Children

In addition to our broad and general script programming, we also have very specific programming about such matters as marrying, having children, and raising children. These programs in turn have an influence on our lives as parents and on the ways in which we raise our children.

Marriage Scripts

Eric Berne talks about different types of marriages, all of which are based upon the scripts of the couple involved. He classifies marriages into a number of different types.

1. The Shotgun or Makeshift Marriage. The couple are far apart, but soon they find a single common bond, perhaps a new baby. As time goes on, they get closer and closer until they finally come together (and then they have a marriage that truly works).

2. The couple starts far apart, but never gets any closer, and the marriage is held together by a single bond; otherwise, each goes where he or she was originally headed.

3. The marriage starts off and ends with the couple forged into a single unit.

4. The couple go round and round in a circle, never getting anywhere, repeating the same patterns until the marriage is terminated by death or separation.

5. The couple wanders around seeking happiness, and finds some degree of it, but never gets farther than that, "leaving both parties disappointed and bewildered and good candidates for psychotherapy, since there is enough for them not to want a divorce."

6. The couple starts off closely, but immediately begins to diverge—perhaps after the honeymoon is over, or even after the first night.

7. The couple starts off far apart, yet at one point there is a single period of bliss. "They wait for it to happen again, but it never does, and soon they drift apart, never to reunite."

8. The couple starts off well, but difficulties multiply. Soon each one finds separate interests, and goes his or her own way.

9. The autonomous marriage in which the couple remain individuals in their own right, each with a strong commitment to the other person, with mutual growth and change throughout the marriage relationship.

The type of marriage (or the arrangement under which a woman has children without being married) is determined by life script. Awareness of script patterns in a marriage can be important in changing the marriage, if the partners wish to do so. Scripting about marriage will also influence decisions on whether or not to have children, when in the marriage to have children, and how many children to have.

Script decisions about having children can take a number of forms: 1) not to have children; 2) to plan the conception and arrival of the children very carefully; 3) to avoid any attempts at conception control; 4) to adopt children; 5) to take in stray children. Each of these decisions only partially influences the outcome of when and how children arrive. There are still matters of fertility, mortality at childbirth, and disease, as well as other acts of fate, which will influence the final family grouping.

Having Children

Until we actually have children of our own, most of our childrearing information is Parent-programmed. That is, it is prerecorded in our head, without the benefit of Adult screening to determine what is effective and what really meets the baby's needs. If our Parent programming is O.K.—i.e., if we feel good, vital, healthy, and happy ourselves—then we have a good base on which to build in rearing children. However, even the most effective program for raising children is in need of updating. Jacqui Schiff points out that one of the functions of rebellion in children is to force parents to update their programming for raising kids.* Therefore, parents need to assess their current Parent ego state programs to become familiar with their own Parent tapes, and to become familiar with what is currently understood about good parenting, growth, and development. All of this information can be used to look at and update our information about raising kids.

Our Parent programming about children includes important information about what it is "supposed" to be like to have kids. This programming may contain phrases like,

"Life is great until you have kids."

"Kids are a blessing and a joy and you should have as many as possible."

"The only way to become completely fulfilled as a woman is to have children."

"Fathers don't know how to take care of children."
And so forth. The programming that we have about raising children includes several levels of information. These levels are: 1) what our own parents *said* about how children should be raised; 2) what our parents *did* in raising us; and 3) how our parents *felt* about raising children.

Thus, if Mama was nervous about toilet training and repeatedly conveyed that message to Mary, Mary's Parent ego state will contain the message, "Be uptight about

* Personal communication by Jacqui Lee Schiff to authors.

toilet training." In addition to such sets of programmed messages from their own Parent ego state, people have often made a set of Child ego state resolutions which they use in raising kids. One very common Child resolution is, "When *I* get to be a parent, I'm *never* going to spank *my* children." When they have children, they may discover to their horror that they are spanking the children just as they were spanked. Other programming includes information on what to do with kids and how to feel about doing it. This programming includes things like what to do when the baby cries, what to do when the baby breaks something, and, perhaps most importantly, what to do when you don't know what to do.

When the baby finally arrives, a new dimension is added. Prior to the arrival of the baby, our thinking about having children was done either as an internal dialogue, or in transaction with our spouse or other grownups. When the baby arrives, there is a real-life infant to transact with. The baby already has unique behavior patterns and specific ways of responding to different stimuli. Besides, baby doesn't have any information about the way that babies are "supposed to act" according to our Parent programs. Baby's lack of programming about our Parent information on babies precipitates an immediate dilemma. Will we parents listen to what the Parent in our head says, or will we gather objective Adult data on this particular baby and do what we think will be effective? Each of us has programming about being flexible, including values about whether it is all right to use innovative approaches, Adult information, and Little Professor intuitions in dealing with the baby.

To the extent that the parenting that is done comes only out of our Parent or Primitive Parent ego state, the parenting will be rigid, unyielding, and poorly tailored to the needs of the specific infant. If our Parent programming allows for ingenuity, we will discover new ways to deal with problems and meet baby's needs in a flexible and adaptable way. A typical problem that parents must deal with is colic.

Andrew's mother had permission to be flexible and creative. When he developed colic, she quickly discovered that the way to help soothe her young son when he was having a bout of colic was to put him in the infant seat and place the infant seat with him in it on top of the washing machine. The vibrations and motions of the washing machine soon lulled him into a peaceful sleep. Other parents may have the message that what they are supposed to do when the baby has colic is to let him suffer.

The "what to do's" around a new infant involve many other significant instructions about what to do with a first child, what to do with a male first child, what to do with a female first child, what to do with a wanted baby, what to do with an unwanted baby, what to do with second and subsequent children, what to do with a menopause baby, what to do with a baby that is not quite "perfect," what to do with an illegitimate baby, and so forth. All of the programming becomes quite complex. The complexity of this programming explains why children in the same family are different from each other. Each parent may have programming about what to do with, for example, an illegitimate third female that is not perfect. Our script programming around the children that we have accounts for a good deal of the individual differences that they show on growing up.

Since script involves a life plan, it includes programming for how to feel and what to do at various ages, and how to feel and think and act when the children grow up and leave home.

Women's scripts commonly define their basic O.K.-ness by the role of being a "mother." When all of the children have "left the nest," such a mother is in a dilemma since she thinks that she must fill a mother role in order to be O.K. In response to this dilemma, some mothers will ensure that the youngest child receives the injunction, "Don't grow up." If the youngest child accepts this injunction mama can continue taking care of Junior (perhaps even to age fifty or so) and maintain her O.K.-ness by keeping a "baby" always around. Other mothers who are scripted to feel O.K. only if they are "mothering" become volunteers at preschools, or script their daughters to become pregnant promptly, so that mama can become grandma and meet her needs from a grandma rather than a mama position. Other women make the decision to give up the script position and define their O.K.-ness in other ways.

Script Foundations

Baby's script begins to be formed long before conception. Each parent's script operated in choosing a mate. The decision to have a baby was determined at least partly by script. Many couples still have babies because they assume that they're *supposed* to have babies, and that something is wrong if they don't want to. Thus they conceive and bear children on the basis of a Parent ego state assumption, rather than as an Adult decision. These Parent ego state assumptions are reinforced by many other people. For instance, the parents or in-laws may ask questions: "When are you going to have a baby (so I can have a grandchild)?" "What, you've been married two years and no children?" The implied message behind such questions is "You are supposed to have children for someone else rather than for yourselves." Such messages discount a young couple's choices. The couple themselves need to decide *if* they will have children, *how many* children they will have, and *when* they will have them. Before our decade ends, they may even be able to choose the sex of the child.

CONCEPTION

Whether or not the parents plan the pregnancy may be an important issue when information about fertility is so readily available. Even when we have so many methods of conception control available, Jacqui Schiff estimates that 50% of pregnancies are unplanned.* More importantly, what messages await baby? "You were an accident" may mean many things. It may mean, "We would rather you were dead," "We're not in control of our own lives," or, "I wanted you but I didn't want to admit it," which translates, "Don't be straight about your own needs."

* A personal communication, February, 1974. This estimate includes pregnancies which end in abortion and in childbirth.

If, in later childhood years, the kid is informed about having been planned, the messages will convey different information, such as: "We just acted like bunnies and hoped we would succeed," which translates, "Sex is fun, we were lucky to have you, you can be lucky in love." "I took my temperature every day for six years except when I was pregnant" or, "We started each of you within a month of when we planned, which translates, "The scientific method is the way to live. Use your Adult in all things, especially reproduction." "We were ready to have kids, so we just expected to have a few," translates, "You get what you expect; be ready." There are many other variations of attitudes about conception which are conveyed to the children. We need to be continually aware that we are giving our children information for their scripts by our sayings and actions.

GESTATION

Most parents have mixed feelings about a pregnancy. Many things can contribute to such mixed feelings, but the scripting information of the parents-to-be on pregnancy has a major influence, especially in the first pregnancy: is pregnancy a joyous fulfillment, nine months of nausea, a time when spouses drift apart, or a time when a couple reaffirms marital bonds? There are also unfamiliar bodily changes for the mother-to-be to deal with, as well as ample time to reflect on what life will be like when the baby arrives. The period of pregnancy is often filled with fantasies about the new individual who will be arriving.

Pregnancy is also a time which some prospective parents use to collect bad feelings by thinking "If only." For example, "If only I hadn't got pregnant now," "If only I had decided to have an abortion," "If only I knew how to be a mother," and so forth. Another way that people use to scare themselves is with "What if?" "What if I have quintuplets?" "What if the baby is born defective?" "What if I stay pregnant the rest of my life and never have this baby?" The "What if's" and "If only's" keep us away from feeling our true feelings here and now. They keep us miserable with ruminations about a past we can't do over and speculations about a future we can't predict.

Often the stroke economy between the couple changes during the pregnancy. Typically, in our culture, a prospective mother gets a great deal of positive stroking from other people, comment upon her pregnancy, and congratulations. (Fortunately the days are largely gone when pregnant women were expected to seclude themselves from the public during the advanced state of their pregnancy.) Prospective fathers are often ignored or jibed at during the pregnancy, and may also find their wives sufficiently preoccupied with the pregnancy so that they receive fewer strokes than before. Concerns about being displaced by the arrival of the infant are common, and may be partly encouraged by both the mother's preoccupation with the arrival of the infant, and the realistic fact that infants require a good deal of time and care. Pregnancy is a time for both parents to keep careful track of their stroke supply and to make sure they get the support and taking-care-of that both of them need.

NAMING THE BABY

The names picked for an infant often embody some of the expectations which the parents have for that infant. For this reason it is important to think about the implications of a name that a person will later carry throughout life. The name "Francis" may cast doubt on the masculinity of a boy, and "Jo" on the femininity of a girl. "Clarence" in England is a perfectly acceptable name. In a tough slum neighborhood in the United States it is likely to cause its owner a good deal of hassle. Children named after their parents, and with traditional family names, get strong messages about the value of tradition. In some instances the messages may also include prohibitions against doing anything differently from the rest of the family.

The sex of the unborn child is important to the expectant parents, and sometimes even more important to other members of the clan. Prospective grandparents have been known to say, for instance, "If he's healthy, that's all that matters" (notice the *he*).

Frequently the parents-to-be are fully prepared to love the child, whatever sex, but they may feel under pressure in their Adapted Child to meet certain expectations. Parents may feel under some pressure to have a daughter for Aunt Sylvia-who's-going-to-leave-her-considerable-fortune-to-the-first-female-heir-in-the-family. When we are in our Child ego states we may believe we can control the sex of our child yet to be born. These beliefs are contrary to the Adult information that there is currently no sure way for humans to control the sex of an infant. The greatest problem occurs when parents allow themselves to take magical ideas (frequently called "old wives' tales") and accept them as Adult information.

The order of birth in the family can also provide important script messages and important influences. Firstborn children may relate better with grownups than with other children. In addition, the arrival of the firstborn changes the parents' status in the community. They may now be considered "a family" rather than "a couple." If Mom and Pop were used to coming and going as they pleased, the new parents may end up feeling trapped by the demands that baby places upon them, with resultant resentment of the child.

Parents awaiting the birth of their first child are usually more anxious than are parents who have had previous children. Parents are more likely to attempt to pass on their own frustrated ambitions to first children. This happens frequently enough that first-born children on the average go farther in school, achieve more vocationally, and show greater incidence of emotional disorder.

All of the information given in this section is designed to make apparent that the parents are laying the foundation for their babies' scripts long before birth. This script-building occurs whether or not parents think about it. We need to look at the messages we are preparing for an unborn child in our families. The more variety in script messages and the more flexible the script messages are, the more options the child will have in later life from which to build a workable and constructive script.

New Sources of Information

Today we have new sources of information available to which previous generations did not have access—information about psychological development, and new perspectives on the needs of people at the various stages in their life. We know now that human development is continuous from birth to death, and that we are all constantly changing. We know that our needs and our expression of them also change many times in the course of our lifetime. Within broad outlines, our development is quite predictable, and our changing needs can be defined and planned for in advance.

While it is true that human development progresses continuously, it also progresses by stages. Understanding the purposes and functions of these stages, as well as knowing ways in which to recognize them, allows us to meet more flexibly our needs and the needs of our children. When we start out in a new stage, we explore certain aspects of our personalities and human functioning. After we have assimilated the necessary information, have the necessary experiences, and accommodate ourselves to them, we are then ready to move on to another new state.

One of the major development tasks of children is the development of the ego states. We are born with a very primitive Child. In order to meet the needs of that Child better, we create for ourselves an Adult ego state to assess reality and a Parent ego state to take care of ourselves. The formation of our Parent, Adult, and Child is based upon experiences we have while growing up in the various developmental stages. Part Two of this book describes the evolution and sequence of developmental stages. We also talk about ways in which parents can respond effectively to children at various stages, and discuss some ways in which parents can take care of their own needs while meeting the needs of their children.

SUMMARY

Life script includes detailed instructions in our *Parent* ego state about ways we are supposed to do things, and how we are supposed to feel about what we do. We have programs that say marriage is supposed to be good or bad, fun or frustrating. We pick spouses to help confirm the truth of our life plan. The life plan also includes expectations about having children. These expectations are often quite specific, such as, "I plan on having two children; the older will be a boy, the younger will be a girl." The Fates do not always comply with our plans and the sexes and numbers of our children may not fit into our script. When actuality does not fit in with the plan, parents then have to make some accommodation to it. In some cases, parents will attempt to make the infant conform to the script. If, for instance, the parents' plan is to have a boy first, and the first baby is a girl, they may unwittingly give messages that say "Don't be a girl." Such attempts to accommodate the child to the script rather than adjust the script to reality are always destructive. The script also includes details about the joys or sorrows of children leaving home and the pleasures or isolation of old age. Since our life plan is a drama that *we* have written, we can revise it if we are dissatisfied with it.

Information about psychological development and the emerging of ego states is useful in helping us to revise our plans about the way in which we want to raise kids.

Human development is continuous from birth to death. We are all constantly changing. Our needs and our expression of them also change. Within broad outlines, human development is predictable and changing needs can be defined and predicted. Shifts from an emphasis on one need to an emphasis on another need apparently occur when we decide to move on. As one child put it, "I'm tired of being five." After we have become familiar with one stage and have explored its possibilities, we are ready to try out new things. An understanding of these patterns of change, both in ourselves and our children, allows us to meet more flexibly the needs of the whole family.

In children, one of the major tasks is the development of the ego states. We are born with a very primitive Child. In order to meet the needs of that Child, we create for ourselves an Adult ego state to assess reality, and a Parent ego state to take care of ourselves. The formation of our Parent, Adult, and Child is based upon the experiences we have while growing up. Part Two of this book will describe the sequence of developmental stages and the evolution of the ego states.

EXERCISES

These questions are designed to help you think about your own programs for raising children.

1. What is the purpose of having children? What are children for?
2. How will/did I decide to have children?
   a. Under what circumstances is it O.K. to have kids?
   b. Under what circumstances is it not-O.K. to have kids?
3. What is it like for mothers to have children?
   a. What is it like for fathers to have children?
   b. What is it like to be grandparents?
4. How did my parents go about raising
   a. boys?
   b. girls?
   c. What does my own Parent ego state say about raising boys and raising girls?
5. What children's names am I partial to?
   a. What do these names mean to me?
   b. What do these names mean to most people?
   c. What do these names say about the person who holds them?

READINGS

Babcock, Dorothy. *Growth, Development, and Family Life*. Philadelphia: F.A. Davis Co., 1972.

Berne, Eric. *Sex in Human Loving*. New York: Simon and Schuster, 1970.

Berne, Eric, *What Do You Say After You Say Hello?* New York: Grove Press, 1972.

Steiner, Claude. *Scripts People Live*. New York: Grove Press, 1974.

PART II

PSYCHOLOGICAL DEVELOPMENT

Growth is the only evidence of life.
John Henry, Cardinal Newman

5

Learning to Trust

(Attachment)

The first stage of psychological growth outside of Mama's body is called *Attachment*. The main thrust of Baby's energy at that time is to attach to (an) other human being(s), i.e., to establish psychological closeness. The process of forming such a relationship is vital to Baby's health. During the earliest months of life, Baby's personality merges with the person(s) * most invested in providing for Baby's needs. The baby's personality structure at birth is primitive and relatively simple.

The relationship between Baby and whoever is there both day and night grows to be a very close one. Over the first several weeks, they re-establish comfortable rhythms with one another, akin to those experienced while Baby was in Mama's body. This relationship is called *symbiosis*.

---

* Seeing the baby and one mother as a unit is a Western viewpoint. There are other cultures in which the infant experiences a small nucleus of interested, loving adults from birth onward.

Symbiosis

In biology, the term symbiosis refers to the relationship between two organisms who live together in close union. Each organism needs the other to complete certain aspects of its life cycle; for instance, we humans need certain bacteria in our intestines to make certain vitamins. The bacteria in turn need the food which we digest. Symbiosis refers to a mutually beneficial union, and not a parasitic one.

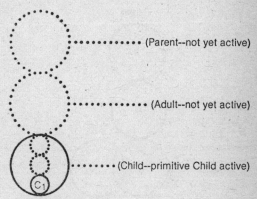

Figure 14. Personality Structure at Birth

Therese Benedek used the term "emotional symbiosis" to mean the early close relationship between mother and child, in which the mother's need for her infant is related to the infant's need for its mother. The baby's feelings of self-confidence are interwined with those of the mother.

Jacqui Schiff and her family have done the most work on defining emotional symbiosis within a TA frame of reference. They have developed a diagram to express this relationship (see fig. 15).

Mama has a Parent ego state which defines what is important and worth noticing, and an Adult ego state which thinks, notices, and solves problems. Her Child ego state is merged with Baby's. Much of what happens to one happens to the other. When Baby feels distress so does Mama; when Mama gets upset Baby grows uncomfortable; when one is content so is the other. Baby feels, and intensely needs, and soon learns many ways to express those needs; but Baby has no available Adult ego state for thinking and figuring out solutions, and no Parent ego state for self-protection, or defining reality.

A satisfactory symbiosis is most clearly demonstrated during nursing.* Baby, experiencing an empty stomach, cries in pain and/or actively roots to find food. Suckling is a very intense experience. Baby flushes, tenses, and experiences an increase in pulse rate and blood pressure.

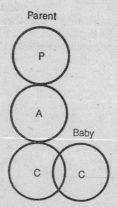

Figure 15. The Initial Symbiosis

As soon as Baby begins sucking on Mama's nipple, a complicated set of hormonal reactions take place in Mama's body, causing her milk to flow and her uterus to contract. Nursing mothers report that their milk begins to flow when they hear their babies' cries, or even think about them. Suckling can be a very intense experience for mothers. While Baby is nuzzling and sucking at the breast, Mama's sensations range from mild arousal to orgasm. While many women in our culture do not expect

* Symbiosis also develops with those who combine tender loving care and bottle feeding.

such sexual reactions during breast-feeding, they are in fact both common and entirely normal.

Within the symbiotic relationship, babies begin to learn about basic trust. They develop trust in themselves that they can cope and be effective. Within a few days they learn to find their source of food. They root around and zero in on the nipple with noticeable improvement.

Babies also learn to trust that their environment will respond to them. The grownups learn to identify the babies' needs more accurately. With each subsequent baby, parents accomplish their part of establishing the relationship with increasing competence.

In some families more than one person enters into symbiosis with the baby. The typical nuclear family is Mama, Daddy, and Baby. Another frequent unit is Mama, Grandma, and Baby. A structural diagram which depicts two grownups in symbiosis with the baby is presented below:

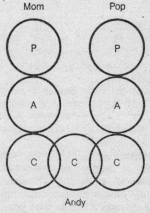

Figure 16. Symbiosis with More Than One Grown up

From the beginning babies demonstrate new aspects of their personalities each day. Infants differentiate light and dark and various shapes and designs very early. They move in response to familiar voices. Within a few weeks they turn their heads to follow bright objects with their eyes. Although they cannot think to solve problems, they actively collect data and learn a great deal. A structural diagram of a young infant even in the first months of life includes some energy in the primitive Adult (see Figure 18, p. 89).

During this early phase of rapid internal and external development, infants need nurturing parents who respond adequately to their needs for food, air, strokes, and protection from overwhelming and painful external stimuli.

The tasks of early parenting are:

1. To think for the baby—to hear distress signals, to notice what is going on, and to figure out what the baby needs.

2. To nurture the baby—to take care of the baby in an effective way so that the baby feels safe, comfortable, and responded to when expressing a need.

Parenting for Different Traits

Babies show differences very early from one baby to another, from one family to another, and from one culture to another. Some of these variations are genetically based, like eye color and nervous system; but many of the differences are learned.

Parents respond to their babies in ways which reflect the parents' beliefs about infants. Such beliefs vary from culture to culture. Their perceptions include answers to such questions as: how delicate, competent, responsible, and aggressive are babies?

First babies, those with handicaps, and babies which remain alive after a number of unsuccessful pregnancies, are usually perceived as delicate. Parents use very careful touching, and sometimes very little touching (incubator babies in the past). Parents who see their infants as delicate, worry and try to anticipate their every need. They pay attention to such things as slight breezes and work hard to protect their offspring from dangers which they perceive (evil spells, germs, changes in temperature, etc.).

Our culture values initiative and independence. We perceive our children as aggressive and competent. Today we expect our infants to let us know when they need something and to become increasingly active. Our Western frame of reference colors our belief about the baby's next psychological task, which is to develop a primitive understanding of the following statement: "By being active I can get my needs met."* This diagram describes the sequence of learning:

Need $\longrightarrow$ Action $\longrightarrow$ Response $\longrightarrow$ Success
(pain, hunger) (cries, roots) (strokes, food) (pleasure)

Babies need to become increasingly aware of their needs, to do something active about getting their need met, and to be rewarded for their efforts. Each time they succeed, they learn how to be effective and increase their competence.

If Baby rides on Mama's body next to her skin, Baby continues to root. Rooting starts as a reflex action. If it is reinforced, it becomes Baby's main way of communicating "I'm hungry!" If Baby is in a crib, Baby learns to cry lustily, and Pop or Mama respond with a bottle of milk. Whatever the circumstances, babies learn something about the world, and which kind of behavior works. When their actions result in a positive response from grownups, then babies feel a sense of power, importance, and competence: "I have impact."

Once the symbiosis is firmly established, we parents should be able to go about our business without getting uptight over our infants' every squeak; we should avoid the extremes of either overprotection or neglect.

Overprotection teaches passivity, and the belief that people are mind readers: "Mother knew, why don't you?" "If you loved me, you would know what I need." If we parents identify our children's needs before they ever feel discomfort, we interfere with their learning how to get in touch with their own needs, and learning to ask.

Neglect also teaches passivity, and the belief that people can't be trusted. The most extreme non-response is to not hear the baby's distress. We can do this by running the vacuum cleaner, watching TV, "tuning out," or "for-

* Pam Levin used this phrase and the following diagram to explain the developmental theory she has evolved in her treatment methods.

getting" to check on the baby. Another way to discount is to let little Lisa herself work up into an hysterical rage with such justification as "It's good for her lungs; all babies cry." Such discounting teaches Lisa that "My needs don't count. I cannot do anything effective about getting my needs met."

Another pitfall to avoid is that of deciding we are helpless, and making our infants responsible for our discomfort. We do that when we take the passive position: "There's nothing *I* can do about that kid's distress." Little Herbie gets the message that Mama or Pop cannot stand his crying. If compelled, Herbie will give up the behavior (crying) and discount his personal needs in order to meet the more vital one of keeping the only source of food and strokes around (Mom or Pop). Under such circumstances Herbie learns to comply with injunctions such as "Don't feel," "Don't cry," and "Don't notice bodily distress."

Pop's Child ego state, upset and desperate, conveys the message that he cannot stand Herbie's feelings and crying (need expressing behavior). Pop needs to energize his Adult ego state to figure out a new solution or seek new information; he also needs to energize his Parent ego state to soothe his distraught infant. Instead, Pop

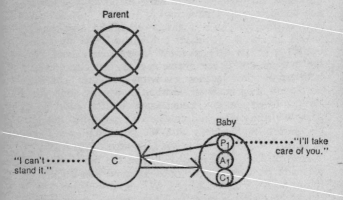

Figure 17. Reversed Symbiosis *

* Jon and Laurie Weiss presented this diagram and the ideas it illustrates at the ITAA Summer Conference, August 1972.

reverses the symbiosis, and expects someone else (in this case Herbie) to solve the problem. Since Herbie's survival depends at this point on taking care of Pop, he cooperates. Herbie prematurely puts energy into the Primitive Parent in his Child ego state. Herbie takes care of Pop by discounting his own needs. Symbiosis is thus distorted, but serves to keep Herbie alive.

Abusive parents also flip the symbiosis. They expect the baby to love them, and they make the baby responsible for their discomfort. They "punish" the baby for being "defiant," "ungrateful," etc. Such babies often die. Those that live learn how to be abusive parents themselves.

Stroking the Baby

Basic human needs include air, food, water, and strokes. Young infants need unconditional positive strokes. They attract the loving positive strokes they need to live. Most grownups, no matter how stuffy, react warmly to sleeping or cooing babies. Their tiny size, velvety skin, outstretched hands, curling toes, and button noses are fun to touch.

Babies are very adaptable. They learn to prefer whichever strokes they can get: holding, patting, rubbing, poking, covering, exercising, bathing, rocking, talking, and singing.

Strokes which help soothe colic include: tilting, resting downhill on Pop's lap, pats to Baby's bottom, rocking chair, auto or buggy rides on bumpy surfaces, etc. Beer or wine or a teaspoon of bourbon and sugar added to a bottle of warm water is the accepted cure for colic in some cultures. (Hot tea or alcoholic beverages can also have tranquilizing effects on tense parents!)

The way babies are nurtured influences their perception of themselves and the kinds of strokes which they recognize as familiar, comfortable, acceptable, etc. Babies who are stroked by only one person gain confidence in their own competence and worth, and develop intense one-to-one relationships. They learn to trust one person deeply. They may or may not choose to trust others. Babies who consistently experience effective nurturing from a small group of loving grownups also feel competent, and they have a head start in learning to trust others. Babies do well when they are cared for by a small group of caregivers who give warm and predictable strokes.

In many cultures the ordinary place for infants is on their mothers' or fathers' bodies, or in the arms of nurturing relatives.

Russians expect strangers as well as relatives to stroke their children. In streetcars and trains strangers frequently place children in the laps of those who are sitting. The grownups automatically start transacting with the little strangers.

Being left in a crib was common in certain parts of Western civilization. This may account for the popularity of sensitivity groups where we get permission to touch again. Fortunately, devices resembling ancient slings and back packs are now very popular for babies.

In our country, baby-sitters frequently help care for infants. Babies who have happy experiences with nurturing baby-sitters from early on develop into children who take nurturing from outsiders in stride. Another mechanism small American families use to enlarge their "clan" is to "adopt" friends and neighbors. Those who live in communes also select their own "clan" rather than inherit them.

Today we live in a very complex, rapidly changing world. We must prepare our children to cope with change and complexity in relative comfort. By offering them various stimuli, we help them learn to adapt to and to enjoy change. Babies who are amply stroked in many ways are most apt to grow to their full potential both physically and mentally.

Babies can, however, experience stroke overload. When some babies are stroked too much they respond by tuning the strokes out. Others respond with irritability, restlessness, and a startled appearance. Healthy babies usually show when they have had enough strokes by falling asleep. Babies know much about what they need, and we parents can learn from our infants.

Psychological Tasks of New Parents

We find fulfillment in parenthood according to our individual scripts. Parenthood validates our sexuality. We have begun another human life with our own bodies in a moment of passion. Our love has borne fruit. It is evident that we have been sexually intimate.

We experience new status; we are recognized as grownups and move into the position with our children that our parents held with us.

We also terminate a stage of freedom and enter into a phase of commitment which lasts from sixteen to twenty-plus years. We parents experience mixed feelings about our babies, more intensely with the first baby, and more mildly with each subsequent baby, depending on how successfully we completed our psychological work regarding our first child.

When we behold our infants we recycle old feelings from our own infancy. Our earliest months were times of nurturing and distress; the bad feelings connected with that distress are aroused once again in some part of our own primitive Child ego state. Such "flashbacks" can be very painful. If we recognize them for what they are, however, we have the opportunity to redo the original problem. This time we can find a better solution; as grownups who can think and talk, we can say what we feel and figure out what we need.

Two common emotional hazards in our society are feelings of rejection in young fathers, and feelings of depression in young mothers. While each of us rekindles our very young Child feelings, our mate experiences a similar upsurge of early childhood feelings.

In our society young fathers frequently feel neglected. A man's relationship with his mate is disrupted by her hospitalization and by the demands of a helpless infant. While Pop's Parent ego state wants to take care of his family, and his Adult ego state is aware that Baby is completely dependent, Pop's own Child ego state remains needy, vulnerably young, and stroke-hungry. Scripts in our society customarily call for the father to be left out while mother and infant establish symbiosis. Maternal and infant care practices in our country have contributed to this isolation. If Pop grew up with brothers and sisters he is also confronted with redoing his original feelings toward rivals. He misses out on sexual strokes. The length of time he goes without sex is unrelated to his needs, and is dictated by the feelings and opinions of others. Obstetricians vary in their opinions about when it is safe to resume intercourse. Cultures dictate various rules, and women vary in how soon they welcome renewed sexual contact with their mates. Men in our culture are discouraged from learning to say what they need, and from learning many ways to get strokes. From earliest childhood, they hear things like, "Don't be a sissy," and "Boys don't cry."

Childbirth completes the reproductive cycle in a very special way for the woman. As she watches her baby, she flashes back on her own infancy. She rekindles the earliest transactions with her own mother, her early experiences with copying Mama, with holding dolls, and singing to them. But that is not all. This baby is not a doll. There is no laying aside a needy crying infant to go out to play, or do anything else when the infant's survival depends on immediate responsive parenting. The most common distressing bad feeling women in our society experience after giving birth is depression, known as "the after-baby blues."

Johanna's account is typical among young families in our society.

I remember the nightmare of weeks without adequate sleep, of quarrels and irritation and guilt feelings: "I love my baby, what's wrong with me?" The temporary after-baby blues that I read about felt like the forever-all-engulfing blacks! I remember the defeat of failing at breast feeding, I felt desperate and isolated. "I have two psychology degrees. I should know what to do, and I should do it all by myself, that's my job," I kept saying to myself.

Somehow, in preparing for parenthood, I had not anticipated the impact of those bad feelings. I was puzzled; I figured there must be something wrong with me. I blamed myself for Tanya's colic, and did not ask for help. Whom could I ask? My parents were two thousand miles away and poor. They couldn't afford to come, and I was not even sure I would want them. Whenever I thought about my mother I felt inadequate and angry. My nearest neighbor was sickly. The cleaning girl was so dumb, she put fingerprints of furniture polish on some of our unprotected pictures. I was better off without her!

What I did about it was what I usually did about problems—research the subject. I followed the advice of the known baby books. Dr. Spock said, "Trust yourself, and try these. . . ." So I observed the baby closely, tried the methods I read about, and eventually figured out what to do for her.

My husband dealt with the problem in his customary way; he worked harder than ever at his job, worrying about our future, and left the baby-tending to me. He figured since I was a child psychologist I probably knew what I was doing. We both agreed that it was my job. The most significant thing he did to help was walk Tanya at night on the weekends, when he didn't have to work the next day. It was hard for me to sleep when I heard her crying in the living room and heard him cuss, but I felt better —at least it wasn't *me* making the baby cry, and he didn't have much better luck comforting her than I did!

As new parents we must also deal with our anger and frustration. Feeling murderous toward the baby is not uncommon. Most parents control such impulses; they take the baby to a sympathetic relative or neighbor— "Take her before I kill her. I'm going to take a drink, nap, pill, or walk!"

Abusive parents usually have experienced abuse in their own infancy. They did not get much nurturing. They isolate themselves from ordinary sources of strokes (friends, meetings, relatives, etc.). They need to take responsibility for the intensity of their bad feelings, and to make safe provisions for their babies in moments of extreme stress. Parents Anonymous is an organization of parents with abusive tendencies, who are helping themselves to control their behavior, and to pay attention to their own needs. Crisis nurseries are available in some communities now, where parents can bring their babies for temporary relief and safekeeping. The treatment of choice is reparenting for themselves and getting many unconditional positive strokes from someone who is willing to nurture and support them.

Needs of New Parents

The basic needs of new parents are similar to those of their babies: good nutrition, good hygiene, and strokes.

Good nutrition significantly affects the mother's rate of recovery. Good diet ensures that the mother's body will heal properly, and that her body can manufacture milk with no burden to herself. Good diet also helps her to feel cared for. Good nutrition is also important for the father. We connect food with our earliest ways of getting strokes, and most of us feel more loved and cared for when we are well fed. Certain vitamins directly affect the nervous system, and promote a calmer attitude.

Good hygiene includes paying attention to rest. Whoever is attending to a new baby does not get to sleep according to the usual pattern. We must lay aside our own rhythms to adjust to the baby's. It is important, therefore, that we use our Adult ego state to figure out ways to cut down on energy output, and to invent new ways to get rest. We need to use our Nurturing Parent on ourselves, to ensure that we are entitled to rest, and to redefine our priorities. (A rested parent and well-tended baby are more important than a neat house.)

Childbirth education courses and organizations like LaLeche (breast-feeding counseling), which are family-oriented, include lengthy discussions of the needs of new parents. They draw on some of the folk wisdom that our immediate predecessors discounted. Traditional cultures still have practices which see to the nurturing of new parents—in some families the new parents go back to their original parents. The young mother experiences the familiar nurturing of her own childhood while she learns to nurture her baby. Some societies have designated individuals called "doulas" who come into the home to do the housework and prepare the meals, leaving the new mother relaxed and free to tend her baby, and the new father well cared for and well fed.

Some important questions for parents to consider when selecting someone to help out include:

1. How do we feel in the presence of that person?
2. Do we feel relaxed, nurtured, important, in control?
3. Does the helper tend to take over and squelch our own beginning attempts at parenting? Or does the helper provide support and promote feelings of competence?

Young families in communes reconstruct their own clans of choice, living right with them. Friends, whose nerves are less frayed (at the moment), provide strokes to the new parents, and help out by babysitting for a while, until Mama and Pop have time to get some peace, take a walk, make love without interruption, or take in a movie.

Men in our society are taught to seek and expect only sexual strokes, and only those available in conventional sexual intercourse. What about giving each other sexual pleasure in new ways? What about giving each other strokes that don't necessarily involve sex, such as brow and back rubs, feet and hand rubs, new kinds of caresses, and simple things like hugs and holding hands?

Other strokes include verbal messages of love and appreciation, careful listening and feedback to what each other is saying. Vera, a young mother, says that she feels especially loved and cared for when Cyd, her man, brings home a sack of toasted marshmallows, her favorite treat. We can be clear, straight, and specific about what we need.

Parents who accomplish the psychological tasks of parenthood with their first child experience subsequent babies with more "know-how" and poise. Those who have not done the psychological work reexperience the unresolved issues, and remain uncomfortable until they sort out their feelings and get what they need.

SUMMARY

Babies need unconditional love and strokes, in addition to air, food, and physical protection. While being stroked, babies learn that they can cope with life and trust the grownups to respond to them when they express needs. This trust usually evolves in the relationship between the biological mother (or her substitute) and the baby.

Symbiosis is the word in TA which describes the close relationship formed between the baby and the prime caregiver. This relationship is vital to the well-being of the baby; within symbiosis, mother and baby re-establish the rhythms they both experienced before the baby's birth.

Babies learn rapidly from the day of birth. Their behaviors initially are based on automatic reflexes, and later develop into learned behavior. They learn which kind of activity is acceptable to the people around them. Parents teach babies to fit into the family stroke system. In our present society stroking patterns differ in each home.

Parental tasks in caring for the newborn involve two major jobs. The first is noticing the baby's actions, and figuring out what the baby needs; such as food, strokes, or a clean diaper. The second task is taking care of the baby in a loving, responsive way, so the baby gets the message, "By being active I can get my needs met."

The needs of young parents count also. Many of us are startled to discover that we are redoing the psychological tasks of our own infancy, and are getting in touch with needy aspects of our Child ego states. This *recycling* of an earlier stage is stimulated by the new infant in our care, which arouses Child needs in us that we had previously ignored. Both parents need special nurturing, and should find ways to get it—from each other, and from supportive relatives, adopted clan, or trusted friends.

EXERCISES

---

1. Trust Exercise (Blind Walk): The purpose of this exercise is to help you get in touch with the original symbiotic relationship between parent and child, and to experience some of the dynamics involved in building a relationship of trust.

Rules:	Purpose of Rules:
No talking———	to re-create preverbal stage
No seeing ———	to decommission Adult ego state, and promote state of dependence

   Read the exercise through before starting.
   a. Choose partners.
   b. Decide who will be blind first and who will therefore lead first.
   c. Blind person: close your eyes.
      1. Stay in touch with your feelings.
      2. Notice all of your sensations—touch, smell, body position (arms, legs, etc.).
      3. Notice what happens to your feelings of comfort and trust as you experience various phenomena.
   d. Leader:
      1. Help your partner experience as much of the environment as it is safe to do.
      2. Protect your partner from being hurt and frightened.
      3. Think about where your partner is moving and anticipate consequences.
      4. Return to home base in five or ten minutes.
   e. Discuss:
      1. Blind person give leader feedback on how safe and secure you felt, what sensations you noticed, and what you did and did not like about your trip.
      2. Leader tell partner what you say and what measures you took to provide stimuli, safety.
   f. Reverse positions.

g. Discuss as in *e.*

    1. Leader, did you lead any differently because of your experience when you were blind?

2. Re-create your original script outline:

a. Describe your family. Think about all of the important members. Include significant aunts, uncles, and pets. Reconstruct the family picture when you were born. Think about the gathering—christening, birth, circumcision—the event at which you were presented to your clan. Give time for your fantasy to develop. In your fantasy have each one of them make two comments about you: one that you like and one that you don't like. Notice your bodily responses as you recall those early messages.

b. How do each of those messages affect your life now? Are you complying with or rebelling against any of those messages? Have you changed any of them?

3. Get in touch with the script you are giving your child:

a. Picture your baby—

    one year from now
    starting school
    ten years from now
    twenty years from now

b. Think about how you want your child to be at each age. Notice how you feel when you picture your child leaving for school, leaving home. Think about what you can realistically expect your child to be at each of those stages.

c. What are the most important hopes you have for your child?

d. What ways can you convey those messages to your baby right now? What are you willing to do about yourself right now, to develop personally those same qualities you wish for your child?

e. What are the most important fears you have concerning your child?

f. What can you do to diminish those fears in yourself right now?

READINGS

Benedek, Therese. "Parenthood as a Developmental Phase." *Journal of Psychoanalytic Association*, Vol. 7 (1959).

Berne, Eric. *What Do You Say After You Say Hello?* New York: Grove Press, 1972.

Children's Bureau Publication No. 8. *Infant Care*. Washington, D.C.: Department of Health, Education, and Welfare.

Fraiberg, Selma H. *The Magic Years*. New York: Charles Scribner's Sons, 1959.

Gesell, Arnold, and Ilg, Frances. *Infant and Child in the Culture of Today*. New York: Harper and Row, 1974.

Ilg, Frances, and Ames, Louise Bates. *Child Behavior*. New York: Harper and Row, 1955; and Dell Publishing Company, 1956.

James, Muriel, and Jongeward, Dorothy. *Born to Win*. Reading, Massachusetts: Addison-Wesley, 1971.

Newton, Niles. *Family Book of Child Care*. New York: Harper and Row, 1957.

Pryor, Karen. *Nursing Your Baby*. New York: Harper and Row, 1963.

⑥

Introduction to Physics

(Exploration)

Stimulus Hunger

Babies enter the *exploratory phase* of psychological development when they show that air, food, and strokes are not enough. They actively seek more stimulation and complain when that need is not met. They show a strong desire for more varied experiences. Their Little Professor, the primitive Adult in their Child ego state, actively engages in data collection. Babies in this phase struggle and fuss until they can see what's going on, even before they can completely support their own heads. Infant seats, modern versions of the cradle board, and back packs are useful devices at this stage of development. Infant seats are very light and portable. They fit into the baskets of supermarket buggies, and can be carried around the house from room to room. Babies receive support, can be placed at partly upright angles, and yet fall asleep with little disturbance. Slightly older babies riding on their parent's backs can look around to their heart's content, and just as peacefully fall asleep.

At about six months of age, or whenever babies start teething, sucking becomes painful. Biting and chewing hurt the baby's tender gums, yet are the same activities which eventually relieve the pain, and help the teeth cut through the gums. Babies experience both pain and pleasure during this phase. This dilemma, having simultaneous positive and negative feelings toward the same person or thing, is called ambivalence. In addition to learning ambivalence, babies learn that not all problems can be easily solved. They have control over whether or not they suck, but they have no control over whether or not they hurt. Nursing also becomes problematical for Mama, until Baby learns how to continue nursing without biting Mama's nipple.

Baby's enjoyment of looking at the world gives way to the need to touch it. Babies first manage to grasp and hold things by accident; occasionally they brush their mouths and automatically suck and chew. Babies are fascinated by this effect and soon learn to do it purposefully. Beginning explorers look at objects they manage to hold, rub those objects on their faces, smell them, and eventually taste them. They carry everything they can grasp to their mouth for oral inspection.

The shiny spoon at mealtime becomes a moving target to track and to capture. A good way to respond to such efforts is to allow Baby to have the spoon. Ambidextrous babies may require two spoons. At this point parents can allow babies to take over self-feeding or they can help out with a third spoon, which rapidly becomes more attractive than the spoons already captured.

Babies are then ready to feed themselves finger food, like string beans and bits of tender ground meat. Puréed foods are nice for squishing and finger painting, but they are not helpful in self-feeding.

Self-feeding helps babies take their first steps to independence and self-mastery. Parents who insist on maintaining control teach the competitive structure, with its emphasis on power struggles. If parents choose to do battle by fastening their babies' hands down, the grownups will win (we're still bigger, smarter, and stronger), but what babies learn is, "It's either you or me, and right now it's you." In the above illustration parents win the battle for power, efficiency, or neatness (whatever Adapted Child need parents are fulfilling), but they win at their babies' expense.

The competitive structure is a frame of reference (way of thinking) which implies that a person who wins does so at another's expense, as in a race or in a poker game.

In life one competes; one either wins or one loses. Only one can occupy the Child ego state position and be needy. Only one can be O.K., etc.

There are alternative ways of thinking. The cooperative structure assumes that both or more can win. Both people count. Both can need, both needs can be met. No one has to lose. Baby can experience increasing mastery and competence. Parents can just as readily feel good about their baby's growing assertiveness, and congratulate themselves on promoting independence, and on being patient with messes, etc.

Speech is another skill which babies master gradually. When we mimic our babies' babblings they are delighted; they respond by increasing their efforts to "talk." At about seven months of age their attention to specific words greatly increases. Verbal transactions change from cooing, gurgling, and babbling to greatly increased interest in specific sounds. Babies listen and pick out words that they hear frequently. They act like they know who mama, daddy, and doggie are, and what "no-no" and "bye-bye" mean. Soon they begin imitating key words. Parents at this phase should notice whatever the baby is attending to and name it: "nose," "toe," "light." In addition, words describing textures and temperatures like "soft" or "cold" can be used when the infant is touching a surface. "Up" and "down" can be used when parent and infant are having fun exercising. The ability to say a recognizable word usually occurs before the first birthday. First words include the names of significant adults—"Mama," "Da-Da"—and things—"ba" (ball or bottle).

Little Missy is forming important early concepts about her O.K.-ness. Her self-image is directly related to her physical abilities, her mastery of her world, and the way important adults treat her.

By eight or nine months of age, the primitive Adult ego state (A_1) has developed to the point that Missy begins to know and remember an object even when it is out of sight. She looks and crawls around corners looking for the source of a noise, especially if she knows the sound: Daddy, or another important person. If Mama puts a pillow over her favorite rattle while she's watching, Missy will lift the pillow and find the rattle.

Babies' intellectual growth also shows in their ability

to distinguish between strangers and individuals with whom they transact regularly. Babies who act "strange" may protest loudly or mildly disapprove of strangers. They include among strangers doting grandparents who do not live nearby, and whom they do not recognize. Their tolerance of strangers greatly increases when they are safe in the arms of Mama or Pop.

Much of what infants learn during the exploratory phase they teach themselves as they touch, taste, turn, chew, and smell everything they can reach. They need time to repeat these activities, to confirm their observations, and to make the connection between cause and effect.

Figure 18. Structural Diagram of an Exploratory Infant

"When I bang it, it makes a noise; when I cry, somebody comes." Their natural curiosity starts the process. Freedom to be curious whets their appetite for discovery. The more they discover, the more curious they become, and the more they desire to learn.

Babies repeat activities over and over, building motor skills. Like careful scientists they redo experiments to make sure. They pull at things and watch what happens. Much of what they learn is brand-new to them. They have no other data to match what they are learning. It takes many experiments to understand a law of physics and many more to "prove" it is really law.

During this Exploration stage the family is constantly reminded there is a baby around. Susie is busy getting into things and usually is learning the rudiments of crawling uphill (climbing). She babbles and enjoys trying to copy sounds. Games like pat-a-cake and peek-a-boo, and "wave bye-bye" are great fun. Nursing is more sociable (after a few sucks she smiles and coos with the milk dripping messily).

Nine months is a very exploratory age. Most infants are mobile in some form or another: seat first, crawling backward, wriggling, one knee and one foot, etc., and jargoning (which sounds like conversation but the words are not English). They develop considerable hand-eye motor coordination; they can approach a small object with thumb and first finger and pick it up. They pull at cabinets and drawers, lamp cords, and diaper pails, and notice different effects. The drawer under the oven usually has a wide variety of drums and cymbals (pots and pans) which are sturdy and make fascinating noises.

While growing, the baby goes in and out of fussy periods. An erupting tooth is a frequent cause of discomfort during the first few years of life. These waves of dissatisfaction interspersed with periods of friendliness allow for small trials of separation and give lessons in learning to tolerate frustration.

Once babies are down on the ground crawling around and drooling and getting grubby, they look less appealing. Their crying gets louder and more demanding. This lessening appeal and restlessness promote gradual and natural separation of the symbiotic parent and child.

The beginning crawler continues to need physical stroking plus a different kind of attention and protection.

A GUIDE LIST FOR PARENTING
A YOUNG PHYSICIST

1. Provide a safe environment.
2. Provide opportunities to experiment with surfaces, sizes, motion, gravity, distance, etc.
3. Allow consequences of experiments within safe limits.

4. Allow increasing independence in feeding and self-entertainment.

5. Allow child to structure some of his/her own time.

6. Evolve a new balance of conditional and unconditional strokes so that the child experiences strokes for doing things. Whenever possible, make conditional strokes positive.

7. Teach beginning problem-solving skills when child is motivated to learn.

8. Allow the child to experience a growing repertoire of feelings: joy, contentment, excitement, anger, fear, frustration, ambivalence, etc.

9. Be aware of the messages your body and face are giving. That is the language your child can understand.

10. Name objects of interest with single words like: "nose," "toe," "ball," etc.

Safety

The parents at this time provide a safe environment to help the Young Physicist experiment safely. From a personality structure point of view, adequate protection allows the child to develop appropriately. Babies who don't get enough protection put energy prematurely into thinking, concentrating mainly on how to survive. When babies don't feel safe, they have less energy to enjoy exploring, which is so important to their development.

In addition to personality structure concerns, it is also important to be aware that accidents are the chief cause of death of children between the ages of one and four. Automobiles are involved most often. Fire, drowning, poisons, and falls are next in decreasing frequency. Bathrooms, basements, and kitchens are the most hazardous areas in homes.

To child-proof the house, put up or away as many dangerous items as possible. Remove the child from danger consistently—that means every time the child goes near it. Save "no" for the very few important things; distraction works well during the first two years. As soon as the child is motivated to do something, show the child a safe way to do it.

Teaching Karen to *do* safely allows her to develop in several ways. She learns about consequences and the laws of nature, she becomes more familiar with her own body and its limitations, and she develops increasing self-control and self-direction. Following is an example of how she can gather several kinds of information while eating. As soon as Karen learns to get her hand to her mouth she starts learning to feed herself. As with all new skills, she misses and messes at first. She learns rapidly as she rewards herself immediately with tasty tidbits. Mama or Pop can improve her chances of success by using foods that are easy to grasp. When giving Karen heated food, Pop says the word, "Hot." Karen very quickly learns to associate the steam with the word "hot." She perceives the heat, and approaches the food gingerly with one finger; this way she learns safely and at first hand what "hot" means. Later, when she approaches the heated oven and Mama says "hot" Karen acts quite aware, and (she has more ability to remember now) makes no mistakes.

Change in Stroke Economy

A new balance of positive unconditional and conditional strokes and independent activity is appropriate at this stage. Explorers are ready to learn about entertaining themselves. Too much attention and protection also interfere with babies learning to be assertive. This concept—expecting the child to learn how to structure more of his/her own time—is crucial at this stage. Too much protection interferes with growth. If babies are not permitted to crawl around (even though drooling, crawling babies get grubby), they may get the message that exploring is bad, not safe, not an option, and end up with injunctions such as "Don't think," or one of its variants: "Don't find out, don't be aware." Some learn "Don't leave, don't grow up, don't be independent." Overprotection teaches children to be passive and to wait. This passive behavior works for infants while they live with doting parents, which is why they learn it; passivity, however, does not work as well when they leave home and expect others to take care of them.

Distractibility is a characteristic of this age, and often is helpful in encouraging babies to attend to something they can enjoy, rather than stay frustrated with something they cannot manage (or may not have). Explorers thus begin to learn the concept of options. "If I can't have/master this, I can have/master that." Some parents overdo the use of distractibility to the point where they pick up babies and play whenever they express discomfort. This parental response interferes with the babies getting in touch with needs, frustrations, and a variety of other feelings. The parents' Adapted Child may be responding to some of their own Critical Parent tapes like, "Good mothers always have happy babies," or, "Don't let your baby cry." Overprotection also protects the parent's Child ego state from the irritation of a crabby infant.

Some parents refuse to move knickknacks. They invest energy in teaching the infant "don't touch." Freddy, being the bright capable infant he is, learns to comply or rebel. This learning takes energy. The problem with such learning is that since Freddy is concentrating on learning to obey, he has less energy to think for himself. At this age he is too young to learn self-discipline. He is freer to develop Little Professor when he can roam, explore, and taste safely, according to his own internal drives.

By the time they have learned to walk, babies have distinct personalities. If they have been allowed choices they know with whom and what they want to play. Outgoing toddlers respond to nearly anyone who is friendly; they go with arms outstretched for strokes whenever they feel needy.

In addition to being able to throw, babies can purposefully release. This skill develops a full six months after they have learned to grasp. Once they learn, they practice letting go with tireless enthusiasm: food over the side of the high chair, toys out of the crib, etc. This is an opportunity for parents to allow the child to learn consequences and to be introduced to the rudiments of problem-solving. Attentive parents who jump too fast to retrieve everything may find themselves exhausted victims in a never-ending pastime. There are actually other options: 1) Let the food or toy lie. 2) Allow Margie to eat and play close to the floor, so she can recover dropped food herself. 3) Tie the toys on strings and teach the game of "fish." 4) Give her just enough food to satisfy hunger (one piece at a time).

Explanation at this point is fruitless. Children still depend on our body language to understand us because their command of language is so limited.

Some programming of family values occurs in the Primitive Parent of the Child ego state (P_1). The little person learns these values from conditional strokes. Families which value activity and vigor allow aggressive, assertive, and noisy play, and they stroke active babies. Families which value neatness and obedience will stroke the children when they are neat and obedient.

Little explorers recognize "no" and will stop when they hear it (at least momentarily).

This is the stage at which some of the most lasting and hard-to-recall programming is occurring. Many messages which are recorded in Primitive Parent (P_1) without words are impossible to reach through ordinary memory which involves language. Decisions made at this early phase tend to occur under duress and some apparent threat to survival. Children who feel generally secure feel less compulsion to make important decisions and spend less energy on P_1. One of the other major difficulties with early decisions is that they are usually based on inadequate and distorted information collected by a very infantile computer (A_1).

Joey, our young navigator, indicates when he's in need of strokes and will seek those which he has learned are available in his family. If he is ignored except when he's in trouble (negative conditional strokes), he may decide that the way to ensure a steady supply of strokes is to stay in trouble and learn the injunctions "don't be happy," and/or "don't succeed." Joey forms important primitive concepts about his own personal worth and adequacy, and his ability to learn.

When he's in distress Joey needs help from Mama or Pop to work at identifying the problem (stuck under a table, can't get a toy out, needing a nap), and to cope with the problem, rather than just be distracted with pat-a-cake or a cookie. As he continues to mature, he needs to learn to cope with problems himself.

One day Joey crawled to the basement stairs and cried because he could see other children down there making happy noises and he wanted to investigate. Mama could have distracted him with treats or a toy; she would have done so if the basement (see paragraph on distraction, p. 90) were unsafe or otherwise off-limits. Joey needs to know that there are times when he can't have what he wants. The basement was safe, however. Managing the stairs was the main problem. If Mama distracts Joey he learns "don't climb, don't explore, don't feel frustration." This takes less time at the moment for Mama, but Joey is robbed of a learning opportunity when he is highly motivated. She can solve the problem for Joey and carry him down. But if she does this Joey learns "whenever I have a problem the thing to do is get agitated and expect someone else to fix it." (Don't tackle problems, don't exert effort.) To teach Joey to be effective Mama turns him around so that his rear end is facing the stairs. Then she puts Joey's knee down on the first step, followed by the other knee, and so on. Joey learns *through his body* at this age.

Energy Crisis

We parents find these early phases very energy- and time-consuming. While the developing toddlers' enthusiasm for living is delightful and contagious, the energy we use to keep them safe without undue restraint is enormous.

Women who keep the traditional role of baby-tender and homemaker in an isolated nuclear family are most apt to feel this energy drain. Their own stroke supply becomes increasingly depleted by typical conflicts (see Figure 19).

Mama is more apt to get into a competitive structure if she bases all her worth on being a mama. (You have to have a child around to be a mama.)

We parents recycle our own exploratory phase along with our children. Those of us who had satisfactory experiences as infants "automatically" encourage activity,

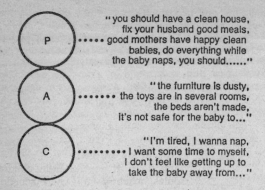

Figure 19. Structural Analysis of Trapped-Mother Syndrome

and provide safety with casual alertness, while we go about our own grown-up lives. Those of us who were inhibited or inadequately protected have some problems. We may redo the scripts handed to us, or we may go overboard in the opposite direction. For instance, a mother who herself felt discounted and neglected may give her young explorer too much attention. A father who was allowed to do unsafe things (and lived through it) may not take ordinary precautions, and pay too little attention to the exploring baby (e.g., he falls asleep while watching TV and Junior pulls out a drawer of knives atop his head).

If our parents anticipated our needs when we were infants, we may continue to expect our mates to show love by "knowing" what we need without asking. If we experienced serious threats during the Exploration stage, we may get in touch with overwhelming nameless fears for which we have no explanation. (One young, competent mother found herself suddenly fearful of driving the car, an activity which she had done for years.)

If we are attempting to raise our children differently than we learned, we are likely to experience internal conflict. We may give our children one message from our Nurturing Parent ego state, and an opposing one from our Adapted Child ego state. Such incongruity does not mean we are bad or liars. It means we have some unresolved Exploratory tasks of our own. Now that we are grownups, we can notice our needs with our Adult ego state, and take steps to get what we need. We can solve the problem various ways: 1) learn from other successful parents whom we like; 2) find a Nurturing Parent who will give us what we need; 3) enter therapy to resolve the issue, etc.

An active, exploratory infant challenges the endurance of a first-class athlete. We have a dual task: recycling our own Exploration stage, and keeping up with our growing infants. Our needs are very similar to theirs—rest, nutrition, strokes, and new stimulation. We need to see to it that our needs *and* baby's needs are met.

Rest: Nap when Baby does. If several little children are on different schedules, teach them a new schedule that is convenient for everyone. Let the house go. It will wait. Ask for permission from your spouse, or a Nurturing Parent your Child ego state will listen to, to give you permission to relax your standards.

Be intelligent with your use of time. Set aside energy-consuming projects until your baby is in preschool. Look around for other parents who will swap baby-sitting with you.

Think about ways to conserve energy and tempers. A house with a fenced back yard or a nearby park is more important when the children are young. Plain meals take less time to prepare. Wash-and-wear clothes need less ironing.

If Mom has been home all day chasing Terry, she may be ready to put him up for sale. When Pop comes home for supper, he's probably tired of work, but not so tired of Terry—and therefore willing to help out. Pop can take Terry out back for a romp at suppertime, or wrestle on the living-room floor. Maybe Terry and Pop can go for a walk. Another possibility is that Pop makes supper while Mom goes for a walk.

Diet: Nutrition is an important tool in the battle of surviving early parenthood. In addition to nurturing ourselves, we refuel when we eat properly. We should feed ourselves as conscientiously as we feed our infants: take vitamins, yeast—whatever we define as nourishing. Give ourselves a glass of juice whenever we give some to our youngsters, etc.

Strokes: When we need strokes we are responsible for

asking for them. Now is the time to relearn OUR responsibility for asking for what we need. Learn to ask for strokes in a way that will get us O.K. ones (not when our spouse is mad or rushing off to a night class, or taking a roast out of the oven). If we're not getting enough strokes at home, now is the time for us to do some exploring. Who else gives good safe strokes?

Stimulation: What do we want for ourselves as persons, at this stage of our life? Look around. Explore. Does the YMCA or local high school teach a fun or stimulating course on a night when our spouse is willing to baby-sit? Confront overparenting. If either of us discount our babies' needs for becoming more independent and growing, we are also discounting ourselves as complete persons.

SUMMARY

Exploratory infants soon tire of lying in their parents' arms or in their cribs. They eagerly struggle to see the world. As soon as they develop coordination of eye and hand, they grasp everything within reach. The first experiments include chewing and tasting everything they grasp.

Teething is a significant event in a baby's life, causing discomfort and occurring intermittently for the first three years. Some of the lessons gained from painfully erupting teeth are ambivalence, various negative emotions, separation, and the knowledge that some things cannot be controlled.

As soon as they are mobile, babies explore every place they can crawl to. Their growing bodily control allows them to explore increasingly wide vistas, learning about their environment. They learn how to structure their own time, and to entertain themselves. They learn about more feelings, such as frustration. The aspect of personality which the young explorer activates is called the Primitive Adult in the Child ego state. The "Little Professor," as it is also called, collects data before knowing how to talk, and figures out problems at an intuitive level. Memory becomes more evident when the child remembers objects which are out of sight, and differentiates faces which are familiar from faces which are strange.

Infants at this phase of development need to explore safely. They need protection from serious injury; they also need to experience small consequences from which they can learn. They should have play space, free from hazards and "no-no's."

We recycle our own Exploration stage with our children, in relative delight or distress, depending on our early experiences. We also re-experience the accompanying emotions: enthusiasm, ambivalence, frustration, etc. We have to redo early unresolved psychological tasks.

Those of us who take care of a mobile baby are continually faced with an energy crisis—our own. This is a phase when fatigue and stress interfere with grown-up communication. It is easy for parents to drift apart.

Our needs are similar to those of our children, though on a more sophisticated level. Basic issues like our rest and nutrition need as much attention as those of our children. Methods for cutting corners, saving work, and getting help from others should be explored carefully.

It is equally important that we pay attention to our grown-up needs for stimulation and fun. Basing our O.K.-ness exclusively on our parenting discounts ourselves as well as our children.

EXERCISES

Crawling. The purpose of this exercise is to help you get in touch with the Exploration stage of your development, and to see what it's like to care for an exploratory baby.
1. Get a partner.
2. Read exercise through before starting.
3. a. Decide who is to be young. Be very young, before you can walk or talk. Crawl around. See what you can see. Touch, taste, pull, and push what interests you. You do not identify people as people yet, rather as interesting objects for your amusement and interest, if they happen to be in your view.
   b. Explorer, notice what each part of your body feels like.

c. Caretaker, check on the environment. Keep tabs on your partner. Keep your crawler safe. Use physical motions to control your crawler. Use language to name things.
4. Discuss your experience.
5. Reverse roles.
6. Discuss that experience.

READINGS

Children's Bureau Folder No. 48-19. "Accidents and Children" (New Edition). Superintendent of Documents, Washington, D.C.

Fraiberg, Selma H. *The Magic Years*. New York: Charles Scribner's Sons, 1959.

Gesell, Arnold, et al. *Infant and Child in the Culture of Today*. New York: Harper and Row, 1974.

Ilg, Frances, and Ames, Louise Bates. *Child Behavior*. New York: Harper and Row, 1955; and Dell Publishing Company, 1956.

Newton, Niles. *Family Book of Child Care*. New York: Harper and Row, 1957.

7

Deciding to Think

(Separation)

The main psychological tasks of toddlers are to gain further skills in speech, to learn more about their own and others' feelings, to solve some of their own basic living problems, to become separate individuals, and, finally, to energize their Adult ego states.

At eighteen months of age, most toddlers can say more than twenty words. They speak in brief sentences: "Sop it, buh!" (Stop getting so big and covering my hands, bubbles!), "Watch me how!" (Watch me while I climb this fence!), and "I show you!" Their attention span increases so that they can sit and look at something in their hands for a few minutes without becoming bored. They also develop more sense of time. They know when "now" is, and that "later" is not "now."

Children at this stage are concerned about what is theirs, as they begin to distinguish between themselves and others. This indicates a dawning sense of separate identity. Those whose Adult ego states are not yet energized play near—but not with—peers. They take a while to deal with each other's feelings. An older child who is willing to use A_2 can do quite well in social relations: conceding, distracting, and being tactful.

Children's increased wrist rotation at this stage means they can manage some of their clothing independently (for example, undressing themselves), and that they can also turn door knobs (and thus toddle out into the streets

101

wearing no clothes!). They become more skillful at such activities as filling and emptying cups, fitting things together, putting in and pulling out. They continue to notice the results of their experiments as they gradually phase into their Adult ego states.

In addition to balancing their bodies better, children gradually learn to walk backward and back up into a chair. This is a major intellectual step. Children have to be able to grasp the idea that the chair (and, by extension, the rest of the world behind them) still exists even when it is no longer in view. They also have to connect the picture of the chair in their head to the sensation of something they feel on the back of their legs.

Toilet Training

Children at this stage begin to get the idea that there is a backside to themselves. They notice their own bottoms and waste products. They show awareness of soiled diapers by walking with feet wider apart. Children learn to pay attention to their colic reflex—this is a slight cramp which signals the arrival of more waste material in the final section of their large intestines, and it stimulates the desire to empty. It takes time and practice to learn how to relax the anal sphincter while pushing in an effective way. Such coordination is best learned in a relaxed atmosphere in the squatting position. Many hemorrhoids have resulted because this skill was not learned effectively.

Toilet training is learned gradually. Children learn to hold onto urine and feces long before they learn to let go purposefully on the potty (as they learned to grasp six months before learning hand release).

When children have some control over bladder and bowels (stay dry for long periods), it is appropriate to consider toilet training. Other important clues to readiness include:

1. Sophisticated levels of lower body control (they can run, walk, climb with ease).

2. Awareness of and dissatisfaction with their own soiled diapers.

3. A communication system developed to a high enough degree that they can tell parents what's going on.

4. They know how to use the potty from watching others.

Toilet training is a part of social growth. In families where bathroom activities are casual and taken for granted, children learn easily. Some of us are influenced by relatives and significant others; we end up adapting to someone else's opinion of when to start, instead of using our own Adult ego state to see when this particular child is ready.

Households vary in general atmosphere. Some are more low-key than others. Some of us react more strongly

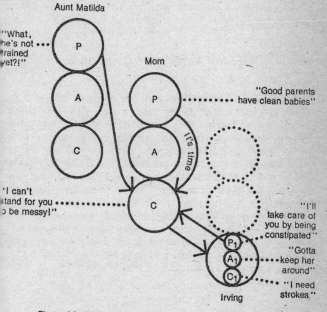

Figure 20. Toilet Training Out of Parent's Adapted Child

to negativistic behavior than do others. In most households, however, there will be a topic around which we resolve the control issue with our children. The bathroom, the dining table, and the bedroom are the three most popular arenas in our culture. We expect our children to do something which seems much more related to our own convenience and pleasure than it is to their whims. We are, in fact, pushing them for a social contract—to give up some measure of their autonomy for the pleasure of our company, and to begin thinking about how to solve some of their own personal problems.

During the *Separation stage* children take over the responsibility of keeping themselves clean and dry, satisfying their hunger, going to sleep, and abiding by certain basic safety rules. A parent who is passing on the competitive structure is apt at this point to turn such tasks into a battle of wills; the little person ends up learning that important events are win/lose situations: "It's either you or me."

"No-No" Vs. Positive Commands

Toddlers have the ability and imagination to get into more and more with every passing day. They are often dissatisfied with what they are allowed to do. They grow grumpy and negativistic, and irritate the grownups with whom they are into symbiosis. They keep doing things they should not do. This penchant for doing forbidden things is one of the reasons we parents find it so easy to fall into the habit of saying "Don't!" every time we turn around.

"Don't!" is very inhibiting. Most of the other injunctions begin with and stem from that base. With some effort and the aid of creative Little Professor, we can change "Don't!" messages into positive commands.

Following is a sample list of possibilities:

Instead of	Use
Don't run	Walk!
Don't hurt yourself	Look both ways
	Use your eyes
Don't be stupid	Think
Don't cry	It hurts (*with hug, kiss*)
Don't go out by yourself	Wait for Mommy/Daddy

Don't get it dirty	Wash your hands
Don't break it	Gentle!
Don't be afraid	Joey's scared (*with hug*)

The recommended statements listed above are all short phrases; detailed explanations at this age are not understood by the child. What Joey needs is to know that his feelings have names, that they count, and that a strong competent parent is around to protect him. Later on his speech will become more developed and his thinking grow more sophisticated. More complex commands and explanations can be added when the child is ready, particularly during the Construction stage.

It is in this stage that children move from experimental physics to experimental psychology. Having explored *things* in their environment for some time, they now increasingly turn their attention to the *people* in it. During the previous phase they had done things in order to see what happened; but now, in the Separation stage, they watch people's reactions to them, particularly those persons with whom they are in symbiosis. As time passes they "bug" us more and more. "No" becomes their favorite word.

Separation = Exasperation

Sally, who has passed her second birthday, is quite bossy with Mom and Pop. When she plays with children her own age they frequently end up in fights and tears: "It's mine! Mine!" She expresses her ambivalence about her own feelings with phrases like "yes–no" and "stop–go!" Mom says (with a good deal of exasperation), "Sally just can't seem to make up her mind!" The Terrible Two's are well-named.

Exasperation is a clue for us parents that our child is nearing the end of the Separation stage. It is important for us to recognize our own feelings about our children and to act on those feelings.

Separating children feel the opposite of their symbiotic partner. Sally, who is in symbiosis with Mom, feels miserable whenever Mom is happy. When Mom's Child ego

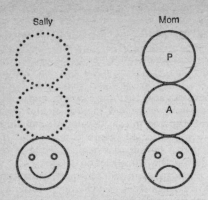

Figure 21. Two Child Ego States

state is miserable, Sally acts quite content. We clearly experience the presence of two separate people when we are both in Child ego state, and each Child is experiencing a different feeling.

The process of separation is usually stormy; one of the main feelings experienced by both children and parents is anger. We also experience irritation and frustration. When we parents name our own feelings, our children put together our words and our body language. They need to learn that each of us has these feelings, that each feeling has a name, that it is O.K. to have these feelings, and that we are supposed to do something about the way we feel. Our children learn by watching us, and by what we do to them.

Purpose of Anger

Sometimes parents who think anger is taboo unintentionally interfere with a child's learning how to deal with anger effectively. We as parents do this whenever we try to suppress or deny our own feelings. Denial of anger teaches a child that anger is bad, dangerous, etc. "If I feel angry, something bad will happen. Mommy can't stand it. Maybe it will hurt her. So maybe I better not get angry."

Others of us feel guilty about acting angry and then "try" to make it up to our kids. They learn to get what they want by manipulating us into persecuting them. Then, the "poor little victims" can get what they want from us whether or not our better judgment says it is wise.

Four important problems arise from this game. Children do not learn how to be straight about their feelings, they do not learn O.K. ways to resolve their anger, and they learn to play all three positions on the Drama Triangle (see p. 46). People learn to become Persecutor, Rescuer, and Victim in an effort to remain in symbiosis: "As long as I can get you to solve my problem, I don't have to take responsibility for my feelings, needs, and actions." People do this to avoid separation, because the players believe that separation is dangerous. The fourth psychological danger to this particular game is that children learn to get what they need while in "Victim." They get rewarded for being not-O.K.

Another way to interfere with the normal resolution of symbiosis is for us to "try" too hard to be good parents, to stand on our heads, expending huge amounts of energy anticipating our children's needs, and working

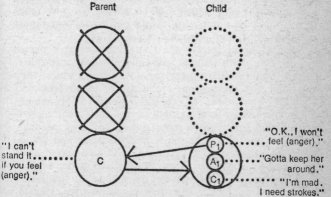

Figure 22. Transmission of the Injunction "Don't Feel" (Anger)

much too hard to avoid conflict. When we behave like this we teach our children that conflict, and being separate, is bad.

To resolve the dilemma we break the symbiosis and insist that the child think for her/himself. "I've had enough. I am tired of solving all of your problems for you. From now on you must solve some of them on your own. I will not go away; I will continue to nurture you, protect you from danger, and help you with those problems you are truly not ready to handle." This reassurance is vital. Children need to be sure that they can be separate and that we will not go away. They need to know it is O.K. for them to think and that they are indeed supposed to think.

Intellectual Development

Learning to think is a gradual process. Exploratory babies mastered sucking, looking, listening, grasping, letting go, vocalizing, and sensory motor skills. With that mastery came a basic sense of competence, and readiness to move on to the next phase. They move on to a more sophisticated level of awareness, judgment, and use of symbols (words and playing "pretend"). Even at the beginning of the separation phase they have some notions about cause and effect ("When I let go of an object, it always goes down!"). At the completion of this phase they will report that they think, and what they think about.

When children resolve the task of becoming separate and thinking, both parents and children experience relief.

Once children start using their Adult ego states, they can think and solve some problems for themselves, and recognize themselves as separate people. This ability requires a certain level of maturity of their nervous systems. Their brains have now grown to most of their adult size, and all of the major and incoming and outgoing nerve pathways to their brains and voluntary muscles are relatively complete. They are in much better control of their body and can devote more time to the larger world. They no longer have to struggle just to navigate.

Children move rapidly in intellectual development. It

is quite noticeable in Jerome's speech. He starts telling little stories about what happened "before," indicating memory and perception of time. He makes statements like "I thinked about a dog," indicating he knows he can think. He can copy a drawing of a cross, but his pictures are still rather difficult to identify.

PARENTING FOR THINKING

1. Encourage bodily freedom and mastery.
2. Allow child to express feelings both positive and negative.
3. Express your own feelings clearly and appropriately, both positive and negative.
4. Consider negative feelings as an indication of a problem to be solved.
5. Teach child problem-solving through action and short sentences.
6. Make demands and commands clear, positive, and realistic in terms of the child's ability to comprehend.
7. Offer labels for objects, activities, people, and feelings.
8. Encourage independence and thinking.
9. Let Kiddo know that Kiddo can be separate and

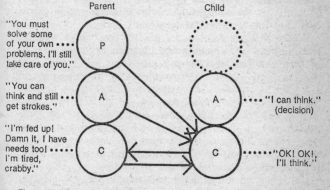

Figure 23. Structural Analysis of Parent and Child Resolving Symbiosis

that you will continue to be available, to protect and stroke.

10. Encourage verbal communication by responding to child's efforts to speak.

Psychological Tasks of Separating Parents

A child's negativistic phase is irritating, tiring, and conducive to producing a set of very grumpy parents. It is therefore important that we direct our feelings appropriately, i.e., get annoyed with our offspring for acting negativistic, rather than begin blaming each other for "spoiling that little brat."

Beginning thinkers often behave quite intelligently around grownups with whom they are not in symbiosis, but don't think at all around their symbiotic partner; for example, Sarah thinks just fine when with Daddy and the baby-sitter, but she thinks very little around Mommy (with whom she is symbiotic). It's not helpful or accurate then for Daddy and the baby-sitter to assume it's Mommy who is doing something wrong.

We may find it difficult to part with a particular child. We are most likely to experience this with our last baby, or one possessing a defect. We may very subtly convey the message that our child is so cute/handicapped that she does not really have to grow up just yet.

Lola and Don expected their first four children to grow up on time, but they were easier on Mary, their youngest. "We're more relaxed with her," they rationalized, putting off correcting her. Whenever Mary pestered her siblings Don scolded them and always expected the older ones to give in. Lola confronted Don when he did this, but finally she let it drop, for Don kept insisting that it was the older ones who should know better. Their friends and Grandma also confronted Lola and Don about their laxity. Still, they continued to make excuses until their oldest child confronted Lola, and Mary herself got very nasty with her dad. Only then did they begin insisting that Mary grow up.

When we are confronted with our children's growing individuality, we recycle our own early efforts to think;

we experience again the scare of being separate and responsible. Our anger and irritability at our negativistic offspring rekindle our own anger.

We parents who find this phase most distressing are likely to have unresolved separation tasks of our own, i.e., those of us with the injunctions: "Don't think, don't grow up," etc. We can handle our pain by discounting it, by passing on the injunctions to our children, or by new creative ways which free us both.

While helping our children resolve their developmental tasks, we can think about giving up old angers of our own which no longer serve a useful function. We can put our rage to work, insisting that our family treat us like individuals, and not just as the Family Rock, Miracle Worker, etc. To succeed at those tasks we must pay enough attention to our own needs. We also must take the risk of stating our needs out loud, and of thinking and doing in new and sometimes scary ways ourselves.

We really are O.K. people. We do not need to justify our existence as Joe's Mom and Pop. Paying attention to our own Natural Child ego state includes finding ways to have fun that fit us as individuals, aside from our obligation as parents. It is much easier for us to turn off old useless messages when our Natural Child ego state is vigorous and enjoying life. What is fun for us? Bowling? Dancing? Sex? Some people need to plan their fun. Others need to go play spontaneously. Either style has advantages; the main idea is to Have Fun!

SUMMARY

"No!" is a characteristic statement which signifies the arrival of this phase of development (*separation*). Children become increasingly negativistic, taking a position which opposes our point of view, no matter what the issue. Children also move from "experimental physics" to "experimental psychology": earlier, at twelve months of age, they drop things while practicing how to open their fingers voluntarily; several months later children release objects to see if the objects always go down; then to see if glass bounces the same way that balls do. At two years of age they release glasses to see what we will do about it.

Children in the Separation stage keep pushing the limits until our own Child ego state gets frustrated enough to call a halt: "That's enough, I've had it!" The aim of these transactions is to push us to insist that they start thinking. Apparently this separation is difficult, and usually is accomplished with a substantial amount of anger.

The part of the personality structure which is evolving during this phase is the Adult ego state. It is still very young, but has most of the characteristics of that aspect of personality.

Children need to hear that they must think, that it is safe to separate, that they can still get their needs met and we won't abandon them. Our kids need to learn that other people have feelings, and that all feelings count. They learn, from watching and hearing us, what to do with various feelings.

Overconscientious parents, who attempt to suppress their own Natural Child anger and who continue to do too much for the kids, interfere with the natural separation which is appropriate at this age. Another danger to avoid is getting into a guilt "racket"—getting mad, feeling guilty, and failing to demand enough of the child.

When children decide to use their Adult ego state, they relax and they think. They have memories which they report, and they tell us about their own thoughts. They are also ready to solve some basic personal problems like how to stay clean and dry, sleep, and attend to their own hunger.

While helping our children to think, we recycle our own early separation tasks. We have an opportunity to redo work which is unresolved from our childhood, and to redecide some important issues with much more information this time around.

We parents who base too much of our O.K.-ness on parenthood are most apt to fall into the trap of failing to insist that our children start to think. We can help each other by insisting on the separation, and by getting our mates into Child ego states with activities that don't include babies: bowling, dancing, sex, movies, etc.

EXERCISES

1. What would you do if your eighteen-month-old son wanted to eat his dessert first?
2. Your two-year-old daughter keeps getting out of bed during the evening and does not want to settle down; what would you do or say to her?
3. Write an original bedtime story with pictures for a two- or three-year-old. Find pictures or draw them. Write the story about something important in the child's life at that time. Try it out on the child. If you don't have your own child try it out on a neighbor, or a little relative.
4. The purpose of this exercise is to get in touch with feelings aroused during conflict and power struggles.
   a. Find a partner.
   b. Join hands. Push against each other, as hard as you can.
      i. Who won?
      ii. How did you win?
      iii. Loser, how long did you struggle before deciding to yield?
      iv. Why did you decide to yield?
   c. Discuss this in terms of a parent and small child.
5. Stand about three arms lengths from each other.
   a. Decide who will take the stance "Yes" and who will take the stance "No."
   b. "Yes" person think Yes absolutely. Think of something you feel strongly and unequivocally positive about.
   c. "No" person think No. Never. No Way. Think about something to which you are strongly opposed. You think it is very wrong.
   d. Approach each other, saying your one word: Yes/ No. Say it loudly and insistently.
   e. What happened?
   f. Reverse positions.

READINGS

Baldwin, Alfred B. *Behavior and Development in Childhood.* New York: Rinehart and Winston, 1955.

Berne, Eric. *What Do You Say After You Say Hello?* New York: Grove Press, 1972.

Ernst, Franklin Jr. "The O.K. Corral." *Transactional Analysis Journal* I, 4 (1971).

Fraiberg, Selma H. *The Magic Years.* New York: Charles Scribner's Sons, 1959.

Levin, Pamela. *Becoming the Way We Are.* Berkeley, California: Transactional Publications, 1974.

Schiff, Aaron Wolfe, and Schiff, Jacqui Lee. "Passivity." *Transactional Analysis Journal* I, 1 (1971).

Spiro, Melford. *Children of the Kibbutz.* New York: Schocken Books, 1965.

8

Script: First Draft

(Socialization)

The major psychological tasks of children during the *socialization phase* include deciding on their positions in their families and society, forming rough drafts of their scripts, improving their communication skills, identifying themselves sexually, learning their roles in society, expanding their imaginations, and gaining preliminary skills in impulse control.

When they become aware of others as separate individuals, children decide on their O.K.-ness in relation to others.

They learn I'm O.K.—You're O.K. in a home which provides plenty of space and freedom of movement, and the furnishings give the message they can touch, sit, and belong. They get a balance of positive conditional and unconditional strokes, and they receive negative conditional strokes when they discount their own ability to think, or discount other people.

They learn I'm O.K.—You're not-O.K. if they live with cruel, abusive adults. They learn to avoid the grown-ups and stroke themselves, until they are so stroke-hungry that abuse is better than nothing.

They learn I'm not-O.K.—You're O.K. in a household which contains a preponderance of beautiful and fragile things which they may not touch (things are more important than my needs). They also learn the not-O.K. stance from getting mostly negative conditional or unconditional strokes. Children who get positive strokes mainly when they are ill or unhappy also learn the not-O.K. stance.

Children learn I'm not-O.K.—You're not-O.K. when they live in an atmosphere of hopelessness and defeat. Their environment is unpredictable or predictably unsatisfying. Their needs are inadequately met, and they seldom experience success.

Considering Future Life Scripts

"When I grow up I'm going to be . . ." is a typical statement children make, indicating that they consider future life scripts. Making (preliminary) decisions about their future at this stage of life is appropriate. Decisions made earlier are dysfunctional; they are hard to expose and to modify.

When our children state that they intend to be garbage collectors, astronauts, mothers, and fathers, they need for us to support their mental explorations. The more scripts they consider the more options they allow themselves. Our responses encourage or discourage such freedom. For instance, on Tuesday Susie announces she's going to be a garbage collector. Pop says, "Well now, garbage collectors are very strong, healthy people. They work outside in the fresh air and sunshine every day; I bet that would be fun." Wednesday Susie notices a lovely ballerina on TV and expresses an interest in that career. Pop tells her she's pretty and graceful, and can go to school to learn how to dance. Thursday, Susie decides she's going to grow up and be a daddy. Pop tells her that she's a girl, and girls grow up to be women like Mommy. Boys grow up to be men like Daddy. Susie insists she does not want to be a mommy. Pop explores with Susie what's not-O.K. about being a mommy, and finds out that mommies have babies. (Susie is less than thrilled with the new baby.) Pop tells Susie that she does not have to be a mommy, that she can decide when she grows up. Pop also confronts Susie on her feelings about the new baby. He explains that when little kids feel jealous it's because they need strokes, and that when Susie needs strokes she's supposed to ask for them.

In the preceding example Pop encouraged his daughter's fantasies, corrected information, and he also noticed when his daughter expressed feelings of distress.

Children can understand slightly longer explanations at this age. They are ready to learn more about various feelings and their appropriate expression. For instance, in nursery school Freddy was crying. Teacher asked him why the tears. Freddy replied, "I want someone to play with." Teacher explained that "Crying is for when you are sad—like if you lost a best friend or puppy, and when you are hurt—like if you fall down and skin your knee. When you want to play you are supposed to ask someone to play with you." Freddy said, "Oh!", and went looking for someone to ask.

When children have mastered bowel and bladder control, and show signs of thinking, they are ready for nursery school. Girls as a group can stay dry during the night earlier than boys. Both sexes have setbacks, under periods of stress, sibling rivalry, illness, etc. Many three-year-olds can use the potty by themselves. They frequently report it, and show that they want strokes for their accomplishments. They may still need to be wiped and helped with difficult clothing. Parents who wish to foster independence buy clothes which separate in the middle, and slip down easily, i.e., pants with elastic waistbands. Youngsters can pull such clothing down by themselves. Experienced parents keep such problems in mind and avoid clothing which has many buttons, etc.

Once the Adult ego state is available, the little person can play with another child with a beginning awareness of the other as a separate person, rather than just a thing. Freddy learns more about compromise and taking turns. He can learn cooperative behavior, and participate in simple group games like "Ring Around the Rosie"; however, he is still not able to see another's point of view or put himself "in the other person's shoes."

Although children in the Socialization stage do not think in terms of distant future, their sense of time has developed. Understanding of time is one of the concepts being accelerated by children's programs on television. They can grasp the idea of waiting for the timer to ring. They understand the statement "when it's time," and they differentiate yesterday and tomorrow. They mix the labels for a while, "Tomorrow I goed to Aunt Mary's." They may also mix the labels between day and evening. Their command of language in general accelerates. They respond to speech better. They can be entertained with language and can themselves entertain with language. They love new words, and are intrigued by statements containing words like "surprise" and "secret." Lowering our voices and whispering is an excellent way to get their attention.

Social scientists put great importance on the ability to use symbols—words. Speech is thought by many to be one of the main differences between us and the lower animals (recent experiments have shown that at least a few of the great apes are able to learn sign language and so we may soon have to look for another way to be superior). Modern television has stimulated young children to grasp symbols earlier than any other generation. They are exposed to many words in appealing ways that are easy to learn; their main speech patterns, however, are still those of their family.

Children ask a lot of "why" questions during this phase. That question serves many purposes. Children exercise their Adult ego states when they ask why. They practice asking the rhetorical questions of the scientific investigator and philosopher, they find out if there are explanations for things, and they find out if grownups know everything. Questions become increasingly sophisticated like: "What's it for?" "How does it work?" "What does God look like?" "Is he a man?" "Where does he live?" Marvella asks many questions. She has many answers. In her answers we can hear her A_2 trying out different theories.

Some Parent tapes are available for quotation but do not necessarily direct behavior. Kirk tells us about avoiding strangers (P_1) and then makes up with the first friendly face he sees (Natural Child). He invokes his own parents when needing a Parent ego state. When hungry, he tells his playmate's mother, "My Mommy says you should give me a glass of milk."

Children incorporate many messages into the Primitive Parent in their Child ego state (P_1), frequently with more extreme rigidity than we would wish. They use their primitive Parent messages to scold others for errors which may or may not be important to us parents. "Please" and "thank you" are used in families where it is valued; i.e.,

Kirk frequently hears them and receives positive conditional strokes when he practices these rituals. Most children enjoy family rituals like birthdays, lighting candles, and the excitement of holidays. They probably have some idea of what to expect at Christmas or Hanukkah, especially with the many reminders on TV. They also learn their families' usual games and ways of discounting. "See what you made me do" is a frequent preschool game. Children enjoy best the family pastimes which allow for the most physical activity, like picnics and visiting the children's zoo.

They are adventuresome and eager to explore the world full tilt. They love gross motor activities such as riding a tricycle. The more practice they get careening around in child-propelled vehicles, the more depth and space perception they have the opportunity to develop. They also learn to notice bodily clues to their feelings, i.e., when Juana gets angry she notices that she feels hot.

During these preschool years there is a general dip in heat production and decrease in appetite. The growth rate slows and children actually need less food. This Adult information may help parents with Parent tapes about "Proper Eating" to relax. Parents who value clean plates (P_2) notice (A_2) their children's decreased appetite, and serve realistic proportions. Children during these years go on food jags; Pamela wants peanut butter for breakfast, lunch, and supper, in addition to sneaking spoonfuls in between trips down the backyard sliding board. Her mother vacillates between "Eat three varied meals of the Basic Four"* and her wish to be less rigid than her own parents.

Children's drawings are affected by what they see, but not too accurately. Rose (a bright three-year-old) could draw a splendid portrait of a person but her milk bottle was a bit difficult to recognize:

---

* Basic Four—whole-grain breads and cereals; fruits and vegetables; meats, fish, poultry, legumes; and dairy products.

Rose's sister with
pigtails

milk bottle

Figure 24. Portraits

This fits with our knowledge that young children respond more to people than to inanimate objects.

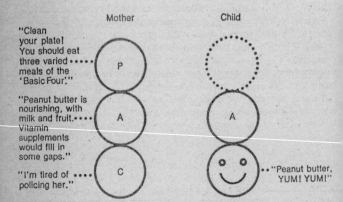

Mother   Child

"Clean
your plate!
You should eat
three varied ••••   P
meals of the
'Basic Four'."

"Peanut butter is
nourishing, with
milk and fruit.••••   A   A
Vitamin
supplements
would fill in
some gaps."

"I'm tired of ••••   C   ••"Peanut butter,
policing her."   YUM! YUM!"

Figure 25. Nutrition: Proper vs. Creative

Sexuality

Children have been receiving messages since birth on what their sexuality means. For example, mothers in our country are twice as apt to nurse girl infants as boy infants, while boys get handled and tousled more than girl infants. One of the major tasks of preschool children is to become aware of their sexuality and what that means in terms of script decisions. "If I'm not part of mother, then who am I? and who is mother, daddy, sister, brother?" They also show more awareness of differences.

In a society unadorned by clothing, children see the differences between themselves, the other sex, adults, pubescents, etc. while they are growing up. In our country genital differences are less obvious. Children use the clues they see (haircut, clothing, activities) to differentiate between male and female. The boy knows he's a male and the girl knows she's a female. If asked, "How can you tell he's a boy?" they are as apt to answer "Because he's tough," as they are to say "Because he has a penis." It will be interesting to see what clues little children use in our culture's trend toward "unisex."

Sex is a broad subject; it covers much more than anatomical differences and reproduction: it includes male–female transactions, male–male transactions and female–female transactions; also various sexual roles, and messages about appropriate sexual pair bonding, etc. Tommy learns his family's taboos and customs regarding sexuality. He experiences competitive feelings as well as identification with his dad. Children frequently express jealousy over parents' showing affection, and order them to stop kissing. Little girls often propose to their daddies. Some girls attempt to urinate standing up, and little boys talk about giving birth to babies. Typically, the little boy proposes to his mother. In the traditional urban home Mom is the center of the world for both boys and girls. Each sex is learning a lot about what it means to be a male and a female, and is making script decisions accordingly.

Children during this phase are usually interested in the origins of things, like "Where do babies come from?", etc. In families where curiosity is encouraged they will be curious: "Why don't I have a daddy?" "Mommy's tinkle is all gone!" "What's that?" (brother's or father's penis). Some children express their curiosity verbally (as above). Others will look, poke, find out for themselves.

O.K. MESSAGES

A list of O.K. messages about sex and social roles includes:

1. You are O.K.
2. Your body is O.K.
3. You are a girl because you have a vulva and will grow breasts, a boy because you have a penis and testicles (balls).
4. You are a sexual person.
5. Your sex is O.K.
6. The other sex is O.K. too.
7. It is not O.K. to . . . (masturbate in public).
8. When you grow up you may (will, will not . . . etc.).
9. Boys (men) are important. They do masculine things like . . . Girls (women) are important. They do feminine things like. . . .
10. Marriage is O.K., an option, expected, etc.

We complete sentences 7 through 10 in many conflicting ways in our society. Few couples today have exactly matching ideas on what males and females "should" be and do.

Girls learn how to be females from watching their mothers and older sisters, from observing how males treat their mothers, and from experiencing how males treat them. Girls copy the models they see; cooking, sewing, going out to work, etc.

Boys learn how to be males from watching their fathers and older brothers, observing how females treat their fathers and from observing how the males treat the females. A boy who seldom sees his father learns that males devalue home life, while a boy whose dad is always doing something around the house learns to value that activity.

Much of the programming on how to be a male comes from what a boy is told by his mother and female teacher, and what he sees on TV. TV is generally more conservative and the young male is exposed to typical male stereotypes: cowboys, detective, superstud. Boys make things, think, compete, and fight. Children exposed to brutality in their neighborhoods, movies, etc., are more apt to behave cruelly than those who are not.

Children over the ages have shown amazing flexibility to learn what is expected of them, even when these expectations conflict.

Typical Banal Scripts

A banal script is a script that is functional within a culture but limiting. "You can be O.K. if . . . (you don't develop certain aspects of your potential)."

The typical banal script in our society allows the male to energize the prejudicial part of his Parent, his computing Adult, and the rebellious aspect of his Adapted Child. The typical banal script for the female allows her to use the nurturing part of her Parent, the compliant aspect of her Adapted Child, as well as her Little Professor (intuition).

Others learn that females are competent and run things while males are helpless and are best treated always as little boys.

STATEMENTS THAT PRODUCE STEREOTYPES

Typical statements which promote the programming of these stereotyped banal scripts include:

	Males		*Females*
CRITICAL PARENT:	Wait till your father comes home. Boys don't play with dolls.	NURTUR- ING PARENT:	Isn't that cute? (the way she cares for her doll) Just like her mommy!

ADULT:	My son's going to be a: doctor lawyer executive. Now, the way to fix a plug is. . . .	ADULT:	She's so silly and flighty. Women are so illogical. They let their heart rule their head.
ADAPTED CHILD:	Just like a boy to be breaking things! I can't figure out a woman. Boys don't cry. Be a man.	ADAPTED CHILD:	Daddy's little girl. Look, dear, isn't that lovely?
		LITTLE PROFESSOR:	How did you know? ("Woman's intuition.") You should feel. . . .

A girl whose mother goes out to work gets a different message than the one whose mother is home during the day, sewing or cooking. Males are generally considered more O.K. in our country. They are the leaders, thinkers, the strong, the powerful, and the protectors. Individuals with the above "masculine" stereotypic traits are generally admired if not liked. Males pay a price for their special status, however: their Nurturing Parent, intuition, and Natural Child are discounted.

Boys in the United States who love babies, dolls, and who cry when they are hurt get negative strokes. Male baby-sitters are still rare in some communities. Men are not supposed to understand women who operate on a mysterious phenomenon called "intuition." Even Freud gave up on understanding them. Adult males are restricted in the amount of Natural Child they may display while in the working force. A male is permitted to cuss and yell when watching sports or injuring himself doing manual labor, but he is not allowed otherwise to nurture himself. He is also permitted to enjoy sex.

The female's Adult (ability to think) and Natural Child are discounted. In general, females are not expected to assume much responsibility. All they have to do is what they are told and be pretty. Many of the men and women who seek psychotherapy are suffering from growth-inhibiting variations on the above theme. Some typical injunctions include:

Males	*Females*
don't feel	don't think
don't cry	don't succeed
don't be close	don't be assertive
don't touch	don't do
don't show your feelings	don't compete
don't be tender	don't be tough
don't be playful	don't lead
don't need	don't explore
	don't leave

Much of the script around maleness and femaleness is formed during these years. Children learn from what they see—the adults in their world (neighborhood, TV) —and what they hear, as well as the reactions of the grownups to what the children do. Frequently these differences are very subtle. Martha realized that she invites her daughter to look at beauty, while she explains things to her son. Men's and women's consciousness-raising groups are helping us to become aware of how we think in stereotyped patterns.

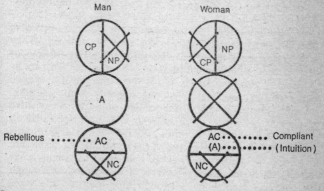

Figure 26. Typical U. S. Banal Scripts Promote Symbiosis and Competition

The real differences between males and females are anatomical. Behavioral differences vary from culture to culture. Various traits such as: aggressive, cold, friendly, emotional, and flighty are masculine in one culture and feminine traits in another.

Position in the Family

Other influences on the script include birth order and size of the family. Martha, the oldest, is an only child temporarily. She is the one most apt to feel the brunt of her parents' scripts. She is frequently expected to develop a compliant Adapted Child and gets the most Critical Parenting. Parents are more apt to hand her heavy programming around "be perfect and be the best." She is more apt to get enthusiastic conditional positive strokes (e.g., praise) for achieving: walking, talking, good grades, etc.

The first child is more apt to be inhibited at the Exploratory stage—parents still have dreams about Martha being a lovely doll-like baby. Later, however, she will be expected to lead and develop much Parent ego state: "You are the oldest, you should know better, set the example." Her parents learn how to be parents on Martha. She's the family pioneer. She's most likely to learn her parents' injunctions and receive more script under pressure.

Middle children are less apt to be programmed like either parent unless they are the first of their sex. They are more likely to inherit the script of Aunt Minnie or Uncle Ben. Middle children find it more difficult to be unique; what they do is less apt to attract the excited strokes that the first one experienced. Some develop special talents which bring them conditional positive strokes (like music or scholarship). Others specialize in Rebellious Child and/or Finicky Eater, which also attracts strokes of a more negative variety. Middle children are parented by more experienced parents. In some ways their programming is less severe. If they are close enough in age and compete hard enough they may get the same privileges as the older ones. Frequently middle children complain about being teased or bullied by older ones and are forbidden to defend themselves from harassment by younger 'siblings.

The youngest child is most apt to receive the injunctions "don't leave," "don't grow up." This is heard in expressions like "this is my baby," even after Sam is quite mature. The youngest child is more apt to be parented by everyone in the family. If parents are tired of Parenting, most of what the youngest gets comes from an older sibling. In many families the youngest gets the most unconditional positive strokes, and is encouraged to develop Natural Child. They have the opportunity to use A_2 and learn from observing rather than having to experience consequences personally. If previous siblings fulfilled parents' ambitions, youngest children receive more relaxed programming. If several others failed, they may feel the pressure of "you are our last chance."

Children from large families report that they have more relaxed scripts with more options on how to be. They also experience less stroking from their parents. They have richer earlier experiences in learning how to cooperate, to depend on each other, to fight, to make up, to compete, to win and lose, and to be loyal. These experiences promote opportunities for confrontation from which it is not easy to escape. Children in large families learn the meaning of group pressure early and learn the importance of interdependence. They often form small units within the family, being especially close to one parent or a couple of sibs to whom they give or from whom they receive parenting. In a large family, children learn more about options, as they see each other selecting which Parental tapes to incorporate and/or reject. They also can learn more about how to ask for strokes. There is usually someone around feeling O.K. enough to give them some Warm Fuzzies. Sex education occurs naturally in a large family and children have more opportunities to form close peer relationships with opposite sex siblings.

An only child is apt to receive a more binding script and experience a tighter symbiosis. John is the only one to fulfill his parents' expectations. He feels special and compelled to measure up. Some children enjoy getting all the available strokes; however, later they may experience difficulty with competition in larger group constellations.

John is compliant. He behaves acceptably during grown-up activities. He receives the injunction "Don't be little"; while his Adult is being encouraged, his Natural Child is discounted. Sometimes an only child is tolerated rather than welcomed; parents were too adapted to consider an abortion, but they really didn't want him. He receives the injunctions "Don't be," "Don't ask," "Don't be close." Hopefully, more birth-control information will encourage parents to have only the children they are ready to love and care for.

Expanding Imagination

The years between two and six are full of magical thinking. During these years children expand intellectually; their behavior and imagination become more elaborate. Three-year-olds climb for the sake of climbing. Five-year-olds climb to "get to the space rocket . . . blast off!"

Many children between the ages of two-and-a-half to four have some kind of imaginary friends. Thinking up imaginary friends indicates an expanding imagination (not necessarily loneliness or maladjustment). Many sociable children from large families have imaginary friends. When selecting an imaginary friend, Jane experiments with new personality traits to see how they fit. She projects bolder, more adventuresome thinking than she would ordinarily admit to. She tries on grown-up behavior that she has observed; she can project a parent who is more nurturing and less critical than her real one. She can also try on complementary roles by being both leader and follower, girl and boy, etc.

As Michael develops, his play with others also becomes more sophisticated. He tries on many roles: Mommy, Daddy, Big Sister, Pirate, Fireman, Doctor, etc. The roles he chooses are influenced by personal preference, the availability of models, and the availability of playmates. For example, during one play session Michael served in two groups. He was called upon to be the groom at one end of the basement, where a "Wedding" was taking place. A few minutes later, at the other end of the basement, he was commandeered to "walk the plank" off a "pirate ship." Each play had a director who told him where to stand and what to say.

During these preschool years children compare themselves with others, i.e., "Jimmy can run better; but I can throw better." Their concept of themselves is big and getting bigger and emerges in conversation. Such understanding is accelerated in a home where children see and hear about their growth and development.

Children do not think like adults, but some of their ideas are found in our superstitions (P_1) and in the ideas of people in primitive tribes and isolated societies, as if they are leftovers of our own earlier thinking:

"The moon and sun follow you when you walk."

"Anything that moves is alive."

"All dreams are real."

"If an idea occurs to me it must be real. It is a fact— also if I am thinking it, you must be thinking it too."

"Stones, clouds, chairs, etc., have feelings and power."

Also, when Phyllis makes up a new word she assumes everyone knows what she means.

Some of the above theories you have probably heard if you have been around young children for any length of time. If you have not done so before, take time to ask and listen.

Figure 27. Structural Diagram of a Young Child During Socialization Stage

When they indulge in magical thinking, children are mentally exploring the limits of their imagination, as well as reaching conclusions on inadequate data or distorted information. Some of their magical thinking stems from magical beliefs: "If I think of it, it is real, it will happen." They have difficulty telling the difference between wishful thinking and reality. One of the magical beliefs which causes the most difficulty is, "If I feel or think something it will cause an event, i.e., if I hate my mother, it will hurt her. If I wish she was dead, and she dies, or gets sick, then I did it."

Children also experiment by expressing various feelings to see what happens. Some children find, for instance, that properly staged temper tantrums (in a store, say) get them extra treats.

Normal children feel ambivalent toward their parents, and have sexy feelings toward them, in addition to myriad other feelings. Death and sex are two of the most taboo areas in our society, so children are most likely to experience difficulty in those areas. They get the message that it is less O.K. to check out magical beliefs on those subjects than on others.

Nightmares result from repressed feelings in the areas of sex and death-wishes, fears of violence, and other fears of loss of control. Usually when children have nightmares, they are scaring themselves about a situation they think they cannot handle. What they need is reassurance that we will remain in control and protect them from violent intruders and their own scary impulses.

Robin was scaring herself night after night, waking up terrified. Her parents went to her and helped her wake up with their Nurturing Parent ego states. Her nightmares persisted. Finally they quizzed her, "What are you scaring yourself about?" She replied with a question: "What would you do if I got in bed with Daddy and no clothes on?" Mom and Pop assured her that they would not allow her to do so. They would tell her to go put her clothes on and then she could rejoin them. They stated firmly that they would not permit her to do things she shouldn't do. Robin stopped having nightmares and started arguing (Construction stage) about why she should have to make her bed before going to school.

Robert's nightmares were related to violence. His

mother and her boyfriend were not getting along. They fought with each other at night. During the day Mom worried a lot. Robert's nightmares ceased when Mom got rid of her boyfriend.

Psychological Tasks of Parents

When we as parents get in touch with our own scripts, we can examine them with our Adults, and can decide what we want to discard, keep, and restyle. Our own psychological tasks around sexual script building include: examining our beliefs, our own sexual stereotypes and script decisions, dealing with our sexual feelings aroused by our children, predicting roles of men and women in the future, and redeciding about our own scripts. See Chapter 12 for more on Scripts.

SUMMARY

Once children start thinking and becoming separate individuals, they decide on a basic position about their own O.K.-ness in relation to other people. Much of the child's O.K.-ness hinges on what happens when the child begins to think out loud and to ask questions. These questions confirm facts and gather new information: "Daddy, why does the phone ring when Michael calls us up?" Other questions are practice in the process of thinking itself. Still others are designed to find out if grownups know everything. Children learn through questions which topics can be discussed and which topics are taboo in their families.

Many questions are rhetorical, through which children express their developing imagination and penchant for magical thinking. Children develop a primitive Parent aspect of their Child ego state, which can be seen when they imitate parenting behavior. The purpose of this aspect of personality is not totally clear. It is thought to be the repository for very early rules and prohibitions which the child has picked up even before speech. Some theorists believe that nightmares and magical thinking are manifestations of this aspect of personality, which children use to scare themselves into behaving.

Achieving sexual identification is an important task at this stage, as are appropriate sexual roles in the society of that particular child. Statements such as "When I grow up . . ." and "I'll never . . ." indicate that the child is making important script decisions and forming tentative life plans. Script decisions are also evident in children's play. After they see people as separate individuals, they can play with others, and begin learning society's rules about how to relate to others.

Children need to know that all of their feelings count, that bad feelings mean they need something, and that they don't have to act on their impulses. They need to know the role of each sex in their society, and that both sexes are O.K.

The programming children receive during the socialization phase is a significant factor in their script. Today's parents need to re-examine the sexual stereotypes with which they were raised. Many of those customs will be very outdated by the time our children are adults.

We parents can benefit ourselves by re-examining our own scripts. We actually have choices about following our scripts automatically, or revising certain decisions.

EXERCISES

1. A script trip. Get a partner to read you the instructions. Close your eyes and imagine the following scene: (take your time until the picture develops)
   a. You are in a theater sitting in the best seat in the house. Picture a stage up front with big velvet curtains. What color?
   b. The curtain goes up and on stage are your mother and father before you were born. They're talking about you. Who and what is on stage with them? What are they saying? (Wait.) The curtain falls.
   c. It's Act II. You're a little kid between the ages of three and five. Picture yourself up there on stage.

Who is on stage with you? Which important grown-ups? What do they say? (Wait.) Curtain falls.

d. It's a scene from now in your life. What are you doing and saying? with whom?

e. The curtain falls again. It's intermission. How does the audience react? Follow them out to the lobby. What do they say about the play so far?

2. Find a group who are willing to participate with you in an exercise in being young. Be five—use small words. Free up your imagination, think magically. Tell tales about what you see and hear right now. Answer the following questions:

a. What's thunder?

b. What's a cloud made of?

c. What happens to the sun at night?

d. What's a bad word?

e. What does dead mean?

f. What's a Catholic? Jew? Nigger? Dingerbummer?

3. Take turns completing the sentence "When I grow up . . ." and let others react.

Return to your current biological age and examine the rest of the questions:

4. What did I learn about maleness and femaleness?

5. What injunctions am I still obeying?

6. Do I wish to pass those injunctions on to my child? What is the reality of now? What does my child need to feel, do, and think about to be a successful male/female now in this neighborhood and era?

7. What do I predict will be the reality of the world twenty years from now?

8. What will be expected of men and women in that future?

READINGS

Burnett, Dorothy, *Your Pre-School Child.* New York: MacFadden-Bartell Corporation, 1963.

Children's Bureau Publication No. 30. "Your Child From One to Six." Superintendent of Documents, Washington, D.C.

Ginott, Haim. *Between Parent and Child.* New York: The Macmillan Company, 1965.

Ilg, Frances, and Ames, Louise Bates. *Child Behavior.* New York: Harper and Row, 1955; and Dell Publishing Company, 1956.

Patterson, Gerald R. and Gullion, M. Elizabeth. *Living With Children* (revised). Champaign, Illinois: Research Press, 1971.

Rosenberg, Edward, and Warner, Silas. *The Pre-School Child's Learning Process.* Chicago, Illinois: Budlong Press Co., 1967.

9

The Little Lawyer

(Construction)

The *construction phase* corresponds approximately to the grade-school years. When they enter school, children show clearly the script decisions they have made. Teachers also make assumptions about the childrens' scripts. Teachers view children from the framework of their own scripts and definitions of losers and winners.

Winners are:	*Losers* are:
obedient	easily led
quiet	lethargic
eager to please	pests
well groomed	sissies
leaders	trouble makers
lively	loud
independent	insubordinate
dressed creatively	grimy

The Grade-School Years

The main psychological tasks of elementary-school children are: to separate reality from fantasy; to develop more fully the Adult ego state operations of memory, logic, reality testing, and problem-solving; to attain numerous skills and become aware of special talents; to gather

135

much data about the world outside their immediate neighborhood; to compare their family's rules and style of living with those of other families; and to firm up their own personal Parent ego states. Some of these tasks are accomplished by much arguing and asking "Why?" and by other forms of lawyering.

Young children are eager to grow. Nothing is more attractive than being older. They are willing and ready to learn how to make things. They realistically appraise their own strengths and weaknesses. They notice differences between themselves and their peers. White children in white neighborhoods take each other's skin color for granted, paying only minimal attention to blonde or brown hair, and blue, brown, or green eyes. Children of other colors—black, brown, yellow, or red—are much more alert to their own skin color as well as to the color of those around them.

Girls show awareness of peer relations in kindergarten; they know who is popular and who the "best friends" are. Boys demonstrate this kind of social awareness soon after the girls, although to a lesser degree. They know who is tallest, fastest, toughest, etc. Children whose scripts contain a lot of messages about competition pay more attention to comparisons, and give these phenomena more importance. Our Western school system promotes individual competition. In some other societies, competition between teams is considered more important. Parents are faced with an important dilemma. We may wish our children to value cooperative relationships, and yet we are aware that our children will live in a society which has a very competitive structure. If we teach our children a frame of reference that is much different from most of their peers, or if we teach them to hold values different from their teachers, then our children will experience much pain and hassling when they are away from home. Today's children need flexible Parent ego states so they can comfortably tolerate more than one frame of reference.

In the first few years of school, children continue to believe that their ideas are valid solely on the grounds that they have thought of them; they cling to some favorite magical beliefs even when they have much data (A_2) to the contrary. Debbie, for instance, at seven years of age, knew Santa Claus's real identity—until it was time to hang her stocking. All her sophisticated knowledge to the contrary, she willingly believed again, and peered up the chimney, peeled carrots for Santa's reindeer, and danced around the house, checking the sky for signs of his approach.

Young children mix fact and fantasy quite freely; they do so for fun, for practice at imagining, and for spicing up conversations. Children need to learn that imagination is great fun and useful for many kinds of thinking. Our society needs these skills to cope with rapid change. Children also need to learn to differentiate fact and fantasy, to know when each kind of thinking is appropriate, and how to tell the difference. Kirk got some instruction on how to detect the difference between reports he heard, and events he personally witnessed in the following conversation:

KIRK: Mom, Moe's been to Africa and his house caught on fire!

MOM: (*smiling*) My, what a fascinating life he's led!

KIRK: (*huffy*) It's really true! I'm not lying!

MOM: (*Nurturing Parent*) Honey, I'm not accusing you of lying. (*Adult*) How did you find out he's been to Africa?

KIRK: He told me.

MOM: Did you see pictures of him in Africa?

KIRK: No!

MOM: Did you see the fire?

KIRK: No, but he told me!

MOM: Then say, "Moe told me he lived in Africa. He said his house caught on fire." It's important to know the difference between what you hear somebody say, and what you see with your own eyes.

Kirk's Mom chose to offer her son some instruction on reporting; he indicated he was serious because he was not using his "pretend" or teasing voice and he got huffy when she smiled.

TEASING

Teasing includes elements of both positive and negative strokes. It is exciting and adds spice to transactions. Teasing is like chili pepper: tastes vary on how much is enjoyable; a little bit spices the meal; too much burns and is painful. Too much can also cause indigestion and discomfort which last for quite a while.

In addition to its stroke value, teasing is a form of mental parrying. Children learn to be more skeptical through the use of teasing. They learn to question Parental statements and to use their own Adult ego state, to examine information before incorporating it. They attempt to get each other to "fall for" outlandish statements and greatly enjoy ridiculing the gullible: "There's a bug on your arm . . . April Fool!"

We parents can use teasing for fun in Child-to-Child transactions with each other and with our children. Mike's Dad, for instance, deliberately mispronounces or misunderstands words that are "soundalikes." Mike gets a big kick out of seeing Dad "make mistakes" and gets a chance to reverse roles, correcting Dad, for a change.

MIKE: Daddy, I read a fun book today in school.
DAD: Oh, was it bright or dark red?
MIKE: Oh, Daddy, not the color! I read the book, you know, I looked at the words.

At this age such "misinterpretations" are fun, and give the little person a chance to act big. Earlier, during Separation and Socialization stages when children are still struggling to learn speech, such teasing would be frustrating and cruel. Children are better able to understand irony and sarcasm, when they have a lot more information on how language is constructed.

Questions during the construction phase have a different function than they did during preschool years. Children in the construction phase ask questions to get information. They can answer some questions by investigation with parents' help. Until young children can read with ease, they need help from a grownup for information that is in books.

Very young children can classify objects (sparrows and wrens are both birds), and they can arrange objects in visible order (rods from shortest to longest). They become aware of various physical laws one at a time and take a number of years learning to generalize, and carry over learning from one area to another. For instance, children before seven or eight will think that water looks the same in a level cup as when it is tilted.

Figure 28. Drawing of a Cup with Water Tilted (by a Six-Year-Old)

Even after looking, children will say, "Oh! it goes up," not getting the connection between the water level and gravitational pull for a few more years.

Concrete thinking persists well into the construction phase. For instance, a child who is nine or ten years old knows that two identical balls of clay have identical weight and amount in them even if one is flattened. The child will, however, still think that one takes up more space than the other.

Children move to understand more logical operations, and other kinds of sophisticated thinking, depending in part on the extent of their knowledge of the practical world, and on the kind of thinking that is rewarded. In our industrialized culture, for instance, logical, orderly, one-track thinking is highly valued. It is the kind of thinking most useful for programming machines and for verifying certain kinds of scientific experiments. Males in our culture are stroked for this kind of thinking. Females are expected to be "intuitive." Multivariant thinking is frequently classified as flighty, and indicates lack of concentration. Artists, dreamers, oddballs, and psychiatric investigators (takes one to know one) are permitted to think "loosely" as long as it doesn't interfere "too much" with behavior acceptable in their particular society. A current trend in the United States is to give more credibility to multivariant, creative thinking, and to alternate frames of reference such as mysticism and other Eastern systems of thought.

Children in the mid-elementary grades are ready to expand their repertoire of skills. As their thinking matures, they also have the attention span necessary for developing special talents.

In general children learn best when new information is presented to them through all their channels of input (ears, mouth, eyes, hands, and body). Children vary as to which channels work best for them, and which channels their environment encourages. A child in a family that values speech learns to talk, ask questions, and listen to conversation. Doug learns mechanics by watching his dad; Doug can now do more to cars than most grownups.

Children's perceptual skills do not develop evenly. For instance, Charlene asked her Dad for some information on dinosaurs. Dad got out the encyclopedia and had Charlene read to him. Charlene read quite well, sounding out the words, but after reading for a while, she complained that she could not comprehend the words. Dad then explained in smaller words and simpler terms what Charlene had read. Charlene learned that the encyclopedia had information; she also learned that Dad paid attention to her, and to her questions. Charlene's ability to say words was ahead of her ability to grasp their meanings.

Children learn to separate facts about the outside world, beliefs, and internal feelings. In the following transactions Lisa and Theresa received some instructions on how to express feelings, without making each other not-O.K. They were angry with each other and Lisa yelled, "You're a dummy!" Their mother, who was nearby, said, "Tell her how you're feeling instead of calling her names. Say, 'I'm mad at you because. . . .' "

We parents are often tempted to solve interpersonal problems for our children, especially when the noise level passes a certain level of discomfort for us. Children learn more from working it out themselves, once they have received adequate instruction.

TESTING FAMILY RULES

In our age of technological change and variety, children need to try new ideas, new behaviors, and to expand their world as soon as they are ready. They need to explore farther with more responsibility and less supervision from us parents. During the construction phase, however, they continue to need a substantial amount of parenting from someone.

Group experiences such as clubs, camping, and scouts provide children with a wide variety of parenting, and opportunities to experiment with new roles.

Katherine's adventure to a weekend camp was accompanied by a certain amount of threat for which she needed support. She used such an event to gain more coping skills and to find out the names of some uneasy feelings. Her mother was helping her to prepare for her first experience away from home for more than one night. Katherine did not have a Parent ego state of her own that she could depend on to take care of herself:

M: (*in a hurry, dashing around kitchen*) Come on in and eat, dear.

K: I'm not hungry.

M: You won't have another chance to eat for five hours.

K: My stomach hurts.

M: Where?

K: Here. (*points to upper abdomen*)

M: What's wrong?

K: I don't know.

M: You don't know if you want to tell me, or you don't know how to tell me?

K: I don't know how to say it.

M: You come over here (*sits down and gestures to lap*) and say what you can and I'll explain it.

K: I want to go to camp and I don't want to go.

M: Oh, that's called mixed feelings.

K: I'm afraid I'll get there and want to come home.

M: That's called being homesick. Do you remember feeling that way before?

K: Yes, on the hay-rack ride.

M: What happened to that feeling?

K: I started having fun and I forgot it.

M: O.K., so you already know that you can be homesick for a little bit and then feel better and have fun.

K: But what if I get lonesome and want to come home?

M: One thing you should know. If you feel really lonesome and want to come home, we will come and get you. If the problem is that you need some strokes, you can ask for them.

K: Yes, I can do that. (*brightening*)

M: It's important to ask for strokes from somebody who wants to give them to you. Look for a grownup with a nice face.

K: Oh, Ms. Smiley; she's going, and she gives good strokes.

M: Fine—and be sure to tell her you need strokes. say, "Ms. Smiley, I'm homesick, will you hold me?" Then she will know what to do. If you tell her your stomach hurts, she may ask the nurse to give you some medicine, and that's not what you need.

K: I feel better now. Can I have some lunch?

Katherine was familiar with the *feeling* of ambivalence. Children learn that emotion by the time they are six months old. While recycling a combination of conflicting feelings at this time Katherine learned a child's *word* for ambivalence—"mixed feelings." It takes time for children, to learn all of the different combinations: love-hate, love-fear, curious-scared, etc. Her mother reminded her of information she already had, namely, that some uneasy feelings are temporary and don't have to interfere with fun. Her mother also went over with Katherine the difference between loneliness, scare, and stomach disorders. It is important to teach children to ask for what they need from people who are willing to give it, particularly as they move away from familiar territory. Children frequently define Nurturing Parents as people who have "nice faces."

Children develop their Parent ego state for over half a decade. They need to incorporate numerous rules, definitions, and values, and reorganize them into a meaningful workable Parent ego state, which will be a good guide for most situations, and which will enable them to take good care of themselves.

In earlier times, when the pace of life was more leisurely and change occurred more slowly, children could just take in their parents' beliefs without question, and get along O.K. in that particular culture. Our children will live in a world that has not yet been invented, for which we could not possibly give them all of the coping skills they will need. It is important, therefore, that we be willing to examine our own reasons and beliefs, and be able to offer our children a Parent ego state which will serve them well. It is important for us to encourage thinking in our children in conjunction with accepting our beliefs and rules, so that they can re-examine their Parent ego states and update them as they go along in life.

Many of us were raised by the rule, "Children should be seen and not heard." That particular belief is in conflict with some of the recommendations in this chapter. "Respect your elders" is another familiar rule. Respect can be defined in many ways. One definition is that elders are O.K. and youngsters are not-O.K. Another is that elders are O.K. and youngsters are O.K. too. Children can show respect by waiting for a good time to bring up their concerns. They can show respect by avoiding Rebellious Child tones of voice. They can show respect to the elders whom they question by listening to answers.

Children's conversations during the construction phase change in character from when they were in the socialization phase. The little "question box" metamorphizes into the little lawyer: arguing, finding loopholes, picking apart our informally constructed logic, finding the flaws in our hastily constructed reasons, and showing a fantastic capacity to notice any other frame of reference which conflicts with ours. Parents of children this age complain that they have become defiant, disrespectful, "lost every bit of manners they ever had, constantly criticizing and comparing us to the other kids' parents." Actually, kids are not trying to do parents in. They are attempting to form a workable Parent ego state, in a changing society, beside neighbors whose frames of reference frequently differ from their own. Many of us were raised where most of our neighbors thought like we did. The few neighbors that did not were considered not-O.K. by the rest of us. In slower moving communities the whole town had the same set of values, and only strangers (who were suspect) thought differently than we did. Arguing is one of the prices we pay for having children who think, and who believe that everybody is O.K.

One very favorite way children have of testing out the family's rules is to bring up a topic with the opening remark, "All the other kids get to. . . ." They may have heard it works in other homes and are "applying some psychology" to us. Their Little Professors find out if "keeping up with the Joneses," the American Dream, is an important issue in their own home. They may also detect that at some level we are vulnerable to being seen as less good parents than our neighbors (the competitive structure used on us).

There are ways to respond to such remarks without feeling guilty, without making the other parents not-O.K., and still stand firm on issues which we consider important. Chuck and his daughter Debbie had such a conversation:

D: Karen has everything and we don't have any-thing.

C: Come on, that's extreme. What did she get now?

D: She got a merry-go-round in her back yard.

C: That's terrific. I guess from your face and voice that you'd like the toys she has?

D: Yeah!

C: I can understand that. How many kids in her family?

D: One.

C: With four kids in our family we have to stretch our money more.

D: Yeah, but her parents are always buying her things.

C: Always is another one of those extreme words. Her parents buy her lots of things, and that's cool. In our family we think education is more

important, and that costs a lot of money. We've
been saving money as we intend to help all four
of you through school. We're not real rich, so we
had to make a choice. We decided to save some
instead of buying more toys. You have some
goodies, you know. What are they?

D: The climbing tower and the sandbox.

C: Yes, that's right. How can you get to play on
Karen's merry-go-round?

D: I can invite her over here to play with my toys,
and go over there to play on hers.

C: That's good thinking.

Children notice other people's homes in terms of their
own family's value system, as well as the value system
they learn at school. They notice others' homes as bigger,
smaller, neater, and messier than their own. They notice
which kids have which kind of toys. They notice if other
parents are friendly or cool. Children who feel deprived
notice children who have much more than they. Children
who feel O.K. about themselves, and don't know the
meaning of hunger, are less apt to notice such discrep-
ancies, unless they are taught to: "We're more O.K.
because we're cleaner, neater, better organized, harder
working, than they."

Children are influenced by what they see and do outside the home. This may occur when they acquire new
friends or travel in new environments. Within a ten-year
span half of our country's population moves, so it is
quite likely that our children will be exposed to such
differences. Parents who have money can control their
children's associates by moving to special neighborhoods
and sending their children to special schools.

Other parents exert control by programming their
children, "We're O.K., they're not-O.K." This kind of
programming has great survival value for helping children
stay winners in neighborhoods populated mainly with
losers. One of the costs, however, is a lifelong habit of
discounting the value of strokes coming from non-family
members. The stroke economy is adequate as long as
the family is intact, but if parents die, and siblings move
away, such people have no structure for learning to get
strokes from a variety of friends and neighbors.

Children's perceptions of themselves broaden throughout the years of middle and late childhood. At age eight years and nine months, Ted described himself:

> I feel like I'm growing up, I'm not a crybaby anymore. I play more softball and stuff, and also acrobatics. I'm trying to catch the ball now, I used to be afraid to. I'm growing up in Cub Scouts. I'm the teacher's pet. I'm wondering about other things and going on adventures—riding (bicycle) to the shopping center and to the park more. I'm just more physical and active. I think about moving, old friends who move away, and how I would feel if I moved away. I think about what I'm going to be when I grow up: a veterinarian or doctor or oceanographer. I remember running away when I was little—from (ages) four to eight. I packed my suitcase and blanket and ran down the block, and I came back. I'm over that now. I think about holidays and building the fort down the street.

Ted no longer believes that dreams are concrete beings which come to his room at night, but he believes in foreknowledge: "Sometimes they come true."

Children and Contracts

Children at this stage of development can make contracts. Contracts encourage the cooperative structure (how can we both get what we want) as opposed to the competitive structure (it's a contest: one of us wins and the other loses).

A preliminary to responsible behavior is learning to be active. Children should be discouraged from being passive, and expecting others to think for them. Real contracts involve mutual consent. Some grownups claim they are making contracts when actually they are making proclamations. It is important to distinguish between them and contract with our children only around issues that we are willing to contract about. If we are enforcing rules then it is important that we take that stance clearly. Structure for negotiating from an I'm O.K.—You're O.K. position:

1. Here is what I want.
2. What do you want?
3. How can we both get what we want?
4. What will you give up so that you can get most of what you want?
5. What shall I give up so that I can get most of what I want?
6. How do you feel about that?
7. Here's how I feel about it.

Children in the early school years are very fond of rules. At first they believe the rules they learn at home are scared. For instance, if two children start playing "Hide and Go Seek" and find their rules differ, each insists "Here are THE rules. Furthermore, if you don't obey them you are bad, cheating, etc." It takes time for them to learn that several different sets of rules can be O.K.

Clubs are popular in middle childhood when kids have some stable rules, and are more comfortable shifting to other sets of rules. Clubs serve many purposes. Children have opportunities to gain information (A_2) about various activities, and skills which are not provided in the regular curriculum. They associate with children other than their regular classmates. They have opportunities to meet children with similar interest, and they have the opportunity to associate with big persons who like little people, in smaller groups than the conventional classroom. Little

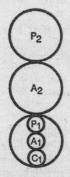

Figure 29. Structural Diagram of Completed Construction Stage

League, Scouts, 4-H, and other clubs provide such experiences.

Late childhood is characterized by a period of greater psychological organization. Children feel better, act more settled and civilized, cooperate in team activities, and start showing signs of self-discipline in school. Joey decided that his restlessness and talking a lot were bad habits. He and the teacher worked out a contract whereby he would get rewarded periodically for good conduct. He was very pleased with his own improvement.

In the process of becoming better organized, children develop their own personal Parent ego state, on which they can rely to take care of them. They act more responsible; whereas, at earlier stages, they could recite safety rules and lecture to each other, now they behave in responsible ways and show genuine concern for others.

Leaders and Followers

Children learn to lead and to follow during the construction phase. They test both roles. Those who succeed at leading already have some measure of energy in their Parent ego state. Leaders entice, convince, intimidate, persuade, or bully others into following, depending on the neighborhood, and their particular beliefs about leading. Leaders believe:

I can lead
I'm supposed to lead
I can get others to do what I say
The way to lead is to. . . .
The way to select followers is to. . . .

Followers assume:

I can follow
I'm supposed to follow
I do what others say
The way to follow is. . . .
The way to select a leader is. . . .

In some neighborhoods the leader will be the kid who has the football, or the kid whose mother is janitor at the high-school gym. In other neighborhoods the leader is the loudest or strongest. In some communities the leader is the one with the most exciting ideas, or is the most popular kid.

When two leaders mistake each other for followers, they reach an impasse. This may be resolved in different ways:

1. Mary convinces Jane that following Mary will be fun, exciting, worthwhile.

2. Mary convinces Jane that following Mary will be less painful than rebelling.

3. Mary gets her gang to convince Jane that it will be safer for Jane if she becomes a member of Mary's gang.

4. Mary gets her gang to convince Jane that it would be safer if Jane leaves.

5. Mary takes over Jane's gang.

6. Mary walks away.

7. Or Jane does the above to Mary.

During the last years of elementary school, as they approach pre-adolescence, girls isolate themselves from boys and make boys not-O.K. Boys return the "compliment." This type of behavior is more noticeable in schools than in neighborhoods. Much of the separation which occurs in the school yard centers around sex-differentiating athletic activities. The boys play football. The few girls who play football play by themselves. Girls play four-square. Very few boys participate in that game.

In the past this type of separation helped each sex to identify with their own sex, and to learn the rules of behavior that were appropriate to that sex. It also served to make parents feel more comfortable, since the separation helps (on the surface) to delay sexual interest in the other sex.

For some time it has been O.K. for girls to be Tomboys. Athletic girls have been welcome in activities where they are an asset—"She's just as good as any boy!" Boys have suffered more ridicule for being "sissies" if they show too much interest in girls during this phase.

It will be interesting to see if making the other sex not-O.K. persists with our movement toward reduction of sex-stereotyping.

Parenting Construction Age Children

We teach our children by what we say and what we do. If our words and actions don't match, they learn to say what we say and do what we do.

Children during this age welcome and need detailed explanation on every important issue. This is quite different from earlier stages when they would be confused by many words, and the next stage when they are often unwilling to tolerate parental advice.

Some suggestions for parenting the construction age child include:

1. Expect children to develop traits of responsibility and kindness.

2. Encourage thinking, questioning, and arguing.

3. Promote discussion of different rules and observations about the world.

4. Make time for each child to do things parents like, and other times to do things children like.

5. Get to know the children's teachers and school system.

6. Acquaint your children with your own Natural Child ego state.

7. Teach the function of rules and the methods by which rules are structured.

8. Teach techniques for settling disputes. Arguing is for solving problems—not just for getting strokes.

9. Define, good–bad, important–not important, non-negotiable demands and areas of freedom.

10. Parents get together on rules. Make policies on agreement and disagreement which avoid double binds and room for manipulation.

11. Give children more complex chores that help maintain the family.

The developmental purpose of our children's arguments is to examine all of the beliefs and values to which they have been exposed, and to decide on the structure of their own personal Parent ego state. The most effective structuring is done by thinking about each rule, the reasons for its existence, and the consequences of accepting or rejecting that particular rule.

Some rules for teaching the cooperative structure:

1. If you don't want to do this particular task you're supposed to say so.

2. If you say no, here are the alternatives and consequences that I can think of.

3. If you don't like my proposal then say so, and offer me an alternative proposal.

4. If you cannot complete the task in the time assigned you're supposed to say so, and tell how much you can do (for younger children), or how much time you need to complete the task (older children).

Children don't tell us, "Hey, Mom and Dad, I need a Parent tape on the subject of weather," or "Hey, I need some more parenting on swimming safety." Rather, children argue until they hear what they need to hear. They may need a certain number of reasons, or a reason which counteracts an opposing debate which they have heard. They may need stronger admonitions to counteract enticing activities; frequently children are aware that an activity is unwise, but their Parent ego state is not strong enough to resist temptation. For example, Nettie already knew what the family's rules were about getting wet:

NETTIE: Mom, can I have a squirt bottle?

MOM: It's not hot enough for a water fight.

NETTIE: But Sid squirted me! Besides, Mrs. Sampoch's letting her kids.

MOM: The sun is setting and it's getting colder by the minute. Mrs. Sampoch's responsible for her kids and we're responsible for you. You may not go out anymore tonight (the temptation would be too great). Put on dry clothes. As soon as the weather warms up again you can have a water fight.

It is important when our children argue with us that we let them know it is O.K. to argue, and to stroke them for logical and creative thinking, with such statements as, "That's a good argument!" "That makes good sense." "How did you think of that?" "Where did you read or hear that?" and to encourage them to report accurately. It is also important to notice gaps in arguments, to stick to the issue, and to not get bogged down on tangential issues.

If they are bringing up issues which were settled previously, they have their reasons, even if they do not say so out loud.

One of the functions of the Parent ego state is to provide a good set of rules which guide responses to routine problems, freeing us to spend more energy enjoying life, and solving new and complex problems. In the construction phase children are ready to learn such rules:

Do the best you know how.
Think about what you are doing and anticipate consequences.
Notice when you do not have enough information.
Ask for information when you need it.
Know your resources for information.
It is O.K. to make mistakes.
When in doubt, do something and study the results.
Learn from your mistakes.
There are reasons for things.
Figure out which part of your thinking or behavior was in error.
Do something about correcting your error.

Children who are high achievers have family scripts with the message "Be successful" in them. In such families, fathers do not dominate their sons, and mothers expect their children to get around the neighborhood a few years earlier than families who don't encourage success.

Children with success scripts receive generalized warm encouragement from their parents and higher expectations: "That's great!" "You can do it!" Children with non-winning scripts hear more specific and urgent messages: "Move this way or that!" "Stop doing this or that!" "Try harder."

During the course of their school years it is highly likely that our children will develop friendships of which we disapprove. Children select friends for good reasons. They may choose to tell us their reasons, and they may not. They gain and learn from every transaction, whether or not we are comfortable with their choices.

When confronted with the problem, we have several alternatives. One is to examine our own prejudices. Is the playmate the wrong color? "They will end up in a mixed marriage!" (They don't have to decide that until they are grown up.) Is the playmate a troublemaker? "He'll ruin my child!" (Not without our child's cooperation.) What need is the playmate filling for our child: do they have interests in common; is the other child fascinatingly different from our family or our immediate neighbors?

One alternative is to insist that our children no longer play with that person. If we make that decision then it is important that we do so firmly, and state our reasons clearly, making sure we have the power to ensure compliance; we are then obliged to notice if our children comply and help our children find friends who give strokes more to our liking.

Another alternative is to express our disapproval and point out the consequences of continuing the relationship. For instance, Doug and Don's dad reminded them that the Roans took their daughters' side in any neighborhood dispute. "If you start playing with them you will probably end up in another fight. I have warned you. You will have to deal with the consequences yourself; I'll no longer rescue you."

Or we may use the undesirable child for a reward, or powerful threat: "Your grades have gone down since you became friends with Ozzie. You have until next report card to bring them up. If you wish to spend time with him then I expect your grades to come up X points! You may have him come stay overnight when I get a note from your teacher that you are all caught up on your work, and are acting more polite in the classroom (no more complaints about horseplay with friends in the classroom)."

We can tell when our children have a reliable Parent ego state when we feel comfortable allowing them to do certain kinds of activities:

Level One—can get the dog to mind.

Level Two—can attend the afternoon movie with a friend and no grownup.

Level Three—can travel to a shop out of the neighborhood within walking distance across busy streets.

Level Four—can travel out of the neighborhood by

bike for a mile or more; and can baby-sit out of the home during the day for an hour or two.

Level Five—can baby-sit in the evening alone out of the home for several hours; and can go on all-day bike hikes with no adults.

Our children can have good Parent structures for certain limited activities well before they are trustworthy in other activities. Part of their level of responsibility depends on their opportunity to develop those structures (practice, etc.).

Early adolescence starts well below the teens for both sexes. Marked increases in the sexual hormones are noticeable in the blood stream of girls from the age of eight on. Boys show evidence of similar increases about two years later. These changes in the blood chemistry are followed by the beginning appearance of the secondary sex characteristics. Girls develop nipples which look like mosquito bites, and pubic down (fine light hair). Boys' testes start to enlarge.

Psychologically, the physical changes are accompanied by a period of breakup of old patterns, "coming loose at the seams," the necessary disorganization that precedes expansion.

We parents are human; sometimes when we are tired we fall back on more traditional responses like: "You'll do as I say, and that's that!" "Don't you argue (raise your voice) with me!" Such a strong Critical Parent approach works because the big person is more powerful and controls more of the stroke economy than the little person. When we overpower our children, we teach them that power is the key to life. Power is more important than what makes sense, than new or different ways of thinking. We also teach them more about rigid adherence to rules and obeying us, than about thinking. That kind of structure works if we intend to continue solving new problems for our children, and if we intend to guarantee them a world which functions according to *our* rules, and which does not change.

We don't always feel up to Adult-Adult or Parent-Parent transactions, particularly when our Natural Child (NC) needs conflict with those of our children, i.e., the youngster may be needing to do some testing when the grownup does not feel like being reasonable or responsible.

A good way to handle this is to be straight.

"Look, I'm tired, crabby, not feeling like a very good parent right now. You'll get a better answer from me if you wait until after I eat, bathe, nap, take a walk, etc., and then we can talk it out when I have more patience."

Sometimes our children spring requests for an answer "right away" on us when we're not thinking too clearly. Thelma says:

Whenever I receive an urgent request for a hurry up answer that the children just "have to have right now!" I have learned to run up a red flag. This is most likely to happen when they are on the phone with another person and don't want to keep the other person waiting. I have a Parent tape in my head: answer the phone promptly and don't keep people waiting. While obeying the tape I neglected to think about the childrens' schedule, homework, colds, etc.

What I learned to do was expect the children to make a statement like the following: "Thank you for the invitation. Rather than keep you on the phone, I'll call back later after I've talked it over with my mother."

We recycle our own construction phase along with our children. Many of us are unprepared for the endless arguments, because such behavior was just not acceptable when we were youngsters. Those of us with strict "respect" tapes may find arguing very upsetting. It is important for us to look at the consequences of the way we were raised, and to look at the future we wish for our children.

When children challenge us we actually have an excellent opportunity to redo our own Parent ego state. We don't have to take the stance: "I'm right equals I'm O.K." We can take the stance: "We're *both* O.K.; here's what I believe and why." "I disagree with you" does not have to mean "You are not O.K."

Psychological Tasks of Parents

When we recycle the Construction stage with our children, we run into earlier personal memories: the struggle to learn to read, the teacher in second grade who restored our self-confidence, the fight we lost with the gang up the street, the time we got to be star in the play we made up, the prejudiced neighbor, etc.

Our children learn things we never knew. Even in grade school they have homework we may not grasp. Many of us want more for our kids than we had (see the American Dream, p. 162), and are delighted with their talent and vigor. We swell with pride when Violet wins a science prize, and Fritz does double flips on the trampoline.

Our Parent ego states are proud of our children—but our Child ego states grow jealous, seeing them get so much that we didn't. This jealousy is also an important feeling to count.

Jealousy is a feeling which results from a competitive structure. It assumes there's not enough to go around. We parents are usually willing to make many sacrifices for our children, but we can overdo it. If we discount ourselves we may teach our kids that being grownup is no fun, and thus without thinking convey the injunction "Don't grow up."

We need to count ourselves as O.K. members of the family, and to find ways to meet our own needs. George, as a child, wanted a bike so bad he dreamt each night about one. As a father, George scraped the money together to buy bikes for his kids. He was surprised and puzzled to find that he did not enjoy their delight more. Finally he realized he was jealous of their good fortune. What he did about it was to decide his turn was next. He used his Adult skills to shop wisely and found a used ten-speed for a very low price. It looks terrible but George knows that he can handle the needed repairs (having learned on his kids' shinier and simpler ones). It works fine and he's very fond of his very own bike.

Our amazement at our kids' energy becomes tinged with the Adult awareness that our own energy will not increase. It is important that we look at our health care more carefully, and take ourselves to the doctor along with our children. This is a good time to review our own health habits, along with the lectures we give to our children.

As offspring go farther and longer from home, we become aware of periods of quiet. Johanna has a holiday in the early fall when her children return to school. At this phase of childrearing, the respite feels good—a breather without arguments, constant demands of fifty cents for softball, a bathing suit to be mended before the bus leaves.

This silence is a forerunner of the time when our children will grow up and go their own way. If we want their companionship, we have only a few years left to encourage it. It is also important that we prepare for their departure. What shape is our marriage in? (See Figure 34 on page 214, Chart of a Marriage Over Time.) What kind of life are we making for ourselves independent of our children? We have separation tasks in this phase of development also (see Chapter 7).

When our children confront us with opposing views and group pressure, we have the opportunity to confront our own beliefs and to retest our own thinking. If we explode, our children learn it is dangerous to discuss outside activities with us. They also collect data on ways to get us uptight, whenever they are in the mood for some "Uproar."

We usually don't examine our own rules; we tend to take them for granted unless they are brought into question. We probably have some rules in our heads that were extremely important at one time, but are already fading in significance for us, and will be irrelevant for our children. For instance, Ricardo says:

I know a lot about the proper way to stoke a coal furnace with coal, to keep the heat the most even and to conserve fuel. Since I was raised during a depression it was important for me to "do it right."

My children never held a piece of coal until their mother obtained an "interesting specimen" of anthracite for them.

SUMMARY

Construction-phase children collect vast amounts of information, both informally and in school. Their Adult ego states mature gradually as their thinking processes become more complex.

Individual talents in areas such as music, mechanics, and sports emerge. Children have longer attention spans and are willing to do the practice necessary to develop skills.

Kids also learn about the construction of rules. They discover how rules are made, what rules are for, and the consequences of disobeying rules. They test their questions about every important issue in their own family. As they move out beyond their block, they hear rules which differ from those at home, and so another round of testing begins.

This construction phase is characterized by testing, arguing, and creating ways to get around rules.

Children spend energy on rules and "Why should I?" questions because they are actively incorporating them into their own Parent ego states. The ideal way to do this is to check out each rule with an Adult ego state before incorporating the rule.

The purposes of argument are to think and to resolve problems. Parents should stroke effective and creative thinking, explain the purposes of rules, and insist on the development of responsibility and other character traits which they consider essential. They should also know what is going on in school, and help their children to deal successfully with the school system.

As parents of Little Lawyers, we are often challenged. Other authorities may take precedence over us: "Coach says. . . ." Our children surpass us in energy and sometimes in specific skills. Our own childhood memories are stirred. We recycle our own fights with the neighborhood bully, our own adventures and risks, and our own triumphs and tribulations in school.

A few hours or days of quiet now and then remind us parents that the child is going to be gone someday. Parents either start dealing with that reality right away and start planning what they will do, or they find ways to avoid the problem.

EXERCISES

1. Construct debates on the following statements. Decide which you favor; if you both wish to take the same side, toss a coin to see who will take *pro* and who will take *con*.
   a. Girls are better than boys.
   b. Black skin is better than white skin.
   c. Rich is better than happy.
   d. Parents should have to stand in the corner when they don't think, the same as children have to.
2. List the ten rules that you live by which first enter your mind.
   a. State the three that are most important to you now.
   b. Exchange with your partner.
   c. Decide who will go first.
   d. Challenge one of the three stated rules of your partner. Find flaws in his or her arguments. Think of exceptions and impossible cases.
3. Each of you decide on something you want your partner to do for you. See if you can get your partner to do it.

READINGS

Ginott, Haim. *Between Parent and Child.* New York: The Macmillan Company, 1965.

Ilg, Frances L., and Ames, Louise Bates. *Child Behavior.* New York: Harper and Row, 1955; and Dell Publishing Company, 1956.

James, Muriel. *What Do You Do With Them Now That You've Got Them?* Menlo Park, California: Addison-Wesley, 1974.

James, Muriel, and Jongeward, Dorothy. *Born to Win.* Reading, Massachusetts: Addison-Wesley, 1971.

10

Firming Up the Script

(Expansion/Consolidation)

I see no hope for the future of our people if they are dependent on the frivolous youth today, for certainly all youth are reckless beyond words. When I was a boy we were taught to be discreet and respectful of elders, but the present youth are exceedingly wise and impatient of restraint.

Hesiod, 8th century B.C.

Adolescence begins with the decision to use our Parent ego state for ourselves. It is followed by several phases of personality disorganization, reorganization, and consolidation. While these processes occur from birth and continue until death, they are particularly evident during adolescence. In our country the usual way to resolve the adolescent phase is to emancipate from the family.

Script Revision

The function of our script is to make sense of the way our life has been in the past and to project some kind of meaningful way to live into the future. In past centuries, when change occurred more slowly, we took our scripts for granted. The future was relatively stable, and we followed in the footsteps of our ancestors. Such an atti-

161

tude is no longer universal. We, who believe in the American Dream, expect our children to go beyond our own frontiers. Black and brown parents hope to see their children live in a society freeing itself of prejudices. Poor parents hope that their children will have more of the good things in life. Working-class parents hope their children will become better educated. If our children are to lead lives which are quite different from ours, then they must modify their life scripts by recycling each of the previous stages of psychological development. They do this while their bodies are changing, and while their ability to think and observe is increasing; they also test out their script decisions in the society in which they are growing up.

The psychological tasks involved in revising the script include:

1. Using P_2 for self and others.
2. Awareness of changing body and physical capacity.
3. Recycling and expanding of previous phases.
4. Development of mature sexuality.
5. Refinement of Adult ego state.
6. Examination of values outside the family (cultural) frame of references.
7. Expansion of Parent ego state.
8. Resynthesizing Parent, Adult, and Child ego states.
9. Modification of script.
10. Emancipation from parents.

Adolescents spend time comparing their own physical changes with others. Those whose bodily changes are similar to their peers are more likely to accept developments with grace and casual interest, as are kids who generally feel O.K. about themselves. If their bodies do not match generally accepted norms they are more likely to invest energy into tracking those changes, and the responses of those around them.

Taller children are perceived as older than their peers. They are seen more easily in groups and get held responsible for what occurs. Boys who mature quickly enjoy their tallness. Manliness is an asset in our culture. Girls who increase in height early are much less apt to be pleased. Smaller children seem younger and often feel discounted. Many complain that they have to work very hard to get listened to and taken seriously.

We parents can help our children who feel out of phase to deal with their discomfort. Early programming is important; for instance, we can teach them that "different" and "unique" are O.K., rather than odd or not-O.K. We know their growth patterns, and we know what our family growth patterns are. If we expect our children to be small, we can give messages such as: "Precious goods come in small packages." If they are likely to be tall, they should hear messages like "Tall is elegant," etc.

When a teenager moans and groans, the least game-y response is Adult: listening and reflecting. Nurturing Parent is useless when the teenager is determined to suffer. If we "try to help," we'll probably end up Victim.

When our children are into "Poor Me" we may get hooked into the game shown in Figure 30. We actually have other choices: decline to play, and withdraw strokes from the young Victim. Another option is to confront, and invite the would-be Victim to figure out what he or she needs to feel better, get out of the not-O.K. position, etc.

Teenagers in our Western world typically experience much turmoil, while their personalities are expanding. Many adolescents exhibit signs of internal distress and upheaval which would be viewed as serious emotional disorder at any other phase of development. Typically, teenagers feel at odds with their environment, particularly authority figures: parents, teachers, police, and the courts. Young people complain about being oppressed.

Much of their turmoil is a healthy adaptation to a changing complex society, with numerous incongruities. We grownups give them mixed messages. For instance, we reward alert, quiet, and passive girls in the early grades of school. We tell them that they have creative options for adulthood, but we get uptight when they start exploring those options. When our boys act aggressive we admire them unless their aggressiveness inconveniences us.

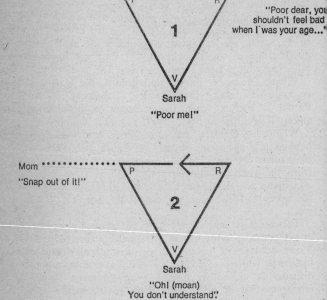

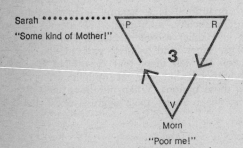

Figure 30. The Suffering of Sarah Heartburn

Recycling

As each previous phase of development is recycled, a number of important and complicated psychological tasks must be accomplished. During this process, young people do not necessarily redo each phase in the original order. With a natural inclination toward growth and health, youngsters continue to recycle certain issues until they resolve whatever it is they need to settle. They also continue to vary themes until they have broadened their experiences to a satisfactory level. For instance, Helen Marie was born with a cleft palate. She was unable to feed normally as an infant, and underwent surgery while very young. Now she is redoing some oral behavior. She spends a long time at the table and eats much more slowly than the rest of the family. She tastes each morsel of food and plays with it in her mouth. Sensing her need, the family has temporarily relaxed many rules around snacking and dawdling at the table.

ATTACHMENT

When youngsters redo the initial phase they display a lot of oral behavior. They develop impressive appetites. Rita eats three enormous meals with her family, another one with her Dad before he leaves for work (on the night shift), and snacks all day in between. Sue, the mother of two ravenous football players, wonders why she wasted her time lamenting their picky appetites of earlier years. Joe talks on the telephone for hours. Herman smokes. Teenagers temporarily revert to earlier agitated behaviors like nail biting, and take up customs like gum cracking.

Kids also redo issues concerned with close attachment and basic trust. Some girls ask for more or less strokes than they used to do. Boys reject physical strokes from Mom temporarily. Young people need to feel they can count on us in predictable ways and to know we are available and care about them. Many kids use this phase to learn more about trusting others.

During their earlier school years, children spent time with outsiders who were recognized authorities or close friends (teacher, softball coach, Joe's father, Susie's aunt, etc.). Adolescents, however, move beyond their perimeters farther and more frequently each year. It is important that they trust wisely. They are well equipped to deal with this expanded phase of trust if they took the ordinary risks of childhood, thought about their encounters, and learned to value their Little Professors.

Kids who grow up in tightly knit clans may not know how to trust outsiders. They may trust everyone, and have little information on how to select people to trust; for example, Sarah trusted Jane. Jane was quite sophisticated, and knew how to talk to boys. Eventually Sarah became aware that Jane was just using her; Sarah's Mom was a handy chauffeur. While they were away on a long school trip, Jane made Sarah the butt of a lot of jokes while she herself flirted with the available boys. Until Sarah "got burned," she had closed her eyes to her classmate's exploitive behavior. Sarah went on to find new friends who treated her more O.K., and kept her relationships more mutual.

Kids who have grown up in a dangerous atmosphere have more difficulty learning to trust people from whom they actually could get good strokes.

Here are some guidelines to offer the young person about trust: you'll be happier if you maintain a general attitude of trust rather than mistrust. Learn to trust yourself and your Little Professor. If you're feeling "something's not-O.K.," listen to that feeling. Kids describe this feeling as, "I just feel like something's wrong, I pick up bad vibes." Adult data include: appearance, behavior, and conversation. How does this person act? ("Weird" is the word kids use to describe behavior to look out for.) What kind of people does this person associate with? Look at the way this person treats others. What does this person say to you about others? "If she bad-mouths others, she's probably two-faced." (Translation: if Jane says mean things about others to you, then she'll probably turn around and say mean things about you to others.) Kids are less likely to trust individuals who talk or dress much differently than themselves. This makes sense, because people who look and talk different are more difficult to predict.

Children set up situations in which to test us parents. Some kids lament, "You never trust me!" while simultaneously behaving in untrustworthy ways. It is important for us parents to note both the words and the behavior, and to confront our children's mixed messages. Kids need parents who are willing to take control when needed. This is not easy because a child may be trustworthy in one area, and not in another. Chuck, for instance, is an excellent baby-sitter. His little customers adore him, and their parents never worry when he's in charge. However, Chuck does not act in a responsible way with money. He spends it as soon as he gets it. If he goes out with his buddies, he treats them with money that he should be saving toward the new baseball glove he wants. Johanna is a lovely girl; she gives good strokes and knows where to get them. She manages many aspects of her life well, but does not handle time effectively. She waits till the last minute and gets herself into binds.

We parents have only limited control over our kids by this age. We help them when we refuse to support irresponsible behavior, confront it, and allow the consequences to occur.

Young people need to have a deep trust in themselves that they can cope with whatever comes, and still know when to get trustworthy grownup assistance for situations beyond their scope. Kids who feel O.K. about themselves trust grownups more easily than kids who feel not-O.K.

EXPLORATION

Exploratory adolescents get reacquainted daily with their changing body and feelings. Paula, at twelve, spends much time looking in the mirror. She tries on various faces and costumes. She feels hurt readily. "I sit and stare a lot—thinking about everything. I wonder what my life's going to be like, what I should be—a doctor or a lawyer. I feel good about that badge I earned in Explorers."

Teenagers also explore the boundaries of their capabilities; for instance, Eric has artistic talent. He likes art classes and draws well. Athletes structure much time on their favorite sports. Carlos and Manuel ride horses. They both have fallen off and remounted, with minor cuts and bruises, and scraped skin here and there. At this point they know how to stay on and guide their horses through intricate drills with one hand. They can execute those drills at a gallop with a heavy flagpole in the other hand. They learned to handle themselves and their steeds competently.

Kids take longer trips and travel farther distances, independent of their families. One of the main goals of Outward-Bound programs is to provide young people with the experience of saying triumphantly, "I didn't know I could do that much!" Parents' definitions of independence vary greatly, as do kids' definitions of fun and adventure. Some kids windowshop with friends; some gangs roam out of their usual neighborhood. Other kids go out of town with the local choir or scout troup.

SEPARATION

"Testing, testing, one, two, three. . . ." During the rerun of the separation tasks, youngsters set up situations to test again whether or not it's O.K. for them to think and to be separate. Their behaviors range from knock-down-drag-out fights to mild Critical Parent statements like, "I don't think parents should live in the past. Times and styles change. Mother and I disagree on clothes. She wants me to dress for the Dark Ages!"

Most kids in our culture are in a bind, because they are feeling more and more pressure to be independent, and yet they still need the support and guidance of the family. They give us mixed messages: "I want to be free and independent" can be accompanied by behavior designed to hook parents to clamp down. Minor shoplifting is one way in which they test us, if we parents consider shoplifting wrong. It is important to notice that our offspring have acquired more goods than their income would indicate and to insist that they make restitution. This will depend on the family and the circumstances, and such factors as how many times this behavior has occurred.

Some options include: returning goods to the manager with apologies, children paying for it themselves out of money earned, etc. It is very important at this phase for youngsters to suffer consequences when they neglect to think. If we parents consistently Rescue our kids from minor scrapes with authorities, we prevent our kids from resolving this issue. They need to hear what we expect of them. They are responsible for thinking about their own needs, for being considerate of others, and for being aware of the reality of the situation in which they function.

Another way teenagers separate is to make us parents not-O.K. (Parents are "old fogies," "ancient," etc.) This ranges from mild disapproval of us to violent discord. Some kids "divorce" their own parents and "adopt" another family. Kids may spend a lot of time at the other home, or actually move in. Some closed societies and clans allow this movement with relative ease. In our heterogeneous neighborhoods, the kids' choice may be downright alarming to the parents. Often moving out is done for just that reason: to alarm the parents. By making us uncomfortable enough, kids get us to look at our own unresolved problems; such confrontations often take place in a juvenile hall, a Good Samaritan Youth Center, a pastor's living room, or an understanding relative's home. What follows depends on how the family defines the problem.

Franklyn ditched school until the authorities intervened. He continued to escalate this behavior until he pinned himself into a boys' center. At the center the counselors helped him to do what he needed to do: namely, stand up to his peers. He was very tiny and had grown up a helpless little Victim. He saw himself as inadequate and his parents saw him as having the cards of life stacked against him. He seemed to carry the worst parts of his dad's script, even after his dad had worked his way out of the worst injunctions: "Don't make it, don't say what you need, try but don't succeed." At the center Franklyn found himself trapped: he had to make it. The counselors continually confronted him with the way he allowed himself to be walked on, but they would not Rescue him. They also encouraged him to learn some crafts and to join the gymnastic team. Finally, Franklyn gathered the courage to confront his peers, and received many positive strokes for his new assertiveness. During the next several months he grew more mature; he developed a brighter and clearer complexion and a firmer-sounding voice (he didn't get any taller). Franklyn's parents saw a family counselor. She helped them deal with their feelings of despair and helplessness. They took a look at how they learned to be the way they were, and how they wanted to live the rest of their life.

Adolescents experience moodiness; they withdraw to sulk, separate, and get better acquainted with their feelings. Debbie says, "When I get in trouble and feel bad, I go to my room and daydream. It takes my mind off it and I feel better." She thinks about herself and who she is. She sits in her room looking into her mirror when she experiences intense feelings, getting in touch with her Child ego state.

Some kids use a diary or journal to practice putting their feelings into words. They can fantasize adventures on paper without actually taking any risks.

SOCIALIZATION

While redoing the socialization phase adolescents clarify their identity as sexual persons. Sexual thinking, sexual behavior, and sexual appearance occupy much of their energy.

By the time he is fertile the young male must come to terms with his sexual drives. Boys in general experience very pronounced and localized genital responses (also known as "getting a hard-on") to a variety of stimuli. An exciting game of basketball, a girl walking by, and/or a full bladder can each cause an erection. One boy feels panicky, experiencing a lack of control over his penis which seems to have a mind of its own. Another boy, fascinated by the amazing responsiveness of one of his favorite parts, spends time learning about its pleasures. When he masturbates, the boy's sexual fantasies are stimulated by what he has seen, heard, and read. Group genital play at a younger age was "Who can piss the highest, farthest?" It changes now to various kinds of mutual masturbation and homosexual experimentation.

Such adolescent experiments are ways of learning about maleness and do not lead to a long-lasting homosexual orientation unless the boy has already decided on that script. The extroverts and group-minded boys discuss together the various myths they have heard, and report on the research they have conducted. Those who prefer solitary activities are less apt to check out their findings with the "local committee."

Girls experience more generalized sexual responses. For instance, a young girl when confronted with an attractive male is more apt to notice "butterflies" in her abdomen, her pulse increasing, and generalized "goose bumps." Both sexes experience flushing and are prone to fits of blushing over the slightest embarrassment. The sexually mature female eventually learns to identify clitoral, labial, and uterine responses with sexual arousal.

Female organs are less available, and sexual caressing frequently centers around girls' budding breasts. Some young females participate in various mutual and group masturbatory activities, the more experienced girls teaching the younger ones. In families where sexual taboos are very strong, girls may not learn to masturbate. Sexual fantasies with solitary masturbation are based on what the girls know about love-making or what their imaginations invent. Their sexual interests are quite wide.

Girls' menstrual cycles are defined by the important females in their lives: mother, older sisters, significant adult females whom they know intimately. All healthy females start to make female hormones which evolve as a part of menstrual cycles. Each month as the hormone balances change, water builds up in the uterus, vulva, breasts, and brain. The way these changes are experienced psychologically varies, according to family scripts. In some families, females are supposed to have premenstrual depression. Others are expected to be crabby, still others experience urges to domestic action (sewing drapes, cleaning cabinets). Uterine contractions which accompany the onset of menstrual flow are defined as cramps in some families, and discounted in others. ("The women in our family are just never bothered with anything like that.") The menstrual flow itself is variously defined as proof of womanhood, "the curse," uncleanness, or a horrible secret. Our beliefs greatly influence our experience of the menstrual cycle.

Girls usually date earlier than boys. They talk for hours, go to local hangouts, and usually get some measure of privacy from grownups. The intensity of sexual transactions varies greatly, according to local customs and family scripts. Parents who consistently welcome conversation hear more about their kids' sexual questions, adventures, and fantasies. Many youngsters, however, in the process of learning to separate, maintain silence about sexual issues. Another aspect is their desire to be independent and retain a measure of privacy. Some teenagers save their most intimate concerns for trusted Adults outside the family. Prying does not work. It convinces our children that their autonomy is actually in jeopardy.

Teenagers like to say radical things to us parents to see how we react. We react with alarm, fearing that our kids are rejecting our values. It may be comforting to know that much of the behavior of younger adolescents from conservative families is talk rather than do. "I'm going to the Springs with a married man," Margaret Anne says. She does not mention until after she has savored our shock that her married teacher is also bringing along his wife, some colleagues, and twenty other students, on a field trip, and that she is holding the permission slip for us to sign. Youngsters do numbers like that for various reasons. The straightest way to find out why is to ask: "Why are you telling me that?"

When we see our children mature sexually we face the task of redefining our own perception of healthy human sexuality. Information gathered by anthropologists and researchers like Kinsey and Masters and Johnson offer points of view which are very different from the Victorian attitude. The advent of modern birth control is effectively separating sexual intercourse from pregnancy. Some of us have always enjoyed sexual freedom and are very relaxed in the messages we convey to our children about the O.K.-ness of sex. Others are very comfortable with more traditional points of view and consider sex a private and sacred matter. Children are most likely to experience difficulty when they get mixed messages from their parents. "Don't do as I do, do as I say" is confusing and breeds conflict. Frequently kids settle that incongruity with, "O.K., I'll do what you do, and say what you say." Some of us parents are caught in the squeeze of changing values. We know we don't want our kids to end up inhibited like we were, and yet we don't exactly feel comfortable with complete sexual freedom. Charlie deals with this problem by sharing each of his ego states with his teenage son and daughter:

PARENT: I care about you, I love you, and I want you to enjoy your body. Take good care of yourself; don't get hurt. Avoid people who want to exploit you. Keep your self-respect. You don't have to have sexual hangups. Sex is good. It is important. Both you and your partner have the right to enjoy sex.

ADULT: There are several effective methods of birth control available. You know about consequences. Don't get yourself into situations you can't handle. If you are stuck, think—solve the problem some way.

CHILD: I'm scared, mad, and jealous. I believed that sex before marriage leads to disaster. I was "good" and now I feel cheated. I wish I had explored more before I married. What if you play around and get hurt? What will people say?

Maturing adolescents need to hear from us what is good and bad about sex, and its relation to nurturing. Two themes are worth pursuing. One is the variety of physical strokes. They do not have to be connected with sexual arousal and seduction. We can learn from Latin cultures which consider it O.K. for men to embrace and to cry. Both men and women can stroke whomever they choose without playing "Rapo." We can keep the enjoyment of physical strokes which we allow little children under two years of age. Teenagers from low-stroke families can learn how to stroke more from the children they baby-sit with, or from the families of friends.

The other theme is the O.K.-ness of sex. Therapists who specialize in the cure of sexual problems invite us to talk and think about our sexual interests more freely, until sexual appetite becomes an O.K. normal appetite, healthy and vigorous, to be enjoyed. Hugging, kissing, skin contact, and other kinds of stroking are O.K. in themselves. They may be just warm and friendly, and they may also be sexy. They may or may not lead to genital contact. Sex is an important part of the relationship between men and women. It is not the whole thing.

CONSTRUCTION

While recycling the construction phase, kids refine their Adult ego states: they develop logical thought, inquire scientifically, collect more data, and arrive at more thoughtful conclusions. Their arguments are much more sophisticated. They can be very enjoyable. We parents have the opportunity to grow ourselves as the kids bring home new ways of thinking. All three of Joe's kids, for instance, are into western riding. "About all I knew was that cowboys in the movies rode western style," says Joe, who grew up in a crowded city. Children who learn to think and to challenge are more apt to see and hear new frames of reference, and to bring them home for discussion.

During their rerun of the construction phase adolescents develop their talents and the products of their effort are more sophisticated. Kids who pursue their interests in cars learn much more than rudimentary mechanics. Douglas has been helping Pop with motors ever since he could chew on a shiny ring. Before he was old enough to get a driver's license, he knew more about cars than most grownups. He can already do minor jobs like change tires, drain oil, and change the filter, and clean the carburetor. Linda is only thirteen. She cheerfully lied about her age and got herself a job after school. She is doing such a good job that her boss is already talking about "assistant manager" training. Certain top athletes are traditionally teenagers (ski-jumpers, ice skaters, and swimmers).

Adolescents form their own ideals and make sacrifices for issues which are important to them. Linda says, "I've told Janee, she can count on me, no matter what." Adolescents' idealism is evident in their interest in issues. They take up causes, and confront the hypocrisy which they see. Sometimes we get uncomfortable when our kids confront us with our own inconsistencies. We have choices: tell them "Shut up! Nobody's perfect!"; or we can accept their confrontations: "You're right. This is what I'll do about that."

Major religions acknowledge the maturing of their young people with rites of passage into full membership: baptism, confirmation, bar mitzvah, and bas mitzvah. Middle adolescents sometimes renew their interest in God and organized religion, especially in the churches which offer programs which are relevant for young people.

While redoing the construction phase, adolescents modify the structure of their Parent ego state, and decide for themselves what is good and bad, what is real and imaginary, and what is important and insignificant. Families with flexible scripts tolerate their kids' new and sometimes conflicting ideas with varying amounts of good will. Sylvia observes: "I am aware that I do fine with my kids' diverse points of view as long as their opinions agree with mine, and as long as the topic is not about one of my basic values."

We parents can help by taking into account each of our own ego states. We increase our Adult reporting and decrease our Parent proclaiming. Our Natural Child is important in every phase of development. The Monroe family does not smoke; their kids complain about the tobacco and marijuana smoke in the school bathrooms and yet toy with the idea of trying it. Their mom says to them:

PARENT: Pay attention to your body. Listen to it when it protests by coughing. I'm glad you kids think it's a bad habit. I do too. It's not O.K. to take chances with the law, especially for a bad thing.

ADULT: I hear you objecting to all that smoke; I stopped smoking when I read the Surgeon General's Report. I am not there to watch you. It's your choice whether and how much you experiment.

CHILD: I don't like it (smoke). I cough and my throat hurts when people smoke near me. I'd like to try grass just to see what it's like, but I don't want to take a chance on getting caught.

If we are wise we will be open-minded as much as we can tolerate, and save our energy for dealing with vital issues.

Script Modification

Adolescents modify script decisions which they made at younger ages; they break out of injunctions they had obeyed earlier. Harry, for instance, is a first child. When he was born, his mother was into complying and suffering. He had "caught" this injunction of "Don't pay attention to your needs" and took the Victim position of scapegoat. Kids would bully him. Instead of fighting back effectively he would do with his peers the same number he had done with his parents, namely, give up his needs, and suffer and whine. Harry decided that when he went to high school he would no longer be a Victim (scapegoat). He made very definite plans for how he would stand up to (and escalate over, if necessary) the first person who attempted to walk on him. This year he says, "I'm just me—Harry. I'm not a 'sissy' anymore." He has decided he's handsome and preens in front of the mirror in a satisfied way.

Girls are still programmed to think about marriage and family. They pick out tentative mates, and dream about their ideal of beginning a home. Boys traditionally do not give much thought to home and family. Many of them in our society have been taught since early childhood to avoid displays of Nurturing Parent ("Ugh! only sissies play with dolls."). The American stereotype is that a boy runs free until some girl catches him.

Adolescents who are career- and education-oriented think about the kind of jobs they anticipate, and the schools they expect to attend. Susie decides that she would not get stuck like her mother: helpless, and unhappily married. Susie is not satisfied with her script about femininity, nor her knowledge of biological functions. She cherishes her religion and wants to express it in her life's career. She figures out an ingenious way to combine her goals in the feminine profession of nursing:

PARENT: I'll do the spiritual and corporal works of mercy. I'll get paid for leading a good Christian life. The better I serve patients, the more respected I'll be.

ADULT: I'll earn a good living. I'll learn a lot of feminine arts: cooking, taking care of sick people, cleaning and being neat. I'll learn about the body, and a lot of science. I can work at nursing to pay for the costs of education myself. If I want to get an advanced degree I can earn my way through working night duty, or get a grant.

CHILD: Maybe if I take care of sick people I won't get sick and need taking care of (*magical thinking*). I'll be able to take care of myself. I won't have to depend on any man. I'll feel safe and secure—I won't have to worry about my future. Maybe I'll find out more about sex. I like strokes. I'll get to stroke a lot of people.

As young people consolidate and reorganize their personalities and make some important decisions about their script, they act more settled and mature. Tom had appeared surly and aloof during his early adolescence. Lisa, who visited his sister periodically, stayed out of his way, because he usually glared at her. This last time when she visited, Tom had become a charming and talkative young Irishman, pastiming in a delightful and very entertaining manner.

Rhonda (age fifteen) tells us why she is a healthy, good-looking, and sexy winner:

> In the first place, I was born healthy, all in one piece without handicaps or anything like that. I live in a healthy environment, a nice house in a clean neighborhood, not the slums. All the people are O.K. in this neighborhood. I was fed a good diet, inherited brains and good looks. The people I associate with are real nice people. My parents tell me that I'm going to college, that girls are just as good as boys. They're always telling me that they love me, and I guess other parents don't do that as much as they should. I'm lucky I got a mother and a father. You can get strokes from both of them. I wouldn't like to be around just one person.

Parenting Adolescents

Some general guidelines for encouraging our kids to be winners include the following:

1. Provide an abundance of warm loving strokes, both physical and verbal. Once boys are over the initial phase of adolescence they will again welcome hugs from Mom.
2. Listen to your kids; respond to their requests. Whether you answer yes or no, explain your thinking.
3. Listen to their arguments. Allow their good thinking to influence your decisions.
4. Expend energy helping them structure their time in activities which consume their energy, which are fun for them, and which fit into your own beliefs about O.K. ways to structure time.
5. To promote healthy sexual identification, let your kids see you and your mate stroke each other, kiss and hug, fight and play. Talk together about problems, and stick together on discipline.
6. Hear with your Adult ego state the messages you are conveying about each sex, about marriage, family, education, etc. For instance, when Donna was pushing the shopping cart, her mother was always ready to say, "That's good training for when you push a baby buggy."

Households with adolescents in them are exciting places. Children become noisier and more demanding. Their confrontations hit square on target. Their arguments become harder to refute. They think more like adults, and their conversations are challenging and interesting. They demand an increasing investment of time and energy, yet we know they will soon leave. Times occur when the house is quiet and the youngsters are gone for longer periods and later hours.

We parents frequently feel out of balance with our teenage children. They act very mature one moment and very young the next, as in "age fourteen-going-on-two."

We find ourselves relaxing over some issues and tightening up over others. We find ourselves being more hard-headed at times than at others. Part of our vacillation is our own ambivalence about relinquishing parenthood; another significant aspect is our children's fluctuations; in addition, we are partly reliving our own adolescence.

It is important that we be clear on which feelings belong to us and which feelings are our children's. We should trust our Little Professor to pick up subliminal clues that something is awry. It is important for parents to stay open to clues for which there are no words. Sol demands to be allowed to go out on an excursion. Yet we pick up some signal that says, "Don't let me go." (Sol's friends plan to rip off a store or bring acid to a party, but he won't squeal out of loyalty to his peers.) "You don't want me to go on that overnight trip (which won't be chaperoned but I'm not telling you), do you, Mom?"

Adolescents in our society are barraged with over-choice; every activity looks great, and, like Don Quixote, they ride off in all directions at once, exploring: football, basketball, baby-sitting, student assistant, choir, softball, dancing, etc. They can reach a saturation point beyond which even the most energetic teenager will not function well.

When they were younger, we parents were responsible for putting on limits and using our own Parent ego state to support the limited P_2 of our children. During adolescence, however, we should do much less parenting, and save our control for issues of very serious consequence. Ordinarily, the way to help is to stand by for consultation, and discuss with our adolescents, Adult-to-Adult, the probable consequences of this or that commitment. They can learn from their mistakes. For instance, Sam and Chuck added softball practice to an already crowded schedule. They ended up in a big mess, with some important conflicts. Dad expected them to solve the problem (i.e., they had to call their coaches and state that they were backing out). He stayed with them while they spoke to their coaches. Afterward he sat down and talked with them about budgeting time.

Psychological Tasks of Parents

Being parents of teenagers is quite an experience. Right when our energies wane their energies and abilities soar. They do exercises to run off energy. They jump and run for sheer pleasure. We do exercises to fight stiffness, and force our bodies to exert themselves. Many of us more vigorous types can keep up, but it's harder than it used to be.

Our children have been growing all along, but when they look us straight in the eye, we are confronted head-long with their approaching adulthood. That growth is hard to discount. In families where growth and growing up are valued, these developments are welcome; still, we are likely to have mixed feelings. Some of us let go of our children with greater reluctance, and give off faint signals, "Don't grow up so fast—not yet." Children who obey these injunctions experience discomfort; their own needs to grow conflict with their parents' needs to hold on too long. They bring us up short on our own script decisions that we pass on to them.

Notice the difference in meaning in the following statements:

If you choose to marry
vs.
When you marry
If you choose to give birth to any children
vs.
When you have children
If you ever finish school
vs.
When you go to college
You never do anything around here
vs.
You have a choice: either succeed in school
or find a good job

Our own adolescent turmoil rekindles in the flame of our children's youth. Any unresolved issues we have left over are likely to produce discomfort in us; in fact, we are likely to experience the most hassle with our kids at the very spots which were troublesome to us.

Our own sexual identity is challenged by the maturing sexuality of our children. While our adolescents are maturing, we parents recycle our sexual development. Dad's little girl, who has always been very special and appealing, becomes sexually attractive as she ripens. Daughter practices on Dad, flirting, and giving him special attention. As she recycles an earlier phase, she competes with Mom, and "knows" that Mom doesn't appreciate Dad fully. This time, however, her weapons are more threatening. Unfortunately, Mom is often going through menopause at such a time and sees all too clearly that her daughter's charm is just blooming when her own begins to sag.

Mom may experience some unmotherly feelings toward her young son, as she admires his broad shoulders and thrills to his deepening voice and tall youthful grace. Dad, watching his son grow (probably taller than Dad), experiences ambivalence—both pride and feelings of threat. An example was what Tony's dad said: "Well, Tony's better than me, now. I just can't keep up with him any more. You should see him handle those turns."

Taboos against father-daughter incest and mother-son incest are very common around the globe. Taboos are usually instituted against attractive options, because they are believed to be sinful or socially disruptive.

When children have or find their own mates as soon as they are sexually mature, the competition is minimized. Some sub-cultures in our society still encourage this. Mothers of many young runaway females admit to hurling sexual invectives at their daughters. In many American families where one of the parents is not the biological parent, incest taboos are less forceful.

We parents defend ourselves in many creative ways against sexual feelings toward our children—and, of course, our children do the same to deal with their own sexual feelings. One is the game of "Uproar." Dad and daughter get into a big fight about her unseemly behavior or obnoxious boyfriends and then each can go their separate ways—slamming the door—to show that "I don't want to have anything to do (sexually) with him/her ever!"

A sad way some of us parents defend ourselves is to shut off exchange of positive strokes altogether. Some of us defend ourselves by discounting the maturing of our offspring. "She's just a little girl."

Our own Natural Child responses count. It's really O.K. for us to know how we feel and to take care of our feelings in ways that count ourselves as well as our children. Following are some options: confront our children's flirtation: acknowledge their sexual appeal. Request that they be sensitive to our feelings. Promote dress codes around the house which will reduce arousal (close bedroom doors, wear bathrobes, no see-through clothes). Respect our children's modesty. Don't go barging into their bedroom or the bathroom when they are occupying it. It is important that parents notice seductive behavior in each other, and protect the children from arousal. Hear and listen to the children's hints and complaints, and do something responsible about it. Pay attention to your own sexual communication. If your love life has become dull, spice it up.

Becoming a Grownup

The final resolution of symbiosis is the parents' job as much as the teenager's. When we give up our children, we also give up the strokes and time structure they provided. We are likely to feel more ready for this if we have been paying attention to our own needs all along, and have gradually built lives independent of them. Those of us who have neglected that task will have the most difficulty relinquishing control.

Young people who are ready to leave do so abruptly or gradually, depending on their style of growing, and the circumstances. Larry, for instance, attended a junior college nearby, then the university a few hundred miles distant, and finally moved much further away on his first job. In Liza's case, she got pregnant and moved out to live with Clarence before she had even finished high school.

Kids who are ambivalent about leaving, or sense our reluctance to let them go, may set up more game-y situations. They do something they know will get under our skin and hook us to push them out. For example, Ron's parents are both extremely liberal. They even acted understanding (and footed the bill) when he got a girl "in trouble." Finally, Ron "confessed" to his father that he was engaged in some homosexual activity, knowing full well that that was about the only thing Dad "couldn't hack." Rose's mom supported Rose's irresponsibility until she started writing bad checks (Mom is a banker). In each case the parents finally responded by saying, in effect, "I've had it! I can no longer take care of you or control your behavior. You're on your own now and must take the consequences for your actions."

Some families do not believe in emancipation. They expect their children to stay on indefinitely and bring their own mates home and into the clan. Our mobile society does not support such a system, although it works in some cultures which are still stable.

SUMMARY

Girls generally move into adolescence before boys do. Their psychological growth generally keeps pace with their biological growth, which is about two years faster than boys' at this time in their lives.

During the Expansion/Consolidation stage, adolescents recycle all of the previous stages of their development in an ascending spiral; that is, as they redo each psychological task, they broaden and deepen their knowledge, feelings, and skills. This recycling also allows them to resolve any unfinished tasks left over from the first time around. Recycling of life's stages is characteristic of human beings as long as we live. While redoing the earliest tasks, kids become more clingy and need more physical strokes. They become all mouth, eating or talking all day long. Adolescents explore farther distances from home. They test the limits of their endurance. In redoing the tasks of separation, they test what happens when they don't think, and get quite nasty. During recycling of the socialization phase, adolescents are dealing with maturing bodies and deeper sexual interest. The amount of sexual experimentation in the early teen years is dependent on peer norms as much as on parental programming. Adolescents redoing the construction phase frequently pursue talents with great vigor. This is the age at which many sports stars become champions, particularly in swimming and skating.

Our kids need to relate to us differently: more Adult-Adult transactions and fewer Parent-Child transactions. It is important that we stay alert, and save our energy to deal with serious crises. While adolescents are redoing earlier phases of development, parents must adjust from day to day, noticing and responding to how needy or responsible their children are at the moment, as in "age fourteen-going-on-two."

We parents recycle our own adolescence along with our children. We experience the most discomfort when we deal with the issues which were troublesome to us originally. Our needs count as do those of our offspring.

The final psychological separation occurs in late adolescence. Some kids do this by taking a job or going to school out of town. Others delay making the break; still others set up an impossible situation to get us to kick them out (by smoking pot, or no longer bathing).

We parents at this point are faced with relinquishing our children and the parenting role which structured so much of our time, and provided us so many exciting strokes.

EXERCISES

1. Have an imaginary discussion with a teenage off-spring. Tell:
   a. What you learned about sex, the mistakes you made, and how you would like to do over your own adolescence.
   b. What you hope for your son/daughter from your
      i. Parent
      ii. Adult
      iii. Child

2. Find a teenager of each sex. Try out your thinking on that young person. Get feedback from her/him.
3. Using the above procedure discuss:
   a. Marriage
   b. Family
   c. Careers
4. Imagine a young person in the neighborhood getting a crush on you. How would you handle it? Would you ask for help from your mate? Why? Why not?
5. Your kids are giving a party. The young people are having fun: dancing, eating, and making a lot of noise. Halfway through the party some uninvited guests show up. What will you do?
6. Your kids tell you that some of the guests intend to bring marijuana to next week's party at your house. What will you do?
7. Your kids tell you they are going to a party at a friend's house and that some of the guests intend to bring marijuana. What will you do? What if the drug is Speed? Hallucinogens? Alcohol?
8. What have you told your children about birth control and abortion?
9. Find out from your kids (both boys and girls) what they know about each topic.

READINGS

Boston Women's Health Book Collective. *Our Bodies, Ourselves.* New York: Simon and Schuster, 1973.

Caplan, Gerald, and Lebovici, Serge, eds. *Adolescence: Psycho-social Perspectives.* New York: Basic Books, 1969.

Erikson, Erik. *Identity, Youth, and Crisis.* New York: W.W. Norton and Company, Inc., 1968.

Gesell, Arnold; Ilg, Frances; and Ames, Louise Bates. *Youth—the Years From Ten to Sixteen.* New York: Harper and Row, 1956.

Ginott, Haim. *Between Parent and Teenager.* New York: The Macmillan Company, 1965.
Ilg, Frances, and Ames, Louise Bates. *Parents Ask.* New York: Dell Publishing Company, 1961.

11

Finding the Cast

(Emancipation)

Inventing New Modes of Living

The period of adolescence has expanded into a new developmental phase. This expansion is an adaptation to our increasingly complex civilization. Extended adolescence allows young people to mature sexually, and to develop peak physical strength and agility, while having permission from society to experiment with various adult roles as "new grownups." They try on many life styles without feeling compelled by society to settle into an early rigid pattern. This extra period of experimentation allows for a more flexible script.

Prolonged experimental living is important to our culture of change. Potent and intelligent young adults, unhampered by family ties, can invent new modes of living. As the pace of change in our culture continues to accelerate, we will need increasing skill at rapid social invention. Young people are inventing this phase of development as they live it. Our culture has only a sketchy script outline for the phase of *emancipation*. Its current definition includes:

1. Termination of the original contract with parents.
2. Shift in roles with parents, from Parent-Child to Adult-Adult.

3. Finding other new intimate relationships outside original clan.
4. Exploring various life styles.
5. Selecting (a) mate(s).
6. Establishing (a) career(s).
7. Making decisions about family life and childrearing.

ADOLESCENT RESOLUTION

The original Parent-Child contract in the family terminates when parents relinquish control of their offspring, by communicating to the new grownup: "We can no longer control your behavior. You are now on your own. We acknowledge your independence and our separateness. You are free to come and go as you please." (See p. 182).

SCRIPTS ON GROWING UP

The family script determines the ease with which young people accomplish *emancipation*. Family scripts vary widely in how much independence is expected. Young people with extended educational and professional goals are financially dependent for many years. Young people from affluent families in general experience more leisure in accomplishing the tasks of this phase. Young people who choose early parenthood experience much less freedom and mobility. From one-third to one-half of teenage marriages involve a premarital pregnancy; young people who follow this script compress the time they allow themselves for the developmental tasks.

Some traditional scripts call for the children to stay nearby and raise their own families within the original clan territory. Sam expects his children to do this. He built an enormous home to accommodate his sizable family. He expects his sons and daughters to bring home their spouses and provide him with his own patriarchy.

Families have various programs for when and how to emancipate. Carolyn told her daughters Rose and Martha:

You are my girls, and you owe me your obedience until your twenty-first birthday. On that day you are women, on your own, and responsible for your own destiny. I know I will be proud of you and that you will do well in what you choose to do with your lives, and wherever you choose to go. I will not interfere in your lives in any way, and I will come to your homes only when you invite me. Until then I expect you to give me your full respect and obedience.

She got what she expected.

On the other hand, Jim's program is much different and seems less planned than Rose's or Martha's. Jim is in junior high school. He's ditching, and will fail if he continues to goof off. He lies around most of the morning yet discounts his mother's admonitions about failing. He says he's going to join the service as soon as he's old enough and finish his education there. Jim's mother wonders, and worries. She's at the end of her rope. She has offered him three choices: work, go to school, or leave home now.

FINDING THE CAST

The original cast of charatcers in our script was drawn from our relatives. As we phase out of our family, we experience the dilemma of finding new sources of strokes. Harry gave up at this point. He went away to a junior college a hundred miles from home. He got so homesick that he returned to his town and married his childhood sweetheart after just one year of college.

We choose our new associates with our script in mind. We can have a Prince Valiant or a Cinderella script and plan to play it out as a winner or a loser. For instance, a traditional winning Cinderella looks for and finds a charming prince who is rich and handsome (whatever her definition of "charming" includes). She goes places where winners congregate, and she falls in love with one who suits her. They will live happily ever after. A Cinderella who's bent on losing looks for a charming prince in the wrong places—bars, prisons—or else she falls in love with a married king, or marries a prince and drives him away by finding his blemishes. In any event, she will lose and live miserably ever after.

A modern Cinderella winner spends time shopping, visiting the castles of various charming princes, being a house guest if they suit her fancy. She goes on various adventures, and works her way by finding employment in various sculleries. She may buy her own castle, hire people to help her run it, and entertain princes as guests when they come to discuss affairs of state with her.

CAREERS

Women who pursue careers in the fields of science and engineering are much more likely to remain single than male engineers and scientists. The women who do marry are less likely to have children, and to have fewer than their male colleagues. Many women who pursue professions still experience more role conflict than men. Couples often start out on egalitarian arrangements until the woman gets pregnant. They both then feel the pull to return to more traditional scripts.

Our scripts contain many messages about careers and schooling: "Get an education." "Knowledge is wisdom and wisdom is Power." "Be a lawyer, so no one can pull anything over on you." "Don't be a nurse, they're just bedpan pushers." "When you get to be a doctor. . . ." "You'll never amount to anything," etc.

Some of us find that our script calls for a career which is no longer appropriate, or even in danger of extinction. Careers are available for which there couldn't be any scripts. They weren't invented yet when we were little; for example, careers in space technology. The doctorate degree, the epitome of scholarship and training in our country, is no longer a guarantee of marketable skills. When the political climate changes, many jobs are affected, such as those industries involved in missile production.

Young people need flexible scripts. They need to feel confident about their abilities and have experience in developing a number of promising talents. They need the courage to make career decisions and the stamina to commit themselves to the discipline required to obtain the required skills.

Many young people are basing less of their O.K.-ness on

accomplishment in the traditional work ethic. The workaholic just does not understand this way of thinking, yet we have old clichés which recognized that wisdom from long ago—"All work and no play makes Jack a dull boy."

Young adults have reached the full level of their biological potential. They have speed, strength, and agility. Full physical strength follows about a year after all of the long bones stop growing and harden on the ends. This phenomenon occurs well into the twenties for tall males. (Football, skiing, running, and gymnastic champions come from this general age range.)

Young adults also have the privileges of legal adulthood. They can drive cars, buy on credit, have checking accounts, rent places to live, and sign legal documents.

They are free to travel; they are knowledgeable enough to find their way around, and see for themselves the societies they have glimpsed on TV or have learned about in school. Many young people travel across the United States. Like a new breed of migrant workers, they travel where their interests take them, and find temporary work wherever they choose to spend time. Many of these young people have marketable skills which are transferrable; e.g., waiters and waitresses who work in the ski resorts every winter. Those who are multilingual can get jobs such as secretarial work and other occupations in foreign countries. With a year or two's commitment to work, they can travel, have all their transportation expenses paid, and receive attractive salaries to boot.

Experimental Life Styles

Communal living takes many forms. Some communes promote the ethic of "back to the soil." Their reverence for the ground approaches that of the brown and the red peoples. "Treat the land well, and it will always be good to you" is a deep basic concept in Hispano culture. "The earth is your mother. Love and respect her" is an ancient American Indian admonition. In such communes young people grow their own food, resurrect organic gardening, and practice a culture of mutual sharing far removed from the affluent middle-class lives of their parents.

Modern communes in general have communal property. They select their families without the usual blood ties. Some communes welcome the use of certain drugs, and experiment with various levels of sexual freedom, while others are monogamous.

A few very interesting communes are consciously setting up systems based on behavioral engineering.

SELECTING A MATE

The traditional Judaeo-Christian script contains strong expectations of marriage. About ninety-five percent of our population currently comply with that expectation. Monogamy or marriage to one person for a lifetime is the ideal held up to us. Many of us comply with the ideal and live together happily—or miserably—ever after.

Couples who live together and who delay parenthood give themselves time to get acquainted. They have the opportunity to pay attention to problems in their communication, if they are willing to notice. Open fighting helps us to get in touch with our own Parent and Adapted Child ego states. When we love someone, we are sometimes tempted to invest too much energy into being polite and not enough into being straight.

RULES FOR FIGHTING EFFECTIVELY

Following are a few guidelines for fighting effectively:

1. When you are upset, angry, say so in an upset, angry tone of voice. Too many people suppress their Natural Child vigor with "Please don't hate me" in their voice, instead of "Hear me, this is important!"

2. Tell about your feeling, and your bodily reactions. "You make me feel" is inaccurate. "I feel" is straighter. Keep the responsibility for your feelings where it belongs —with you.

3. State your beliefs out loud; this gives both of you the opportunity to get in touch with your Parent tapes on important issues.

4. Give your partner direct feedback on what you saw, heard, etc. "You're a liar" hooks your partner to respond

in Rebellious Child. You will have a very exciting war, but you won't solve anything. Rather, say "Yesterday I heard you say you would . . . and what I see you doing now is . . . I feel . . ."

5. State what you need from your partner. It is not fair to expect your mate to read your mind. If you don't know what you need then it is your responsibility to figure it out.

6. Count what you get when you ask for it. Strokes we ask for are just as weighty as those offered to us. They are also more likely to be just the kind that we need.

We are responsible for learning to be thoughtful and considerate of one another. Discounting ourselves and our own feelings to "protect" our partner's feelings is being irresponsible.

Many emancipated young adults live together uncommitted. They agree marriage is an important and binding contract, and they are unwilling to "tie myself down—yet."

Some segments of our population have lived in alternate family styles for generations. Among the poor of every race and ethnic group in our country a common pattern has been mother and kids, no permanent father. Desertion has been the poor man's divorce route for a number of decades.

About one in four married persons participates in serial monogamy. That means they marry one person at a time, but they do not stay with their partners for life. They separate (through divorce or death) and remarry once or several times.

The pattern of mother and kids and no permanent father is no longer confined to the poor. Many more couples today who are dissatisfied with their marriages, separate. Society is allowing women to exercise more freedom in the jobs they hold and the incomes they earn, but society still expects women to keep their children when they separate from their mates. Fathers get the kids only if mothers are willing to relinquish; women who do so face the risk of public censure. "What kind of a mother could leave her kids?" Fathers can also get their kids if they are willing to prove that their former mates are unfit mothers.

Consensual adultery can take the form of "swinging."

Married adults get together and exchange sexual partners while remaining legally married, and maintaining a more traditional marriage in other parts of their lives; i.e., housekeeping, childrearing, etc. Others, by mutual agreement, may form "intimate friendships" while maintaining the primary marital relationship.

Some who live in communes may keep traditional family patterns; others develop group marriages, similar to those in the early history of our country.

Emotional Maturity

How do you now when you are grown-up? Terry says he could tell he was grown-up when he stopped worrying about whether or not he was grown-up. We are emotionally mature when:

1. We are in touch with and enjoy our own Natural Child ego state.
2. We feel our emotions accurately and deal with bad feelings as problems to be solved.
3. We pay attention to our own needs and feelings, and we take constructive action to get those needs met.
4. We can delay meeting our own needs when some issue of higher priority is urgent (crying baby, hard job).
5. We form satisfying intimate relationships with others.
6. We find satisfaction in giving and receiving from all three ego states.
7. We structure our time creatively.
8. We have learned to adapt to the society in which we choose to live. We care enough about other people to respect their needs and feelings.
9. We contribute to our intimate, local, and political community.
10. We have a flexible and winning script from which we build our lives, select our goals, and evaluate our actions.

Thus, emotional maturity represents an ideal to work for rather than a status conferred. The resolution of the Emancipation stage occurs when we decide to commit ourselves extensively to a particular life style.

SUMMARY

Emancipation begins with the termination of the original contract with parents. The young adult moves out from home and becomes independent and legally free to explore.

"Post-adolescence" is a relatively new term. This phase is not a separate biological phase. Rather, it is a culturally determined phenomenon; young people themselves are defining it. The culture of the young adult is spreading rapidly across the globe beyond Western civilization, to wherever mobile young people choose to go. They are seeing for themselves the societies that their parents only heard about, or saw on TV. They are resurrecting experimental life styles based on very ancient traditions (as in communes). They are inventing various careers (mod and head shops). Many persons are living together in sexual union without long-term commitment. Among this group, the age at which they marry is getting older again, averaging in the middle to late twenties rather than in the late teens.

This phase of experimentation, unencumbered by family responsibilities, may be crucial to our survival as a civilization. We have moved from an era of superabundance (in the Western world, at least) to population, energy, and food squeezes. It may be up to this age group to invent new ways of living which address attention to our major ecological problems.

EXERCISES

The following questions are designed to help the participants look at some important issues regarding maturity and mate selection.

A. Find a partner.

B. Interview each other on the following questions; discuss them with each other.

1. Self awareness:

a. What are the most important values to you in life?
b. What do you believe about money, religion, sex, birth, death, truth, and goodness?
c. What do you know about making money and daily skills (cooking, shopping, cleaning, budgeting money)?
d. How do you divide up the work if you're both males, females, one male and one female?
e. What fun/silly things do you like to do? What are you too old to do?
f. What do you need to feel loved, secure, and happy?
   How willing are you to talk about and experiment with lovemaking?

2. Time structure:
   a. What are your favorite ways to withdraw? How much of your time do you like to spend that way?
   b. What are your favorite rituals? Which are sacred to you? (For instance: trimming the Christmas tree on Christmas Eve—will no other time do? Does it also have to be trimmed in a certain sequence—lights, big balls, little balls, tinsel, etc.?)
   c. What are your favorite pastimes? How much time do you like to structure partying, coffee-klatsching, yelling at football games?
   d. What are your favorite activities? Working, sewing, cooking, painting? Do you like to do these activities alone, together with someone, or only with people as expert as you?
   e. What are your favorite psychological games? How painful are they? Do you wish to continue them? At what degree of intensity? What are you willing to do about that?
   f. What does intimacy mean to you? What kind of intimacy do you cherish?

READINGS

Bach, George, and Wyden, Peter. *The Intimate Enemy: How to Fight Fair in Love and Marriage*. New York: Avon Books, 1968.

Berne, Eric. *Sex in Human Loving*. New York: Simon and Schuster, 1970.

Boston Women's Health Book Collective. *Our Bodies, Ourselves*. New York: Simon and Schuster, 1973.

Erickson, Erik. *Identity, Youth, and Crisis*. New York: W. W. Norton Company, Inc., 1968.

Kincade, Kathleen. *A Walden Two Experiment: The First Five Years of Twin Oaks Community*. New York: William Morrow and Company, 1972.

Rogers, Carl. *Becoming Partners*. New York: Dell Publishing Company, 1973.

Skinner, B. F. *Walden Two*, New York: Macmillan Company, 1960.

Toffler, Alvin. *Future Shock*. New York: Random House, 1970.

12

Living Out The Script

(Creation)

During the *creation phase* we settle down to a pattern of mating, living out a career. We express our creativity in our children, in products, in work, and in other ways of being productive. We enter this phase by making a commitment to a life style.

Getting Enough Strokes

We need strokes throughout our lives, from ourselves and from others. We expect the kind of strokes we experienced in our original families. There, we learned what kind of strokes exist, what kind are O.K., and which are available. We also learned how to give strokes, and how to show our love and affecion for each other.

In most families the rules by which we ask for strokes and by which we give them are so taken for granted that we hardly notice them. It is quite difficult to bring the rules for stroking into Adult awareness. When we were little children, our relatives seemed to read our minds, tell what we were thinking, and what we needed. We frequently come to equate "mind reading" with "real love." (Mother knew, why don't you?) "If you really love me, you would . . . without my having to ask." That frame of reference is possible if: 1) we are raised by the same

198

parents; 2) we have identical personalities; 3) our needs never change; 4) circumstances never change; and 5) our own needs are so well met that we always have the time to notice each other's every mood change.

In addition to learning different ways to express our need for strokes, and to acknowledge that we have been stroked, we learned what kind of strokes were O.K.

In general, male scripts contain narrow boundaries for seeking, getting, and noting stroke needs. Males learn that it's not masculine to ask for strokes. They seldom turn their own Nurturing Parent on for themselves. When a man needs strokes, he is allowed to seek sexual strokes, or get sick, and need to be taken care of. Much of his nurturing and responsive warmth was discouraged as bordering on the "feminine." Many of the men who complain of unsatisfactory unions make it clear that they don't know how to ask for strokes. They act very embarrassed when they are asked to show affection.

Women in our culture are allowed more freedom in the area of strokes. They are allowed to hug and kiss their mates, each other, older people of both sexes, and children of both sexes. They are also allowed to ask people to do things for them, to talk to them, and to pay them compliments.

Many of us of both sexes are programmed to discount strokes. When we received our scripts we also received little "but" brushes, with instructions to brush off any verbal compliments: "Gee, your hair is pretty!" "Thanks, *but* I should wash/cut it." "I like your paper." "You're very kind, *but* I know you can do better than me." "Your house looks so shiny." "*But* that's because I keep the lights low."

Actually, we do have another choice: to take the strokes which are offered to us, and acknowledge our good feelings.

Learning New Stroking Patterns

One of our important psychological tasks, therefore, in building our union, is to figure out how to give and get enough strokes from each other, in a variety of ways. Enough means that our Child ego state feels well taken care of. Enough is not a number. Mary Jane needs to hear "I love you" when she and her mate get up, before they part for work, when they reunite after work, and before they fall asleep. Harry needs to "see" strokes and smell them. He needs for Mary Jane to smile at him when he cooks breakfast, pucker for a kiss before they part, and smell something good cooking when he returns.

In order for us to establish adequate stroking patterns, we need to feel O.K. about our needs, and not compare them with the Proper Standard Stroke, on file with the Government Bureau of Standards. We can tell each other every kind of stroke we ever heard of, and decide which ones we wish to experiment with. It is quite likely that we will run into some injunctions: "If I have to ask, it doesn't count," and, "If it doesn't feel right, then it's wrong." That's like saying, "Riding a bike is wrong," because when we first started we felt awkward. Most new behaviors admittedly feel awkward, until we have practiced them for some time, and until we can do them without expending a lot of Adult energy.

Those of us who grew up in families where positive physical strokes were not-O.K. need to become desensitized to the script injunctions against touching. Sarah and Charlie broke her injunctions through simple teasing. Charlie would move close to Sarah, and she would immediately grump, "Don't touch me!" He teased her, by just touching her on the arm quickly once, and then a couple more times at each of her complaints. Eventually they would both get to laughing and wrestling.

Enjoying sexual satisfaction involves psychological work. During the first romantic months of living together, we enjoy the excitement of a new adventure; we hope for a perfect match from our Child ego state, even though our Adult ago state recognizes such a hope is "magical thinking." We take risks when we level with one another. As in other aspects of our union, we have our ready-made notions about how males and females should participate in love-making: length of foreplay, Standard Number of Intercourses for Newly United Couples, etc. Sexual communication involves permitting ourselves to talk about our needs and feelings, and to experiment.

Finding sexual satisfaction is a mutual task. It means

letting our partner know what feels good and finding out what we can do to satisfy our partner.

Women still have a lot of programming in their scripts that sex is for the man, even though their Adult ego states have evidence to the contrary. Our Victorian myths are giving way to current knowledge. While this attitude of relaxed O.K. sex is new to our culture, it is not new to many societies, who have long wondered about us Westerners and our sexual hangups.

Meshing Scripts

The traditional scripts in our country are variations of: *he* goes out to work for the family, while *she* takes care of him, their home, and his kids. The traditional marriage is very symbiotic. In money and worldly matters it is he who does the thinking and the managing, while she remains the helpless childlike dear. At home, the reverse occurs. He can't find his own socks or a Band-Aid, and she makes the decisions on how the cupboards are to be arranged, always "knowing" how her man feels more accurately than he does himself. In fact, a good woman tunes into her man's feelings when he walks in the door

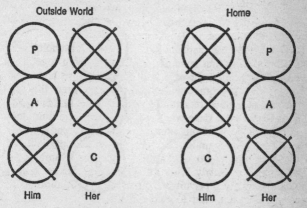

Figure 31. Traditional Symbiotic Marriage

at night, and plans her strategy for the evening based on this assessment. The refrain "Hey, Little Girl, Time to Get Ready for Love" is recent evidence that the above-described tradition is still cherished even in this "emancipated" decade.

Other couples combine the more experimental life styles of the emancipation phase with marriage. Egalitarian couples share the chores, and work out arrangements for taking turns. They decide on the tasks that each finds most agreeable or least distasteful, and each person is responsible for his or her own values, thinking, and feelings.

In an "ideal" relationship, the couple communicate and exchange strokes along all of the possible transactional vectors. In a stable union the couple get enough strokes from one another to continue their relationship and have strokes available for many people. Types of stroking change in importance through various phases of the relationship.

The process of building a stable cooperative union includes consideration of all the ego states of each partner:

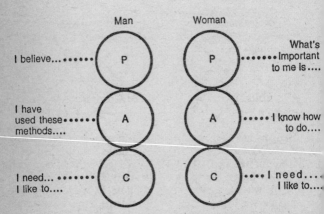

Figure 32. Optional Cooperative Marriage

PARENT

1. Working out our belief about God's existence. Worshiping God together or showing mutual respect for one another's beliefs.

2. Becoming aware of our definitions of good, bad, right, wrong, important, unimportant, etc. Finding ways to deal with our differences.

3. Deciding if, when, and how many children, and who's responsible for birth control.

ADULT

1. Finding ways to get money and deciding how to spend it (with respect to our Parent rules about finances).

2. Dividing the work.

3. Finding a place to live together.

4. Agreeing on major time structures.

5. Finding compatible ways to solve problems.

6. Figuring ways to negotiate needs of both parents.

CHILD

1. Building sexual satisfaction.

2. Structuring fun pastimes together/separately.

3. Dealing with parents, in-laws, and other authorities who impinge on our life together.

Establishing New Patterns of Communication

Each of us has Parent assumptions in our head for solving problems. Those ways of thinking have value (they have worked for us thus far in life). We get in trouble when we follow those assumptions without questioning. We have difficulty when we allow these beliefs to hold us to "the only right way" to think, solve problems, etc. An example of such difficulty is illustrated in the following discussion about buying a coat. In the process of deciding on such a purchase Kristine and Kirk consider similar Adult questions:

1. Do I really need it?
2. Can I use or alter what I have?
3. What kind of coat will be the most appropriate (sturdy, warm, versatile, etc.)?
4. How long will the weather be this cold? Does it last long enough to justify the expense?
5. Where do I need to go, that I need this kind of coat?
6. Which stores have it?
7. Which has the best price?
8. Are any sales coming up soon?

When Kristine says, "I'm thinking about buying a coat," she means that she has been thinking about questions 1 through 8 for as long as a year, and has found a coat which meets her criteria. She is ready to buy. When Kirk says, "I'm thinking about buying a coat," he means he is ready to start thinking. Kirk likes to think out loud and he is ready to begin on question 1.

If Kristine goes out and buys a coat, Kirk thinks she's being impulsive—not knowing about her long process of thinking which she has not shared. When Kirk talks about buying a coat Kristine gets very upset with his stalling around, unaware that his statement is not a commitment to act. They get into games innumerable times: the opening transactions are diagrammed as follows:

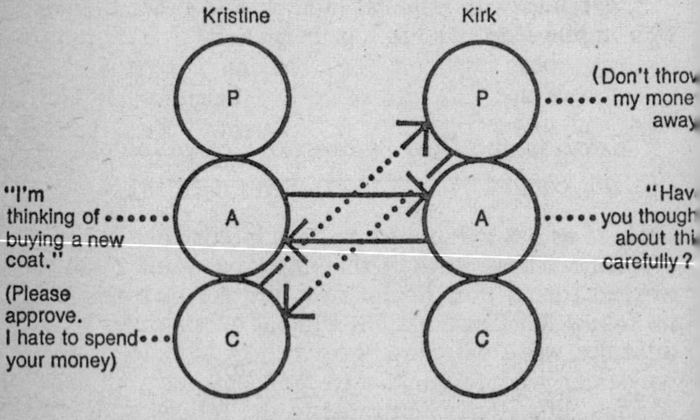

Kristine

Kirk

P

A

C

P

A

C

"I'm thinking of buying a new coat."

(Please approve. I hate to spend your money)

(Don't throw my money away)

"Have you thought about this carefully?"

Figure 33. Marital Ulterior Transaction

Adult-Adult Stimulus: "I'm thinking of buying a new coat."

Child-Parent (Secret Stimulus): ("Please approve. I hate spending your money.")

Adult-Adult: "Have you given it any thought?"

Parent-Child (Response to Secret Stimulus): (Don't throw money away.)

Payoff: Anger and depression

She—Kirk doesn't trust me.

He—Kristine doesn't ask. She tells me!

Much of the process is out of awareness of the Adult of either partner. The games provide them with topics to pastime about. Kristine complains at the coffee-klatsch that Kirk is wishy-washy and never makes up his mind. Kirk bitches at the bar to cronies that his "old lady" is too headstrong and impulsive. Their fights gave them something to talk about but eventually they got tired of the pain.

To solve the problem, they both must examine their Child needs and Parent beliefs, and come up with an Adult solution. Kristine admits to Kirk: "I hate being dependent, asking you for money. I feel uncomfortable not making my own way." Kirk replies: "Honey, I love you. I wouldn't have married you if I didn't want to share with you. You do stuff for me. I do stuff for you. We're a team. I just hate to spend money; when you ask me about a coat and then walk out the door, I get shook."

Kristine learned to say more of her thoughts out loud: "I have been thinking about buying a coat for a year now, here are the criteria used. I have found one, and I intend to buy it today or tomorrow." Kirk learned to say, "I'm just starting to think about doing something; I'm not commiting myself. I haven't decided, etc."

Starting a Family

In our culture more people marry now than ever before. Birth rates, however, have been steadily declining for the last two hundred years. Until very recently "Marriage and Family" was a single concept. Couples who did not pro-

duce offspring experienced pity and pastime about
(Parent): "Who's blemished (infertile)?" "No children?
What a pity!" Couples who had the audacity to choose to
have no children were disapproved of as "selfish."

The traditional definition of marriage and family is
being challenged in our lifetime. Groups such as ZPG
(Zero Population Growth) present an alternative frame
of reference. Opposing Parent slogans include: "Population Control," "Human Pollution," "Quality rather than
Quantity." Their propaganda includes data (A_2) to support their point of view.

Since this book is written for those who wish to be
and/or help O.K. parents, the focus of this chapter will
remain on couples with children. We fully recognize that
many couples today are choosing other options—and
thats' O.K. with us, too.

Pregnancy

Our psychological work of pregnancy begins when we
start another life. "I'm pregnant," "She's pregnant," and
"We're pregnant" are frames of reference which show
different script orientations.

A woman's physiological symbiosis with her newly forming baby is very clear; within a few weeks her body under-
goes tremendous hormonal change. Women in the past
have been led to believe that nausea and sleepiness are
efforts to escape and reject the pregnancy. Actually, these
symptoms are related to hormone changes. Her distress
subsides as the life within her takes hold and grows.

Ambivalence and puzzlement are normal to pregnancy.
Frequently women feel out of control—some other life
force is now indeed directing their destiny in ways un-
known. They do not yet know if the tiny being will turn
out whole. The chances of losing a first pregnancy are
high enough for some to be alarmed. If they manage to
maintain the young life they nevertheless do not know
the hour or the day when they will deliver it. They cannot be sure that they will welcome it. They experience
irritating discomforts, like having to urinate very often,
and feeling nauseated all day (*morning* sickness is a

joke), or whenever they get into a moving vehicle. That's a bit inconvenient for those who drive to work, or must use transportation to get groceries. Such physical discomforts do not make pregnancy an ecstatic "mystery." Each woman experiences pregnancy in her own unique way. She is in a way insuring her own immortality. She is completing the life cycle that she started within her own mother's body. We humans have very few instincts to guide us. We must learn what foods are good for us and our babies. Women do not automatically know what is going on inside them. Rapid mood swings puzzle them as much as they do their mates.

During the first months of pregnancy a woman becomes more interested in the baby as a person. She withdraws from the outer world, to get better acquainted with her inner world. She recycles her own infancy and gets in touch with her young Natural Child. She spends time thinking of her mother and the nurturing she received. This recycling helps her to prepare for the nurturing she will do for the baby.

Men experience their mates' pregnancy in many ways. With their manhood now confirmed, they feel the obligation to measure up to whatever their definition of manhood and fatherhood entails. This usually generates a good bit of anxiety.

Men are also frequently at a loss how to deal with their mate's changing moods and unusual behavior. When they ask what's going on they get such unsatisfactory answers: "I don't know!" "It's your fault!"

Men must shift from seeing their mates as lovers to mothers. All of the feelings they held toward their own mothers are rekindled as the baby's presence becomes more and more prominent. As the woman's figure changes, her mate no longer sees the shape which filled him with desire. He may find her new shape very appealing, or he may find it downright repulsive.

Man is dependent on his mate to bear him his own child; there is no way he can do it himself. Both society and his mate expect him to meet her emotional needs. If he does not satisfy her she may leave, and take his child with her. Her needy Child ego state (which society condones) activates his own young Child ego state, but his male script does not allow him to show it, or even recognize that he is also needy.

A man frequently feels left out as his wife withdraws to concentrate on her inner life and her original family.

A substantial number of men enter into such a close symbiosis with their wives during pregnancy that they also experience disturbances of the digestive system. They gain weight and exhibit other symptoms similar to pregnancy.

Parenthood as a Psychological Phase

Parenthood in our culture sets in motion a series of script outcomes. We have script patterns for Young Family, Teenage Family, Empty Nest, etc. A very real reward is our own capacity for growing and developing along with our children. ("The Child is father of the Man"—Wordsworth.) Each of us brings with us unfinished business from our own childhood, as well as pet ways of transacting. As we experience the growth of our children, we have the opportunity to rework our own early developmental tasks, finish our unfinished business, and learn new rewarding ways of transacting. We also can reactivate the good parts of the Nurturing we received from our parents. "While sitting up at night rocking my daughter who was ill," Eda recalled, "I remembered that my own mother rocked me and sang soothing songs."

Some families consider childbearing and rearing as a side issue. We take it for granted, and focus on other issues, such as our professional practice, mother's and dad's taking turns helping each other through school, or location of this year's crops.

Others consider childrearing the main focus of attention for a specific period of time, i.e., from birth of the first infant to eighteenth birthday, or marriage of the last child.

Another important difference among families is the *value* of children: all children, specific children, a specific number of children.

While Moses was traveling through Northern Europe with four children in the 1960's he noticed that observers disapproved (Critical Parent) of such a large number of children, but his *bambini* were welcome and a source of delight to the smiling (Nurturing Parents) Italians.

Throughout history abortions and infanticide have been acceptable in various cultures to control numbers and types of children. The most common reasons were to get rid of unwanted pregnancies, babies of the "wrong" sex, and infants with obvious defects.

Much time in our culture is structured figuring out which sex the baby will be since one sex may be valued over the other. Methods include astrology, pendulums, and other forms of ESP. ("My Aunt Millie guesses right nine out of ten times.") Now we have more scientific ways; i.e., heartbeat and amniotic fluid analysis. In a few decades we may be able to choose the sex of our babies, but it may be hard to define which are the wise choices.

We tend to see our children, biological or adopted, as extensions of ourselves, and expect from them qualities that meet our own needs. Since young humans are flexible and can develop within a wide range of potential, they often oblige us.

We parents also find negative feelings within ourselves. Chester observes:

When my wife and I first married we were "playing house," enjoying one another. We ran into games, but the payoffs were easy to dodge—both of us went to work in our chosen profession and I received plenty of strokes at work around being competent, friendly, a good researcher and teacher from a wide range of colleagues. My wife and I transacted Child-to-Child for the major part of the time and we talked Adult-to-Adult in ways that we had learned in school. The real crunch occurred for me when she stayed home. (A child needs one full-time relationship to get a good start in life. Mothers belong at home with their children. Fathers who really care provide for the families.) She became more and more dependent on me for strokes at the same time that I was studying for final exams and needed extra strokes myself. It seemed that more of our transactions were colored by our own old messages about strokes.

I experienced running into problems for which I did not have solutions, and I did not have the time to think about them. I also saw myself upset and angry much of the time. I had thought that most of the anger I experienced as a child was caused by my parents, and that I had left it behind when I left them. I was very disconcerted to re-experience those same old bad feelings toward a woman I had selected myself and toward my own son.

Matilda was raised to believe that a good mother automatically has a good baby, and there is only one best way to raise a baby. The message she had heard from her mother included:

Parent—You were a wonderful baby! So husky! (Husky is best.)

Adult—You slept all night from the day you came home from the hospital.

Child—See what a good mother I am?

Matilda's Adult heard in the maternity clinic class that babies differ, but when her baby was born she reverted back to her script:

I saw my colicky baby was miserable. So I felt like a lousy mother. The social worker talked like I would ruin the baby if I didn't take care of him right. She said that colic was caused by tension in the family. Willie Jr. had colic, so I blamed myself and big Willie. I felt awful but I didn't know how to make myself feel better.

I went to a mother's group. They said a lot of things that helped. A lot of other mothers had feelings exactly like mine. They talked about normal babies. Willie Jr. was just like they said. (I thought to myself, "Thank God, he's normal . . . I'm *not* ruining him!") I also decided that the house was less important than the people in it. I told big Willie either to help me with the housework, or else shut up.

I walked with little Willie in all kinds of weather. Even on winter nights I wrapped him up and took him for walks. He calmed down as soon as I started the buggy, as if he knew he would feel better soon. The walks were good for both of us. I felt less nervous too.

"Out of the mouths of babes. . . ."

Johanna was unprepared for learning from a two-year-old, especially for seeing a two-year-old child do better than herself at dealing with her mate:

> I grew up hearing that feminine scheming was bad, so I did not learn to do it. I made a virtue out of being direct and to the point. When I wanted something from Fred, I said so. He often said no. Each time he did that I got angry and hurt.
>
> When I saw Suzan Anne wrapping her father around her little finger, I became jealous, felt betrayed (he would meet her needs but not mine), and had other miserable feelings. I hated to face the fact that I held so many bad feelings toward my daughter, my own flesh and blood, whom I also loved very dearly.
>
> After I felt bad long enough, I decided to learn from little Suzie. I watched her deal with her daddy. If he said no, she did not get upset and angry. Rather she would switch to another approach. Since she was only two-and-a-half I could follow her thinking. She also learned early to phrase her requests in ways that were most likely to succeed, and I could hear her sometimes stop in mid-sentence and take a different tack which to her appeared more likely of acceptance. She was usually right. It was hard for me to change my approach and learn from a kid—but I did it!

Living Out Our Marriage Scripts

Those of us who marry while still in the Consolidation or Emancipation stages of development find that our needs change as we drift away from the value system of our early life. We rethink our existence and form value systems which diverge from those given to us. The reasons for which we marry in earlier phases of development are likely to shift along with our maturation. Couples who marry before completing these developmental tasks run the risk of finding themselves moving separately toward different goals.

Throughout our lifetime, as we recycle our earlier stages

along with our children, we continue to change. We are also affected by moves to new jobs and new neighborhoods, as well as by the impact of our changing society. When we grow our needs change. Self-awareness is a continuing process. We don't become completely self-aware all at once, or once and for all. We need continually to nourish our Natural Child ego state, to periodically take stock, and see how much fun we are having together and/or separately.

Communication is not a skill like learning to ride a bike. It's more like running a computer—the basic skills are important, but major changes occur which require new learning and practice on our part if we wish to remain current.

Psychological Distance

Our psychological distance from one another shifts during the course of a long-term relationship. If our scripts allow for only so much distance, and our partner needs more or less distance, we may feel the need to discontinue the relationship, or get our closeness needs met by others.

Art and Anna are both professional people, who have moved from a traditional marriage to a more open structure. Anna was able to shift only after she modified her script. Art's script allowed for both styles of marriage. They love each other, and meet some of each other's needs. They maintain an exclusive sexual relationship, but get other kinds of strokes from their children and people outside their home. They see their current status as temporary, and expect to modify their relationship many times.

Figure 34 depicts psychological distance over a period of time.

Problems arise when we insist on clinging to a structure which no longer works, when we lose strokes we need, or when our need for strokes shifts. Our distress is compounded when the ways we are used to solving problems no longer work.

A STRUCTURE FOR SOLVING STROKE HUNGER

1. Get in touch with my stroke hunger: an increase in feelings of discomfort, tenseness; an increase also in physical symptoms (bodily distress frequently signals stroke deprivation).
2. What, specifically, do I need that I'm not getting?
   a. More physical strokes? From myself? From another?
   b. More attention strokes? From whom?
   c. Change in time structure?
   d. Feeling in a rut?
3. Find a remedy:
   a. Use known solutions
   b. Explore resources:
      i. A trusted sensible friend or relative (who does not Rescue or Persecute)
      ii. New institutions: library, classes, etc.
      iii. Professional counseling
   c. Release Creative Child Ego State:
      i. Squish finger paints
      ii. Play with kids in the sandbox
      iii. Throw a ball; play with clay or play-dough
4. Decide on a Plan of Action.

Martha and Moe solved their problems using the parts of the above problem-solving structure which fit for them.

Moe and Martha married during the emancipation phase as was customary where they grew up. They had three kids and lived in their hometown. Moe worked at a local mine. He worked with the chums he had always known. Their roughhouse strokes were familiar and hearty. They all worked hard and stayed in good physical shape. Moe went to school nights and studied much of his spare time. He didn't want to spend his working life in the mines. He wanted "out of this burg."

Martha took care of their home and children. When she had problems, she felt guilty interrupting Moe's studies, so she went looking for strokes from familiar friends and relatives. It wasn't perfect, but she could get what she needed from Uncle Pat, Mom, and the others.

Moe's hard work paid off. He got a chance to get a

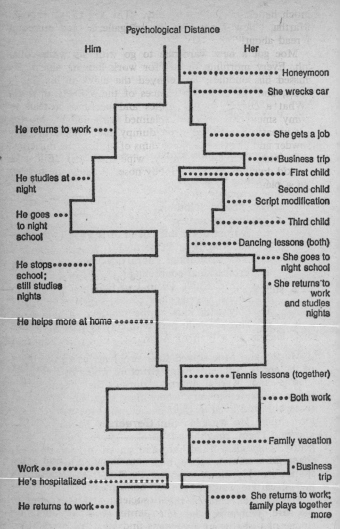

Psychological Distance

Him	Her
	•••••••••••• Honeymoon
	••••••••••• She wrecks car
He returns to work ••••	
	•••••••• She gets a job
	•••••• Business trip
He studies at •••• night	••••••• First child
	Second child
	•••• Script modification
He goes ••• to night school	•••••••• Third child
	•••••••• Dancing lessons (both)
He stops•••••••• school; still studies nights	•••• She goes to night school
	• She returns to work and studies nights
He helps more at home ••••••••	
	•••••••• Tennis lessons (together)
	•••• Both work
	••••••••••• Family vacation
Work ••••••••••	• Business trip
He's hospitalized ••••••••••	
He returns to work ••••	•••••• She returns to work; family plays together more

Figure 34. Chart of a Marriage Over Time

much better job in the big city. "The Big City!" thought Martha. "Now I can visit the art galleries and museums I read about!"

Moe got a new wardrobe to go with his white-collar job. Every morning he left for work looking sharp. He missed his buddies, but enjoyed the envy of his flabby peers, and the admiring glances of the women at work. "What a change, pretty smiles and perfume instead of grimy smelly dudes!" he exclaimed with delight. Martha felt uneasy. She looked a bit dumpy and smelled of baby powder and detergent. Her dreams of visiting the museums were interrupted by "Mommy, wipe me!" and "Bill gave the kid down the block a bloody nose." Finally she figured out a plan:

Problem:	Solution:
The other women look good	Daily exercises Better grooming
I'm lonely and tired of babies	Make friends with the neighbors, join church, co-op nursery
He's still going to school two nights a week	I'm taking a course on two other nights
I want to see those museums!	Find another friend who does, too; trade baby-sitting with still another friend who wants to go to hairdresser in peace

Living Out Careers

Most grownups enjoy creating something. We find satisfaction in what we do, whether we are professional bricklayers, carpenters, teachers, or homemakers.

We live in a work-oriented society, and thus tend to measure our worthwhileness in terms of our productivity. Those of us with winner scripts find jobs that are satisfying. We find jobs with our kind of strokes, or we find jobs with enough money that we can afford our kind of strokes after work.

Women have more options than in former decades. Women can have full-time careers, and marry or stay single. They can also combine marriage, parenthood, and childrearing. Today women are more likely to stay in the working force, to have fewer children, and to return to full-time work when the children reach their definition of independence, or the women themselves reach their limit of tolerating isolation from the working world.

Young people in today's emancipation phase show less affection for "the work ethic." When they reach the creation phase, it remains to be seen what they will do about deciding on careers.

The resolution of the creation phase occurs when we become aware that we have met a number of script goals.

SUMMARY

Creation is the stage of settling down with a mate, living out a career, and creating a family, a book, parts on an assembly line, money; i.e., whatever creativity means to each individual. Until recently "everyone" married and had a family. It "happened" to everyone except the leftover unfortunates, martyrs, or very selfish ones. Today that attitude is changing. Adults can choose whether or not to marry, and if they marry, whether or not they reproduce. If they choose to bear children, women can decide whether or not they will be the primary caregivers. If they choose to "stay home" women still have many options about if and when they will return to work, and about part-time or full-time employment.

This chapter addresses those who choose to create families, and concentrates on the joys and tribulations of parenthood, as well as discussing what parents can do to pay attention to their own needs.

Some of the psychological tasks of parenthood include: finding as much satisfaction in giving as receiving; forming permanent loyalties which involve give and take; using leisure time creatively; contributing to the improvement of home, school, community, nation; and work. Parents must deal with many major problems and be able to separate those which can be solved from those which cannot be solved. They must also decide how to respond to crises over which they have no control.

EXERCISES
_____

1. Find a partner. Make a list of all the strokes that both of you can imagine. Allow yourselves to be silly, indulge in "magical thinking." Enjoy the mental trip.
2. List strokes in the order of appeal for you: most appealing first and least appealing last. If you've never tried a certain stroke, put it down in the rank you think would apply.
3. Exchange your lists, discuss with your partner.
4. Pick out three strokes you want but are not currently getting. Negotiate with your partner. Settle on a stroke that you want; exchange it for a stroke that your partner wants. Figure out a specific schedule and method for getting the stroke you want, and some way of acknowledging that you have gotten that stroke. (Keep refining your negotiations until you have a clear behavioral statement about what, specifically, you expect, i.e., "You never notice how I look" is both negative and extreme (never). Restate: "Each morning before we leave for work I need for you to say something nice about my appearance like, 'Your shoes match your purse, your hair's shiny, you look sexy in that suit, etc.' When you give me that stroke I will acknowledge it by. . . .")

   Partner, confront any discount you see or hear. You must say "yes" to one of the three strokes, and you may qualify or negotiate the circumstances under which you will give it, and what stroke you want in exchange.

   Notice if your partner acknowledges your stroke and confronts any discounts.
5. Make a chart (see page 214) depicting the life course of your parents. If they separated and remarried, adapt the chart to describe that part of their life which involved you, i.e., the one you lived with or heard the most about.

6. Describe the life chart which you expect to happen to you.
7. Discuss your chart with a partner. Ask questions, get at differences. Discuss how much psychological distance and/or closeness you think you need.

READINGS

Bach, George, and Wyden, Peter. *Intimate Enemy: How to Fight Fair in Love and Marriage.* New York: Avon Books, 1968.

Berne, Eric. *Sex in Human Loving.* New York: Simon and Schuster, 1970.

Berne, Eric. *What Do You Say After You Say Hello?* New York: Grove Press, 1972.

Colman, Arthur D., and Colman, Libby Lee. *Pregnancy: The Psychological Experience.* New York: Herder and Herder, 1971.

Comfort, Alex. *The Joy of Sex.* New York: Crown Publishers, 1972.

English, O. Spurgeon, and Foster, Constance. *Fathers Are Parents Too.* New York: G. P. Putnam's Sons, 1951.

Friday, Nancy. *My Secret Garden (Womens' Sexual Fantasies).* New York: Trident Press, 1973.

Ginott, Haim. *Between Parent and Child.* New York: The Macmillan Company, 1965.

Pryor, Karen. *Nursing Your Baby.* New York: Harper and Row, 1973.

Radl, Shirley. *Mother's Day Is Over.* New York: Warner Paperback Library, 1974.

Read, Grantly-Dick. *Childbirth Without Fear.* New York: Harper Brothers, 1944.

13

Script Revisited

(Evaluation)

The psychological tasks of middle age include recycling with our adolescent children, relinquishing them, reevaluating our scripts, dealing with reductions in energy, and preparing for our future old age.

The way we respond to our children's approaching adulthood is related to our own scripts. Joe gets in trouble in high school. The school officials are at their wit's end with his defiant pugnacious behavior, and they bristle when he cusses out the teachers. They are ready to kick him out. Joe's Mom and Dad come to school for a conference. Joe's dad (who left school in the seventh grade) does not act worried about his son. "He's just like I was at his age, and his older brother. Joe's still a boy; what he needs is to go to work and be a man. I got in trouble for a while, too, then I found a job and settled down, got married. He will be all right."

Miguel and his son ride motorcycles whenever possible. His son, Juan, is now taller than Dad. Miguel says, with much feeling, "Juan beats me hands down on the hill. He can ride better and faster than I. He can take longer jumps than I can. The kid's really good!" Juan is asserting his manhood and Miguel is recognizing his son's new status.

Jan comments on the differences between her girls and herself: "When they were younger I took their agility and energy for granted as that of healthy youngsters, but now I see them surpassing me with their own special talents. Both sing well; when I sing with them my voice cracks. They have won prizes for their horseback-riding skills. I still have to hold onto the saddle horn. They can do backbends and difficult feats on the trampoline. I struggle just to climb on and off. I am both proud and jealous."

Recycling Our Own Uncertainty

We enter the *evaluation phase* about the time our children mature sexually. We recycle our own adolescence as we watch our children struggle through this period, which in our civilization is a time of turmoil and tribulation. We feel again our own discomforts, mood swings, tremors of uncertainty, doubts, and changing body image. Not only do we re-experience our own sexual awakening, but we are also confronted head-on with the maturing sexuality of our own offspring.

Marian shared the following: "My children are all females. Two are now teenagers. I'm experiencing mixed emotions. They are ripening and growing more luscious daily. I'm getting a bit dried-up around the edges. While they plump out in the right places, gravity pulls at my curves, I see more lines in my face and spots on my hands. I feel pride and pleasure when they flirt so confidently, and when young males turn around as we walk through the shopping center. I'm happy that they can exchange warm, loving strokes with their father with absolute trust and lack of fear; and yet, all the same, I experience terrible tinges of jealousy when he lights up in response to their attentions. For his part, when interested young males come hanging around his daughters, Dad credits them with all his own early sexual interests and adventures (real or fantasied). He views all these young men as predators."

Some fathers respond by discounting their daughters' maturation, and continue to treat them as little girls. Other fathers are particularly protective of their daughters, resisting the freedom and independence their daughters demand.

We parents see our adolescents enjoying more freedom —sexual, mobile, financial, and academic—than we ever had. But we find it easier to rave and carry on about drugs, cars, money, and school than we do about sex. We were raised with taboos against the topic, and sex seems to be the topic over which most of us still get uptight. Some of the energy behind this dilemma is our own ambivalence. Misty says: "My Natural Child ego state would like to run around experimenting sexually like today's kids do, but my Adapted Child would be horrified. My Parent is bound and determined they won't have any more freedom than I did. My Child would like to see how much they can get away with (ha! ha!). My adult is aware that available effective birth-control methods remove the fear of a girl's getting 'in trouble'; it no longer serves as a reason for 'waiting until you are married.' "

As we hear our children talk about sex and behave as sexual people, our own early struggles with sexuality are rekindled. We are most likely to experience the greatest impact with the maturation of our first children of each sex, but other factors from our own scripts are also important.

Luanne complains about communication problems with her daughter, Sally. "I weathered our first daughter's and son's adolescence O.K. We had our problems, but not like with this one. Sally's impossible; she won't talk to me, she sneaks out. I'm sure she's going to get into trouble!" Luanne's discomfort had increased several months before Sally was seventeen.

During counseling Luanne recalled her own illegitimate pregnancy at age seventeen and her own regrets that she had left school and married too young—"to give the baby a name." Luanne saw that she was expecting Sally to repeat her own script. A prime goal in treatment was to help Luanne and Sally disentangle their respective scripts. Sally succeeded in completing high school—unpregnant.

A man who had to fight for his own manhood by doing battle with his father and/or brothers is likely to expect similar challenges from his son. The competitive feelings he experiences in the outside world begin to bother him at home as his own son equals him or surpasses him in size and strength.

Paul grew up in a competitive household. He and his

next brother vied constantly for their dad's favor. Paul's brother was perfect in his father's eyes; whenever the boys misbehaved, Paul was the one who always got in trouble. He became aware of the competition component to his script when Paul Jr. was born, and has succeeded in exerting Adult control over it. He and his wife are raising lively, friendly, and responsible boys, who like each other. They feel O.K. about themselves and their parents. When the boys reached adolescence, however, Paul seemed to lose his perspective. He re-experienced intense rivalrous competition with his first son, Paul Jr., and saw himself in his second son, Danny. In addition Paul kept expecting his sons to relate toward one another in the same way he and his brother had. Kate, his wife, noticed that he was changing in the way he treated the boys: he was always harping at Paul Jr. while constantly defending Danny. When the boys felt Mom's support, they confronted Dad on not being fair.

During the course of family therapy Paul got in touch with what he had needed and not gotten from his own dad. He is getting more for himself now, including better Parent messages regarding his own basic O.K.-ness.

Climacteric

Women's hormones decrease, reversing many of the physiological processes our daughters are experiencing. We age, our ovaries make less hormones, our circulation slows, and our blood vessels lose some elasticity. In time, other glands take over and substitute for the loss of sex hormones.

In some women the redistribution of hormone production takes place gradually and rather smoothly. In other women the adjustment period is much more jolting. Adrenalin overflow produces "hot flashes," and sets in motion the body's alarm system: increased pulse, blood pressure, heart rate, deeper breathing, dry mouth, and pounding heart. A woman may be very puzzled at feeling alarm "for no reason." Actually there *is* a reason: her body is experiencing an excess of adrenalin, but it is not caused by external threat.

We respond to our changing bodies according to our individual, family, and cultural scripts. In societies where women die soon after their childbearing years, they anticipate impending death. Many of our more traditional scripts offer little guidance for later years because middle age used to be the end of life. Existing cultural traditions have not quite caught up with our current life span.

Some typical script messages in our country about menopause include: "When Mother went through 'the change' she almost died. She had a nervous breakdown, became unbearable, tried to kill herself, and stopped caring about everything." "Menopause is horrible. It is the end of the road." "When you stop being fertile, no one wants you. You are no longer a woman." "The women in our family have never been bothered by anything like that— we just stopped menstruating in our fifties, and that's all there was to it."

Breast tissue and vaginal tissue do, in fact, alter in the absence of hormones. They shrink and become drier. Skin tissue changes and bones get more brittle. Intercourse can become uncomfortable, unless various lubricants are used to promote comfort during love-making. Women can also take artificial hormones (birth-control pills) which delay these changes. Such medications are powerful and have side effects similar to pregnancy.

Men do not experience the same kind of dramatic hormonal shift, or cessation of a bodily process. They continue to produce sperm for many years. Eventually their sperm count subsides as they continue to age, but they experience no abrupt bodily change. Sexual vigor for them is related more to general health and attitude than it is to fertility. Men whose scripts call for early loss of sexual interest may comply, but they don't have to. Men who equate their virility with performance may confuse retirement from work with retirement from intercourse; actually there is no biological connection. The way to continue an active sexual life is to continue an active sexual life.

Retirement from Parenthood

Some people from more traditional sub-cultures do not recognize emancipation as a phase of development as we know it. Children do not go away; they grow up, mate, raise their own offspring, and remain children (albeit grown-up) as long as the elder parents live.

Generally, we expect our offspring to declare their adulthood by leaving, going out on their own. It is a profound step for us as parents as well as for our children. When we relinquish our children we give up all of the exciting strokes which they provide. We give up the ways we used to structure our time around them; many of our familiar activities are no longer functional. We give up the influence and control we used to have. We give up the Parent-to-Child transactions we used to have with our offspring.

Fathers experience many different feelings as they notice their sons' waning interest in father-son excursions and hear their daughters talk incessantly about other males.

The task of relinquishing children is very important for the full-time homemaker. Women who have the Parent Tape "You live for your family" find themselves out of a job and a script as the family grows up and leaves. Hogie Wyckoff calls this script "Mother Hubbard." Mother Hubbard counts her self-worth only in terms of her family. She perceives her reason for existing as leaving with her children. Many women rush to the family doctor saying, "I don't know what's wrong with me." They cope with their confusion by making up reasons: "My husband neglects me, my children never come around, they don't appreciate all I have done for them." Many convert their rage, depression, and stroke hunger into physical symptoms, and report to the doctor, "I have headaches" or "It must be menopause" instead of, "I am mad as hell at my dilemma!" They often get tranquilizers. Some women who maintain the not-O.K. position medicate themselves on alcohol. They become the silent drinkers, and slowly suicide.

Women who reach the end of their script at this point face existential crisis. This crisis is accompanied by the usual characteristics of crises: they suffer extreme psychological distress, none of the coping mechanisms they know work, and they continually feel a need which they cannot discount. People in crisis are people in flux. It is a time when they are most likely to change with a minimum of intervention.

Lori was sent to the mental health clinic by her doctor, who insisted her headaches were caused by bottled-up feelings. In the clinic she admitted that she was losing control over her children, and realized it was just a matter of time before she could no longer depend on them for strokes. Her husband kept his distance by repairing trucks in the garage during his spare time.

In group therapy Lori got in touch with her rage. Then she faced a choice: either learn how to get more strokes from her husband or start seeking them elsewhere. She decided to do both. She joined a "great books" club, a bowling team, and began a night class. Her husband growled objections and made not too subtle hints about her possible infidelity. She countered this with, "I didn't know you cared!" and acted more seductive with him, along with delivering straight communications about her needs. The group confronted her on how controlling she was toward him. As she relinquished some of this control over her husband he responded more, and their relationship improved considerably.

Women who decide to remain with their original script and who want to feel O.K. again sometimes find other children to raise: foster children, grandchildren, etc. Women who alter their scripts slightly go out and find a "little job" which will reward them monetarily for their homemaking skills; e.g., baby-sitting or housecleaning. They can also perform certain tasks like dressmaking and selling preserves at home. "Homemakers" serve families in crisis. These women come for the day, clean house, cook meals, stroke little children, send them off to school shop for groceries, etc. They are vital to the families they serve; they prevent family collapse and are paid in both money and satisfaction for doing what they know how to do best.

Careers

Men and women who work reach the peak of their careers during middle age. They are in positions of power and prestige. Susan, a psychotherapist, states: "At work I began noticing statements made by younger clinicians which were superficial and showed lack of experience. I'm beginning to feel wise. I take great personal satisfaction in knowing that most of the time when patients share their lives with me, I can say with conviction, 'I've been there. I know how that feels.' I am aware that I have not experienced extreme external trauma (loss of child, war), or extremes of wealth and power, but I *have* experienced most of life's everyday events."

Chet, an auto mechanic, was a terrible rabble-rouser at work in his younger days. He was a good enough mechanic to hold his job and now he has moved up to night supervisor. He is one of those "pencil pushers" he used to castigate. Chet has improved the work output markedly on his shift, and is well known for the way he manages the employees. He has a knack for keeping things running smoothly. Rebellious and lazy behavior have diminished and morale is rising noticeably. Chet feels proud of his crew and his skill at "practical psychology."

In some industries professional men sometimes are unsettled in their careers until they reach their thirties. Definitions of middle age are related to economic grouping. Men with smaller incomes tend to see themselves as old and middle-aged earlier than men from higher income brackets. For instance, some men are just completing professional degrees around twenty-five, whereas poorer men have already been in the labor market for ten years. Some professional men are just settling down to a career around the age of thirty.

Forty is a magical age for men and women in our society. Men in business are expected to move up to administrative levels. For them to be considered successes, the script of the system calls for all men to move up. If they don't move up they usually experience pressure and disapproval from the system. In some institutions, a person who is passed up for two or three promotions (or chooses to pass them up) is a "dead duck." Being passed over means they have not won—even if they stay in jobs they like. "If you are a winner, you climb."

One of the dilemmas faced by organizational men is the expectation that they will rise by becoming administrators. For those who failed to fulfill scripts of "success" or otherwise did not meet their own expectations, this can be a time of depression, irritability, and renewed effort. Conflicts arise when an individual's script leads one direction and the company's script leads another. A person has several options: drop his own script and accept the company's; cling to his own script and become increasingly out of phase with "management"; shop for a company whose script is more compatible.

Harry, a teacher, was studying for his Master's degree in counseling when the school authorities told him to switch his major to administration. Their script called for his becoming a principal. He complied for twelve years. During middle age he decided that he was miserable doing what others wanted, and he chose to return to his own script. He's back now in a training program, learning what he needs to fulfill his own script, rather than the script he allowed the school system to impose. "I'm damn scared. A man at my age, changing jobs like this; but, scared or no, I am determined to do what *I* have wanted to do for a long time!"

Men who are dissatisfied have several choices; some include: redoubling efforts on the job, taking the risk to change jobs, or changing one's career. Another option is to give up and start growing old.

Script Revisited

Middle age is a time for taking another look at our life scripts, and asking questions like: Am I satisfied with my script? Did I choose the one I really wanted to live out? Where do I want to be twenty or thirty years from now? Am I headed that way? What will it cost me to get there?

What plans and decisions do I need to make for my immediate future? My old age?

Jake re-examines his script thusly:

What's it like for me right now? I'm past forty, my health and vigor will never be as high as they used to be. There is no hope of my energy level returning to that of my early teens, when I could work full-time nights, go to school full-time days, get my homework done, sleep enough, party a lot, and even gain weight!

Until the last few years I felt like I was assaulting life. Now it feels more like a holding action (that's on a physical level), as I see my chest move down to my belly. Sexually, I'm feeling freer and enjoying my senses more. Even as I do, however, I already notice the difference in my ability to see—fine print in the paper is now more difficult to handle. It's also harder to see while driving at night. I spent years looking forward to the future. I do that less now. The future holds freedom in some ways, but it will also be accompanied by less energy and older muscles. Part of what I will be free from (children) was what I dreamed of obtaining in my youth (home, family, children).

I don't enjoy my parents. I have a long-distance relationship with them. My father, an alcoholic, has every intention of continuing his recreational pastime of "High and Proud" as long as he is able to lift the cup to his lip. My mother, who has restricted herself to a few lifetime friends and her clan, lives very much the same way she did when she stopped working to marry forty-four years ago. She has lived in the same neighborhood for more than sixty years. She still does a little housework, goes downtown every week, and cooks good meals.

When redoing a script we weed out aspects which are no longer functional, just as we give away old furniture. We also invest less energy into aspects which become lower on our priority list. We can re-invest energy in parts of ourselves that have lain dormant for years. We can look at our script from a new point of view and decide we already have permission to do something we wish to do. We can dispose of whole sections of our script, or throw out the whole and start from scratch. But the older we are, the more difficult and scary it is to throw away the investment of a lifetime. Following are some examples of script revision.

Michael has become a noted academician. He raised his children and supported his wife while he did what he was supposed to do. He reached the level of administration a very "successful"—and unhappy—man. After his last child became independent, he divorced his wife and married a woman who did not hold traditional values. They worked and saved enough to go overseas. Michael is living now as a gray-haired hippie on one of the islands he used to tell his students about. He makes some money by teaching in a local school.

Alfreida ran out of script after her second child. She had done everything she was supposed to do: get an education, write a book, marry a professional man, buy a nice home, have children (including a son). Now she had no direction. She drifted anxiously for a while, and then made a few tentative plans, finally settling into volunteer work at a nursery school.

Aging

We middle-aged people find ourselves relating to helpers who are younger than we are—the high-school counselor, the dentist, the young nurse. We notice our parents looking older and moving more slowly. ("I realize that someday they will die.")

When parents die, adult children may experience relief. If our parents die before their time we adult children may not be ready. We usually find it easier to terminate if our parents live to an old age or die after a lengthy illness. Those who have intense unresolved ambivalence toward parents are apt to suffer longer and more intensely than those who have mostly good or mainly bad feelings.

Doris is well past sixty. She was hospitalized for an emotional disorder for several months. She returned home to her husband and a father-in-law who was senile and incontinent. She attended counseling regularly and gained some insights but she never mentioned her father-in-law in group except to say that her husband was adamant about his dad not going to a nursing home. Shortly after her father-in-law passed away, Doris started making notable changes in her life: accompanying her husband on conventions, going out on her own to sight-see in strange towns, and becoming more aggressive about what she wanted.

SUMMARY

Parents enter the *Evaluation phase* about the time their offspring mature sexually. As we watch our children ripen, we parents recycle our own adolescence, which was and still is a period of trial and turmoil in Western civilization. We women see our daughters' lush young beauty unfold, while our own is beginning to droop a bit. Women respond to their sons' broad shoulders and deepening voices. Men see their daughters, whom they've loved and held since babyhood, become disturbingly attractive. The competitive feelings fathers experience in the outside world begin to bother them at home as their sons equal or surpass them in size and strength. We parents feel disappointment when our children don't do well, and pride complicated by wistfulness when they do.

As children leave, we parents face the task of learning to restructure our time. This task is more significant for full-time homemakers. Parents engaged in demanding careers focus much of their energy on work.

Middle age is a time of reevaluating our script: did I choose the right career, the right mate? did I succeed at my life plan, do I really want to follow the script I chose? Couples who have buried themselves in separate interests may find very little left in common. They have several options: to just room together, to part, or to build a new script together.

Those of us who are satisfied with our careers and marriages pursue them with vigor and satisfaction. Those who are not face choices of continuing to feel stuck, or taking risks in new directions. Middle-aged people notice the repetition of the life cycles in their children and grandchildren, enjoying the babies with fewer anxieties than the first time around. We also become aware of the aging of our own parents. One of the important tasks of this phase is to plan ahead for a meaningful old age.

EXERCISES

1. Learn natural ways to tune into yourself:
   a. Yoga
   b. Music
   c. Meditation
   d. Soaking in the tub
   e. Drinking hot tea
   f. Listening to the conversation at family gatherings
   g. Experiment to find out what helps you:
      i. Examine your feelings. Notice what you do.
      ii. Fill in a script questionnaire (see *Born to Win*, p. 210).
2. Accept permission to change your script:
   a. Change a few odds and ends
   b. Make some important changes
   c. Re-activate a permission you have always had but seldom used
   d. Do serious architectural redesign on your script
   e. Throw out the whole thing and start from scratch
3. Decide how you need to start, and when.
4. Initiate Search Behavior
   Examine new frames of reference, learn about new possibilities; for instance, study a different religion or Eastern philosophy.
5. Learn about new possibilities:
   a. Travel
      i. to the library, and read a different kind of book
      ii. out of your neighborhood, take a bus ride across town, to a new shopping center, or a park listed in the phone book
      iii. to a different kind of vacation spot—a new state, or country, or continent (depending on your pocketbook)
   b. Join a consciousness-raising group—they offer new

frames of reference, group support in examining injunctions, and group support (permission and protection) to challenge those injunctions.
c. Take up a new activity which stimulates a new part of you. For instance, if you have spent years immersed in diapers and sewing, which are Parent activities, join a Bridge or Famous Foods Club— rediscover your thinking ability.
d. Join a militant group (NOW, Chicanos, Black Panthers, Gray Panthers).
e. Join a special interest group, one involved in something you have wanted to do since you were a child.
f. Spend time in messy child activities every day: play in a sandbox, draw pictures on the bathroom mirror with shaving cream, etc.
g. Find yourself a permissive atmosphere which will offer you the permission you need, plus help you to look realistically at consequences of change
   i. Therapy: family, group, individual
   ii. Total imersion
       Walden Two-type commune
       A Parenting House

6. Keep a diary. As you plan new risks, write down your fears, whether or not they seem ridiculous. Write down exciting feelings and uneasy feelings. Then record what really happens. Does the world fall apart? Does your family stop loving you? Do you look different? Feel different?

Do this each time you take a risk. Then when you are scaring yourself, reread your previous struggles, and what actually happened.

READINGS

Bach, George, and Deutch, Ronald. *Pairing*. New York: Avon Books, 1971.
Boston Women's Health Book Collective. *Our Bodies, Ourselves*. New York: Simon and Schuster, 1973.
Castañeda, Carlos. *The Teachings of Don Juan: A Yaqui*

Way of Knowledge. New York: Ballantine Books, 1968.

Comfort, Alex. *The Joy of Sex*. New York: Crown Publishers, Inc., 1972.

Gray, Madeline. *The Changing Years*. New York: Doubleday and Company, 1967.

James, Muriel, and Jongeward, Dorothy. *Born To Win*. Reading, Massachusetts: Addison-Wesley Publishing Company, 1971.

Janeway, Elizabeth. *Man's World, Woman's Place*. New York: Dell Publishing Company, Inc., 1971.

Mead, Margaret. *Blackberry Winter, My Earlier Years*. New York: Simon and Schuster, 1972.

O'Neill, Nena, and O'Neill, George. *Open Marriage*. New York: Avon Books, 1973.

Radl, Shirley. *Mother's Day Is Over*. New York: Warner Paperback Library, 1974.

Saxe, Louis, and Gerson, Noel. *Sex and the Mature Man*. New York: Gilbert Press, Inc., 1964.

Schutz, William C. *Joy*. New York: Grove Press, 1967.

Steiner, Claude. *Scripts People Live*. New York: Grove Press, 1974.

Wyckoff, Hogie. "The Stroke Economy in Women's Scripts." *Transactional Analysis Journal* I, 3 (July 1971).

14

Epilogue

(Resolution)

Old age is the last stage in our development. It begins with our retirement from "work," and ends with our death. It is not a disease. Old age is a stage of life, with additional developmental tasks: recycling life's stages, reviewing our script, making peace with significant others, dealing with losses, and coming to terms with death.

Most people in our society discount the fact that we are aging. We tend to avoid thinking about it—yet we, more than any previous generation, can expect to reach old age.

Our life span has doubled in one century. We Americans can expect to live until our mid-seventies. Those of us who are fifty can expect to live twenty-four more years. Those of us who are sixty-five can expect to live at least twelve more years. White women live the longest. Black men live the shortest lives. Since women generally marry men older than themselves, they can expect to spend close to a decade as widows.

Retirement from Work

Retirement from conventional work is a developmental task peculiar to our society, and not a universal one. In

234

some ancient societies, an old person continues to be an active part of the usual work of the community. Many people in our society feel forced to retire at age sixty-five or even younger. This arbitrary age has little to do with individual vigor and ability. Many people this age express bitterness at a culture which considers people over a certain age as no longer welcome in the labor market. Others just refuse to stay on the shelf.

Pete was sixty-five when he retired from the post office. He retired for six months and then obtained a job as a bank guard. He found himself gaining weight and growing very bored. He then switched his political affiliation and managed to come up with another job. By the time he was almost seventy, he was working for the highway department, going to blueprinting school every winter, and getting praise for his vigor and problem-solving ability on the job. In order to get the job he bought a car and started driving thirty miles a day to and from construction sites.

Older people with power and prestige can sometimes influence arbitrary cutoff, by retaining ownership of the business, or by designating themselves as consultants to the company and deciding to work part-time, gradually relinquishing the most tiring aspects of the business. Val's father turned over the usual affairs of the business to his subordinates, and started traveling, to open up subsidiary businesses in other countries, using the connections and experience he had acquired over a lifetime of work.

Retirement may be welcomed or dreaded, depending on how it fits in with one's script. Bad feelings go with decisions like, "I'm no longer useful, I'm on the shelf, I'm not-O.K." Good feelings would go with decisions like, "I've done what I was supposed to do. Now it's O.K. for me to do what *I* want to do."

Recycling

Grandparents usually report that they enjoy their grandchildren. Katy says, "I can just enjoy Lonny, Larry, and Lottie and not worry about them. Their parents can't do that. I relax, and play with them when I'm in the mood.

If I'm not, then I send them home, or not go to visit. It's so pleasant to be with them when I feel like it, and not, when I don't."

Oldsters review the cycles of life from the unique position of having been through them all:

> We who live seven or eight decades are life's experts; we have had the most experience in doing and reworking each developmental task, and have the most experience in surviving. We have endured several economic depressions, and rebuilt our lives.
>
> We are earth's experts on change. We were born at the turn of the century. We watched gaslight give way to electricity and now to solar and nuclear energy. We have watched telephone poles go up around the world, and be replaced by buried cables that stretch across the seas. We have watched our neighbors travel by horse and wagon, then horseless carriages, then by planes, and now by lunar modules. We grew up making jokes about the man on the moon and have lived to see Man on the moon—in "living color"!

Reviewing Our Life Script

Reviewing our life script is another task of the *resolution phase.* It is important and mentally healthy in reviewing our scripts to find meaning and value in what we have done, and to come to terms without regrets over what we failed to do. It is important to give ourselves credit for our accomplishments and to recognize that we did what we needed to do under the circumstances. "I should have . . . if only . . . and what if . . ." are various ways to make ourselves discontent, and interfere with resolution.

We have completed our obligations to our family traditions. We have raised our children and lived to see our children's children. We worked for the prescribed number of years. Now what?

"Now what?" can be a scary question as well as an exhilarating one. We have more than a decade of living after we retire. How do we wish to spend that time?

Old people, like young people in the Emancipation stage, are expanding and developing this phase as they continue to live.

Winners, oldsters who feel O.K. about themselves and the world, are inventing various styles of aging. Organizers exchange new activities and interests for old ones. Pete is an example of a reorganizer (see p. 235). Reorganizers place great value on being active. They go from work to other meaningful activities such as community affairs, church activities, or various associations.

Another pattern chosen by winners is that of being selective of their activities, and structuring their time around roles which are important to them. Margaret is the wife of a retired minister. She took her role as the pastor's wife very seriously and gave to her mission tirelessly. Now that they have retired, she is changing her focus: "I looked forward to the day when I would have free time to do *my* things. Now I do have that freedom. Sometimes I feel guilty about refusing to do the things I can do, but I have decided I will keep myself free to follow my own pursuits this time."

José is a musician; to retire, he slowed down and became a consultant. Helena, his wife, is a professional writer. She now does only free-lance work. Some old people choose to disengage. Fred belongs in this category. He does not race around to all of the senior citizen activities; instead, he spends his time at home, chatting with neighbors, puttering around the house and garden, and taking walks every day to buy odds and ends at the little shopping center. The roundtrip to the store is well over a mile up and down hill. Fred cordially declines rides from well-meaning neighbors, and continues to preserve his independence and his circulation.

Many oldster carry around scripts which dictate that they can only be O.K. if . . . "you keep busy." This type frequently are obeying the injunction, "Don't be satisfied." Some people in this category restrict their thinking to very elaborate health rituals. "I'm O.K. if . . . I drink Foothills pure drinking water every three hours, take my Regitol with my morning and evening meal, and . . . etc."

Some oldsters are into the "I'm not-O.K.—You're O.K." script position. They constantly seek reassurance from others. Margaret's mother is like that. She is forever badgering Margaret with statements like: "You must hate me." "I know I'm a burden to you." Recently Margaret's mother had a severe accident. At the age of ninety-six she recovered, and after months of struggle in a wheelchair, she finally got upright and took a step in a walker. She was as triumphant as if she had stopped the war single-handed. Margaret remarks on her will power, "I don't know how you keep going!" She replies, "It's not will power, it's fear! If I don't keep going you'll put me in one of those places!" As far as Margaret's mother is concerned, the Nursing Home is the Poor House, and she won't have anything to do with it.

Those who have maintained the stance that "I'm not-O.K.—you're not-O.K." are apathetic. They complain that "Life is hard, but wasn't it always?" and "There never was much that could be done about it, anyway." They include about five percent of the total population of people over sixty-five who become disintegrated, disorganized, and grossly deteriorated. People who fit this category are not necessarily those greatly advanced in age.

Myths of Old Age

Old people who choose to disregard the "characteristics of old age" are exploding many of the myths in our scripts about how we are supposed to act when we are old:

1. *Our brains become sieves through which recent events slip.*

Forgetfulness can be caused by high blood pressure, "little strokes" *, grief, and poor nutrition. Better diets, more Warm Fuzzies, and controlling one's blood pressure can do wonders for one's memory.

2. *Like old dogs, we cannot learn new tricks.*

Old people can continue to learn as long as they live. They need a more leisurely pace and adequate support from others who give them permission to keep learning. Bessie and Butch sought marriage counseling when they were sixty-eight, stating that they were dissatisfied with their relationship. They subsequently decided to let go of

---

* Cerebral hemorrhages.

their kids, modify their scripts, and change their marriage. They learned how to stroke each other better, and have a lot more fun. They also made plans for their advancing years.

3. *Flexibility, creativity, and curiosity are gone.*

With adequate emotional support, and permission to loosen up, old people can be very creative and spontaneous. Many need permission to free themselves from the stereotypes they are obeying on how old people are *supposed* to be. Dorothy and Dan valued home ownership. They have now decided to sell their home at a profit, rent an apartment, and take their first trip to Europe.

4. *Old people live in the past.*

In this instance, there is much factual evidence to support the stereotype. Virtually all people beyond the age of fifty-five are past-oriented. It is a mechanism to avoid the future, which may include disability and will certainly include death. There comes a time when we have more to look back on than we have to look forward to.

5. *Old people lack energy. They are slow and plodding.*

Speed is relative. It depends on the pace around one. The pace in New York would be overwhelming to a young, vigorous adult who was born and raised in Abiqui, New Mexico. For example, Rudolpho remembers being irritated at the slow pace when he walked his aging grandmother home. "To amuse myself I started looking around and noticed her feet. They were flying! She was taking three very rapid steps to every one of mine. (I was a foot taller than she.)"

6. *Old people are ultraconservative.*

Many old people are more sympathetic to the viewpoint of their grandchildren than the generation in between. The Gray Panthers are militant groups of senior citizens who have declared themselves America's most neglected minority. The admission requirement is an interest in old age.

Eric is a retired petroleum geologist. When the oil spills occurred at Santa Del Rio, Eric started visiting civic groups, lecturing to businessmen, and taking an ecology position on the problem. He suggested solutions which were good for the ecology, but less profitable for the big oil interests. They were furious, but because Eric didn't work for anybody they couldn't touch him.

7. *Old people are unattractive and sexless.*

The "old crone" look is usually due to poverty, poor dental care, poor nutrition, poor medical care, and unbecoming wardrobe. Sexual interests do not necessarily disappear. One gentleman at age 112 decided he became old at 102. When asked why, he responded that that was the year he had resigned from sexual activity.

Making Peace with Significant Others

Another developmental task is making peace with whomever we need to make peace. One of the advantages of old age is that it is easier to see things in perspective. Older people report that they overlook petty faults more readily than they did earlier. The most important relationships to resolve are usually with relatives. We can adopt the "I'm O.K.—You're O.K." attitude without sacrificing our own integrity. We can love our relatives, and still find ways to resolve differences without feeling like we lose. "I'm O.K.—You're O.K." implies that I consider myself responsible for what I do, feel, and think, and that I own up to my past mistakes, knowing I did the best I knew how at that time in my life. It means also that *you* count too, that you are responsible for your feelings, thoughts, and actions. And that you must reckon with your own past mistakes. (I will give you credit for doing the best you knew how under the circumstances as you perceived them.)

Dealing with Losses

Coping with stroke deprivation is one of the most difficult tasks of old age. The longer one lives the more friends and relatives one loses. No one can live without strokes, and much of the senility which we stereotype as hopeless can actually be reversed with adequate stroking. Many old people, in the midst of normal appropriate grief over yet another loss, stop eating. Their forgetfulness and confusion, aside from that which normally accompanies grief, is due to malnutrition, and can be corrected.

Other signs of "senility" may be due to such ailments as insufficient oxygen reaching the brain due to arteriosclerosis. Americans in general tend to eat too much. Food is one way a stroke-hungry person can survive. Improper diet can cause many problems, particularly of blood circulation, which can produce symptoms which we classify as "senility" and which are preventable through good eating habits. If a person is going to give up some of the strokes from food then he or she must find another source.

Some people who have experienced repeated losses refuse to take the risk to reinvest in new people. Sam says, "I'm so lonely for my friends. No one can replace them. No one else shared the good memories we did. No one else knows exactly how I'm feeling from just a glance at my face or the way I walk into their room. Sure, I can make new friends, and I do, but the energy I must spend to get them to understand me, and the effort I must make to understand them, increases each time. I have become selective of the people in whom I am willing to make such an investment."

Loss of financial security is a severe threat to the elderly. Unexpected problems, like serious illness and rising costs, may deplete what seemed like a good amount of savings. Larry has decided he will not scrimp. He is going to live well, and if he eventually runs out of money he will present himself to the Department of Welfare.

Our bodies tire more readily, and we take longer to "bounce back" after physical setbacks. We accumulate wrinkles and sagging muscles, and lose some of our power. Decrease in hormonal output makes our bones more brittle, and thus more susceptible to fractures. Our senses grow less acute. Robert has noticed that, since he was forty, he has increasing trouble seeing. "I can still see, but it's harder for me to focus, and I get uneasy driving at night, trying to make out the edges of the street. I still *think* and *feel* the way I did twenty years ago. I get so frustrated when I can't *do* like I used to!"

Older people in our culture declare a religious affiliation more than any other age group. Most elderly people read religious literature regularly and believe in a hereafter.

Older people swell the ranks of the traditional churches in our country. Those with a living faith find it a source of strength in their hours of trial. They experience their God as a source of unconditional positive strokes.

Old people need strokes as do humans of all ages. Those who are well-stroked and who stay physically active delay much of the decline we associate with old age.

One way of continuing to stroke ourselves is to practice good grooming. Grooming takes time, energy, and a continuing interest in our appearance. The oldster has plenty of time. Many of us resent graying hair and wrinkles. If we become so ashamed of our appearance that we don't go anywhere, this leads to further isolation and quicker aging.

An older person runs short of energy more quickly. Even getting into and out of the tub may be a struggle. When we need help from others, we respond accordingly to our script messages about dependency and the O.K.-ness of being needy.

Millie was a passive dependent woman throughout her life. As she became very elderly she grew even nicer and very thankful for all that was done for her. She died in peace after a long illness and much attention from her family. Mike, her widower, eighty-three, is ill. He has always been independent, vigorous, and in command. He's so weak now that he can't even finish his own bath. When his nurse helps him he remarks, very cynically, "O.K., where's the diaper?" He has driven his children away from him, and continually crabs at his favorite daughter. Anything that she suggests, he does the opposite. He feels only frustration and despair. Mike's script does not allow for him to be needy.

An important need at any stage of life is to maintain control over ourselves and how we choose to live. Martha worked at a large women's residence for a number of years. She noticed that those women who had decided to move in of their own volition were well-liked by their apartment neighbors, and remained healthy and active well into their nineties. Those who were put there by their families deteriorated much younger, and died sooner.

The need to feel needed, important, of value, is a need which also runs deep. Abe says of his father: "Dad did quite well, in spite of poor hearing, faulty vision, and a serious heart condition. His doctor decided that Dad was a menace in a car, and urged me to stop him from driving. Dad was the only man in a suburb of thirty or forty women. He was their friendly neighborhood chauffeur, driving them all to the doctor or grocery store each day. When I insisted he stop driving, Dad said I was taking away his life. It turned out he was right. He started going downhill immediately and died within a year."

Coming to Terms with Death

Old age is the only developmental stage for which there is no next phase. Lack of a future orientation is therefore an appropriate adaptation. Old people often feel the pressure to do something while there is still time, like communicating to others what they have found to be of value, "before it dies with me." Those who refuse to face their impending death, by remaining future-oriented, discount important tasks such as making wills or settling important issues in their family, leaving those who remain after them bitter and angry over their irresponsibility.

Coming to terms with death is difficult in our Western culture. We consider death an enemy to be avoided at whatever cost. Medical personnel are taught to be fanatics in this fight. Nurses and doctors on Intensive Care Units in hospitals can now keep people "alive" when their heart, or brain, or kidneys stop functioning. The definition of death is no longer simple. Physicians are asking the courts to help them redefine "legal death."

A hospital is not the best place to end one's life. The ideal final scene is in familiar surroundings, attended by our most important loved ones, with time to say good-by, and time to pass on all the important messages we may have left unsaid until now.

SUMMARY

The tasks of old age include retiring from regular employment, restructuring time, dealing with losses, maintenance of health, deciding how to spend what time is left, and dealing with physical decline and death.

Old people vary—in their personalities, in their health, in their acceptance of their aging, and in their flexibility.

Much of this variety can be explained in terms of their scripts, and by the interplay between life's exigencies and their own particular script. Frequently old age brings the script as originally planned to a close. The individual may then feel free to choose a new life style or go back to school to get a long-desired degree. Others will feel at a loss and retire to the nursing-home porch and wait for death. Some follow typically American ways to structure their time by joining Golden Age Clubs. The Gray Panthers are declaring themselves the most oppressed minority group in the country.

Others remain rigid in their thinking and isolate themselves from the changes they are unwilling to accept.

The aged person comes to terms with the meaning of life, what life has meant, and what it is like to die. The longer one lives, the more losses one incurs. Parents, close friends, and maybe even children die, removing one by one all of the familiar sources of strokes. The older person faces the ever more difficult task of finding new strokes.

Being allowed to die with dignity is an important issue that is currently being reassessed.

EXERCISES

1. You have just been in a car wreck, you are far out in the country and there is no hope of speedy rescue. You can't move your legs or right arm and you can't see.
   a. Do you want someone to find you?
   b. Do you want to live or die?
   c. Whom do you want to talk to?
      i.   What do you say?
      ii. Do you have any unfinished business?
      iii. Errors to correct?
      iv. Do you have some advice you wish to convey?
   d. Think of the things you own and cherish most. To whom do you want them to go?

e. Suppose you recover after giving your things away. Then what?
2. How will you know when you are old?
3. What concrete steps are you taking now to prepare for your age? How do you learn to be old?
4. Compare your religious faith with your faith thirty years ago.
5. Are you thinking about death? How do you cope with it?
6. Think ahead to your funeral. Who will come? What will they say about you? Is that what you want?
7. What other topics do you need to consider?

READINGS

American Association of Retired People Publication. *Modern Maturity.* Available from Amer. Assoc. of Retired People, 1225 Connecticut Avenue, Washington, D.C. 20036.

Bitrren, James E., et al. *Human Aging* (Public Health Service Bulletin No. 986). Superintendent of Documents, Washington, D.C.

Butler, Robert. "The Life Review." *Psychology Today* (December 1971).

Kaslenbaum, Robert, ed. *New Thoughts On Old Age.* New York: Springer Publications, 1964.

Kutner, Bernard, et al. *Five Hundred Over Sixty.* New York: Russell Sage Foundation, 1956.

Neugardern, Bernice. "Grow Old Alone, With Me." *Psychology Today* (December 1971)

Tayter, Robert B. *Feeling Alive After Sixty-five.* New Rochelle: Arlington House Publishers, 1973.

Wolf, Dale. "Dying With Dignity." *Science* (June 1970).

PART III

TROUBLE-SHOOTING

. . . He makes his sun rise on the evil and on the good, and sends rain on the just and the unjust.
Matthew 5:45, RSV

15

Troubleshooting

Why Problems?

Problem-solving involves effective thinking and behavior. In the first sections of this chapter, we present ways to think effectively; in the second section, we present some problem-solving behaviors.

Day to day problem-solving in the family is usually so thoroughly ingrained that we do not even identify that we are solving problems. However, every time we make demands on each other or express needs, we are posing a problem which needs to be solved. This level of problem-solving is taken for granted. At times, however, our resources run thin; that is a time to look for new and different ways of dealing with the problems. It is not possible to raise children without problems. First of all, nobody's perfect, and secondly, there are times in a child's development when he or she needs to set up problems in order to learn things from the grownups about problem-solving. The dilemma of parenting is very well expressed by Henry T. Close in an article called "On Parenting" *
He says:

There is no question but that your parents failed you as parents. All parents fail their children, and yours are no exception. No parent is ever adequate for the job of being a parent, and there is no way not to fail at it. No

---

* Reprinted by permission from *Voices: The Art and Science of Psychotherapy* IV, 1 (1968).

parent ever has enough love, or wisdom, or maturity, or whatever. No parent ever succeeds.

This means that part of your task—like that of every other person—is to supplement what your parents have given you, to find other sources of parenting. You need more mothering than your mother could give you, more fathering than your father had to offer, more brothering and sistering than you got from your siblings.

. . . The problem is complicated by the demands our society makes on parents to be good parents. They are supposed to be 100 percent adequate, and it is a terrible disgrace if they are not. If they are successful, their children will reward them with devoted love, obedience, and success; if they are not, their children will turn out to be unloving, disobedient, and unsuccessful. This is the prevailing conviction of our society. But when parents buy this notion, they put themselves in an impossible position. They try first to be 100 percent adequate, and then when they inevitably fail at this, they try to appear 100 percent adequate. In either case, they cling to you, demanding that you get all your parenting from them, thus reassuring them that they have been good parents. They may also demand that you be loving, obedient, and successful, since this would be living proof of their success as parents.* They thus find it difficult to let you grow up— that is, to find other sources of parenting. This means that you will have to grow up in spite of them rather than wait for their permission. They will not make it easy for you, and you must do it on your own.

To grow up, it is necessary for you to forgive your parents. But you must forgive them for your sake, not theirs. Their self-forgiveness is up to them, not you, and they cannot afford to wait for you to forgive them any more than you can afford to wait for them to forgive you. When you do not forgive them, it means that you are still expecting all your parenting from them. You are clinging to them in the hope that if you can make them feel guilty enough, they will finally come through with enough parenting. But this is impossible, and in order for you to be really free to find other parenting, you must forgive.

---

* Such parental concern about children's "failures" can be understood in part as an attempt to force the children to succeed, and thus reassure the parents that they have been good parents.

I hope you will not be embarrassed at your need for parenting, and that you will be humble enough and determined enough to find effective ways of getting it.

What's Wrong?

When faced with bad feelings or difficulties between people, the first question to ask is, "What's wrong" Many difficulties are compounded because the source of the predicament is misidentified. For example, if two-year-old Annie is being stubborn, negativistic, and cranky, she is probably behaving that way out of the need to test her separateness from Mother or Father, If the parents feel that she is acting that way because they aren't good parents, and decide to feel not-O.K. about themselves, they have misidentified the problem. As a result, they are unlikely to stand up to Annie in the way she needs. Their bad feelings about themselves will interfere with Annie's need to learn that she can think and still be taken care of.

The basic question, then, is: "What's wrong?" Does what's wrong reside with me or the other person, and what do my Parent, Adult, and Child have to say about what's wrong? What do other people say about what's wrong? Problems are often presented in circumstantial ways that are designed to hide the true source. One place that this is apparent is in tattletale behavior. The complaint, "Roger's pickin' on me!" is not an accurate identification of the problem; in fact, it's an invitation into a game. When George complains that Roger is bugging him, George is taking the Victim position in the Drama Triangle, and inviting parents to Rescue by Persecuting Roger (see Figure 12 in Chapter 3). George has not asked for anything and has merely made a statement; teasing takes at least two persons. There is reason to suspect that George has done something to invite being teased. If things are not going well between George and Roger, *they* need to take responsibility for the problem. The hidden problem is that the kids are not being responsible for their behavior. To deal with the problem they need to be thinking about what they can do in order to get along.

How to Analyze Problems

REVIEW OF STROKE ECONOMY

Families function most effectively and cooperatively in a free stroke economy. When there are restrictions on strokes and family members act on the fictions about strokes, there will be strife. Our most common fiction is that there are not enough strokes to go around. We maintain this fiction by declining to ask for what we need, rather than stating our needs all of the time. The "scarcity" of strokes gets perpetuated by our assuming that all people in the family do not have equal rights. In a family everyone has the same rights to satisfaction, and equal responsibility in the process of cooperation. The rights and responsibilities of every member need to be recognized.

Are people using power plays (e.g., manipulation) in attempting to get strokes?" Power plays assume that strokes are scarce and must be competed for. Many of us have been thoroughly trained to use power plays to get what we want. In many families threats, sulking, yelling, banging doors, and discounting are acceptable substitutes for discussion and negotiation. Any child after the age of three has a functional Adult ego state and can be an active party in discussion and negotiation. Children need consistent training in discussion and negotiaton, and they learn this principally through the examples set by their parents. Methods for establishing cooperative discussion and negotiation will be presented later in this chapter.

In order to develop a free stroke economy, everyone in the situation must ask for everything they want one-hundred percent of the time. In asking each other for what we want each and every time, we do not grab, out-fox, or cajole others; instead, each of us must state our position and our wants. When everyone's wants are known, we can cooperate and negotiate around meeting them. Cooperative negotiation will not always get us what we want immediately, and so we are also responsible for working out priorities. Many of us have the Child fantasy that if we don't get what we want immediately, we'll never get it. Many times parents encourage this fantasy by responding to requests with, "We'll see," or, "Maybe later," and never following through. Our children's rights are respected when their requests are responded to thoughtfully. If we cannot meet a need immediately, they need to know when. "I can't hug you right now, Jane, because I have to get the carburetor back on and the grease off my hands; I'll come and find you and we'll hug in about half an hour."

In order to cooperate, we cannot keep secrets about what we want. When we hide our wants, we assume some sort of scarcity and act as if it is not legitimate to expose our needs.

We can avoid getting into power plays by confronting extreme statements. Statements such as, "You never let me have any ice cream," "Why do I always have to take care of you?", and "Nag, nag, nag, that's all you ever do!" are ways of justifying the idea that cooperation will not work.

WHO'S O.K. AND WHO ISN'T?

When people maintain mutually O.K. positions, cooperative living is possible, and effective problem-solving occurs. When we take an I'm O.K.—You're O.K. position we get on with solving the problem and doing what needs to be done. If our position is I'm not-O.K. and You Are, we do things to get away from the problem. If we take the

Figure 35. What We Do About Problems from the Four Basic Positions

position I'm O.K. and You're Not, we attempt to solve the problem by getting rid of someone else. And if we take the position, I'm not-O.K.—You're not-O.K., we go around and around and get nowhere.

Games and Time Structure

"What keeps happening over and over again in our family that results in bad feelings?" This question is useful in identifying psychological games. Games are often somewhat difficult for us to identify because we keep them a secret from our Adult. Often persons outside of the family are in a better position to identify games than we are. A knowledge of some of the typical games is also useful. There are typical games which are played from the Persecutor position, the Rescuer position, and the Victim position in the Drama Triangle.

The Persecutor in a game takes the attitude I'm O.K. —You're not-O.K. A frequent game played by the persecutor is "Now I've Got You—You SOB." This game is designed to justify being angry, and the NIGYSOB player invites others to show their faults in order to kick them. The Rescuer also takes the position I'm O.K. and You're Not, and "therefore I have to do your thinking for you." The Rescuer frequently plays "I'm Only Trying to Help You" and frequently ends up frustrated and tempted to become an angry Persecutor or a depressed Victim. The Victim's most common game is "Kick Me," in which the Victim invites a Persecutor to be angry. Another common game that a Victim plays is "Why Don't You—Yes, But." In this game the Victim invites a rescue and stubbornly maintains that nothing will work.

CHILDHOOD GAMES

Robert Zechnich describes several games which occur in infancy and childhood. A game played around newborn infants is called *Let Me Show You*. In this game, the baby has arrived home from the hospital and the new parents have kindly accepted an offer of help from someone (often a grandma). In this game, the helper, who is really a Rescuer, is "only trying to help." The helper "patiently" explains and re-explains procedures for feeding, bathing, etc., with barely concealed contempt. Thus the Rescuer is also Persecuting the new parents in the guise of helping them, and the parents wonder why they feel like Victims. The new parents' confidence in their ability to care for baby is undermined, and they become anxious in dealing with the baby. In response, baby may develop colic, having "caught" the parents' anxiety. Colic can then be taken as further evidence of the parents' incompetence. This type of colic can often be miraculously and instantly cured as soon as someone has the good sense to send the Rescuer home. The bad feeling payoff in "Let Me Show You" is that the parents are declared dunces and Rescuer acquires a smug feeling of adequacy at their expense.

All of the games in infancy or childhood share this same theme: someone is, or appears to be, incompetent, and someone else is made, or made to appear, competent at other's expense. The way out of the game is either to decline help from persons who want to take the Rescuer-Persecutor position, or to insist that they take care of chores around the house other than the direct care of the baby.

It Makes a Difference. In this game, after Rescuer goes home, someone replaces that person in proving the parents inadequate. This someone is generally the pediatrician. The pediatrician becomes the Only Competent Person and takes a Rescuer-Persecutor position, with the parents in Victim position. In this game, the parents ask for pronouncements from the pediatrician on issues that they pretend they could not possibly think about themselves. Zechnich describes one form of "It Makes a Difference":

> *It Makes a Difference (Stool Variety) is played this way: Mother notifies the doctor daily on all data pertaining to the baby's bowel movements—color, shape, consistency, frequency, odor, and so forth. The pediatrician quickly calculates a medical-aesthetic value for each production and for the composite. He generally does this by comparing it with the Standard Stool kept at the National Bureau of Standards in Washington. Then he issues a judgment about the overall health status of the baby. He*

is proud of, and Mother is grateful for, his Superlative Wisdom about the things that really count.

The way out of this game is for pediatricians to reassure parents that these matters do not really make a difference and insist that parents limit their consultations to things which are important.

Indispensable. In this game the Drama Triangle shifts, and the parents who were previously the Incompetent Ones now become "Indispensable." Anyone else who might conceivably undertake some of the baby's care, thus allowing breathing space for the parents, is defined as Incompetent. (In much of our culture Mother is the Indispensable One.) Since only the Indispensable One can be with the baby, he or she must be present and busy all the time. There is no time for other activities, and Indispensable Ones soon become exhausted and grumpy. They get strokes from other people by pastiming about "My baby is more demanding than your baby" or "I'm a more conscientious parent than you." The way out of this game is to recognize that babies can be adequately cared for by other people, and for parents to recognize that their needs count too.

Mommy, Don't Leave Me. Up to this point in the sequence of infancy and child games, the baby has been an onlooker. In "Mommy, Don't Leave Me" the baby begins to actively support the parents' claim that they are Indispensable. In this game the child begins to play a hand in the game that has been learned. At about 12-18 months of age baby learns to support the parents' Indispensable position by registering a strong "protest" whenever they go anywhere. Now and then they may "try" to get out to a movie but they allow the child's strenuous objections to prevent it. The way out of this game is to decline to respond to the child's protests, and to give reassurance that others can take care of the baby.

School Phobia. The four games previously mentioned progress to a game called "School Phobia." The child is actually afraid of separation from the parents, not of going to school. This game can begin at age five or sooner and continue indefinitely. In the game of "School Phobia" teacher takes the Victim position and is defined as Incompetent, and parents play the Persecutor-Rescuer position as the Competent ones. Thus the parents gain importance at the expense of the teacher. This is characteristic of all these childhood games: someone becomes important at the expense of another, through the actual or pretended incompetence of the other person. The way out of the game of "School Phobia" is to insist that the child go to school and remain there. It is essential that this permission come from the parents in addition to anyone else who says so.

IDENTIFYING GAMES

One way to identify your game position is to notice if you frequently end up righteously indignant or asking rhetorical questions (i.e., ones where you already know the answer). For example, when you ask Mary, "Who took the last of the cookies?" when she has cookie crumbs all over her face, you already know the answer, and thus are playing the game of NIGYSOB. If you take the position, "I am the Only Competent One around here," and feel *angry* about it, you are likely to be into Persecutor games. If you take the position, "I'm the Only Competent One around here," and feel *self-righteous,* you are likely to be playing Rescuer games. If you are giving help when no help is asked for, and if you are not checking to see that your actions are useful, you are playing Rescuer games. If your helping never quite works out, you are probably Rescuing.

You probably play Victim games if you try hard and get nowhere, if you feel sorry for yourself and feel woeful.

The way out of games is to turn on your Adult. One of the ways to turn on your Adult is to make use of the types of information we are describing in this book, to get your Adult back into commission. We get into games because we discount some need or some feeling. We assume that the need cannot be met directly, so then we engage in a game position to get strokes or express the otherwise unacceptable feeling. People who play NIGYSOB often feel that it is not O.K. to be angry. As a consequence we save up minor irritations and annoyances until we feel "justified" in having a temper tantrum. Then the anger is displayed all out of proportion with the event we are responding to. The fact that we overreact with our anger, of course, confirms the basic position that being angry is not O.K. and only bad things happen from expressing such anger.

Real Helpers	Game Helpers (Rescuers)
1. Listens for request ••••••••••••••••	1. Gives when not asked
2. Presents offer •••••••••••••••••••	2. Neglects to find out if offer is welcome
3. Gives only what is needed ••••••••	3. Gives help more and longer than is needed
4. Checks with person for results ••••••	4. Omits feedback
5. Feels O.K. Does not depend on •••• others for O.K. feelings	5. Feels "good" being a "helper" and "bad" if turned down

Figure 36. Helpers

Passive Thinking and Passive Behavior

When we play games we are being symbiotic. When we play Persecutor and Rescuer games we are in our Parent ego state, making ineffective use of our Adult ego state, and discounting some Child ego state need. Thus, if we find ourselves frequently into Persecutor-Rescuer game positions, an important question to help us get out is,

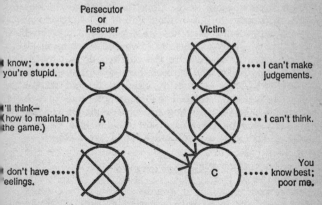

Figure 37. Games Are Symbiotic

"What does my Child need that I'm not letting myself know about, and what can I do to get it?" When we play Victim games we do not use our Adult to think effectively, or use our Parent to make judgments. Thus we discount our ability to think and judge.

Because grownups have more experience in thinking, and because they more frequently have injunctions against expressing feelings, they are most likely to take the Persecutor-Rescuer position around their children. Since the Drama Triangle positions are not stable, parents also end up being Victims who are Persecuted by their kids: Children above the age of three are quite capable of using their Adult ego state and thinking about things. Their thinking initially may be naive and magical, and yet they still are capable of some problem-solving. If we discourage our children from exercising their Adult ego state, we encourage them to maintain a symbiosis with us which will create problems for everyone concerned as time goes on. The goal of raising kids is to raise them to be independent. Prior to age two-and-a-half or so, children have not yet broken the primary symbiosis and it is not realistic to expect them to do a great deal of independent thinking. The most common premature expectations occur in attempting to toilet train a child before the physiology and willingness to use Adult ego state to think about the problem are adequately available.

Children who are in the Construction stage are looking for information to put in their Parent ego states. In order to get information they test what will happen when they don't think. Many parents are frustrated by children in the construction phase because the children do not make use of information to take care of themselves that the parents know they have. Ordinarily, children do not start consistently making use of this information until they have completed the Construction phase. Completion is signaled by a decision on the part of the child to use Parent ego state to take care of the child's Child ego state.

Ego State Inventory

When you are faced with a particular problem, find out what information is available in each of your ego states about that problem. Muriel James has developed a useful outline for finding out such information.

The problem Is

_____

_____

Mom would say	Dad would say

Mom would say
_____

_____

and do
_____

_____

and feel
_____

_____

Facts I already have
_____

_____

My hunch is (A_1)
_____

_____

_____

_____

Dad would say
_____

_____

and do .
_____

_____

and feel
_____

_____

Facts I need to get
_____

_____

The feelings I learned

to have about things

like this are (P_1)
_____

_____

My basic uncensored feelings about this are (C_1)

_____

_____

Figure 38. Ego State Inventory*

* Adapted from *Transactional Analysis for Moms & Dads*, by Muriel James.

The Think Structure

Another method for analyzing a problem is to make use of Pam Levin's "Think Structure." As Pam points out, simply telling someone "Think!" to solve problems is not enough. There is a whole sea of information which may or may not be relevant to solving a particular problem. Therefore a structure (method of organizing) is needed to look at the data.

I am _____
                              (Feeling)

Because I think that if I _____
                              (Behavior)

I will be _____
                       (Unhealthy Parental Response)

Instead of _____
                        (Healthy Parental Response)

So I _____
                  (Games, Rackets, Problem-Justifying Behavior)

Figure 39. A Think Structure (devised by Pam Levin)

Seven-year-old Lucy was angry and nasty much of the time toward her mother, who, after her divorce, had become overprotective of Lucy. When she started looking at the problem Lucy filled out the Think Structure this way: "I am *mad* because I think that if I *do what I want* I will *not get any strokes or else get stopped* instead of *stroked,* so I *get nasty to Mommy and mess up things she wants me to do.*" Thus Lucy identified her need to be responded to positively while showing independent behavior. After the problem was clarified using the Think Structure Lucy and her mom arranged for Lucy to get more strokes for doing things she wanted to do. After several weeks Lucy's mother reported that she was more independent, more pleasant, and more cooperative around the house.

The Think Structure emphasizes the logical reasons for feelings and behaviors, provides a statement of the reasons, and offers immediate alternatives to unfruitful behaviors that perpetuate the problem.

The Think Structure is most effective when:

1. The feeling is expressed in Child words; i.e., a five-year-old understands scared, mad, or sad, and does not understand depression, guilt, anxiety, remorsefulness, etc. (The bad feeling you keep having over and over again is probably a racket rather than an authentic feeling.)

2. You state what you will do, not just what you will stop doing.

3. You take some time to enumerate all of the racket feelings and behaviors.

4. You don't work at filling out the structure, but play with it until it feels right. Solving problems can be fun.

How to Change Behavior *

I can reveal
The way that I feel
By the things that I say and do.

By changing the things
I say and do,
I can change my feelings too!

Jennie Lou Vance

When we are changing to solve problems, there are several things that we can revise: our thinking, our feelings, and our behavior. We can demand that other people act differently—and the choice about changing is still one they must make. We can also change the situation; e.g., moving bedrooms around so that two squabbling youngsters will each have more privacy.

The decision on *what* to change rests on our understanding of the problem. *How* we change involves learning. We learn new behaviors, we learn to do some things more often or less often. Whenever we learn to do something new, or whenever we stop doing something that we used to do and do something else, we are following laws of learning, even though we don't think about it, and even though we don't know what these laws say. When following these laws of behavior, we accomplish several things. First of all, we develop new behavior; that is, we learn how to do things that we previously did not know how to do. We maintain behaviors that have certain functions for us, we give up certain behaviors, and we increase or decrease the frequency with which we do certain things.

Learning theory answers these questions: "How do we get to do the things that we are doing?" "How does that behavior get developed?" "Once we are doing something in a certain way, why do we keep on doing it that way— and if what we are doing is undesirable, how do we stop it?" Such questions have nothing to do with identifying what should be learned and what should be unlearned. In this sense, learning theories are neutral, and only define and describe processes. This is why we need to know the behaviors that are important to our culture, and see to it that our children learn them, too. We need to consider thoughtfully which behaviors in our culture are truly desirable, and which ways of doing things are not good for us as individuals nor for our society. Many men are taught to be workaholics; they get lots of strokes for working themselves into exhaustion and not playing. People can be taught to be workaholics or they can be taught to be free and spontaneous. If little Georgy is only stroked for being responsible and doing things well and does not receive strokes for being free, playful. and spontaneous, he is learning how to be a workaholic. In the same way we can train daughters to be "nice" suburban housewives (this usually includes training on how to be depressed), or how to be self-directed and think effectively.

Types of Learning

Theorists in psychology have argued for years over the question, "How many types of learning are there?" We will describe three types of learning here, since we are convinced they are separate ways of learning, and that they are useful in thinking about what goes on in all learning.

OPERANT LEARNING

In *operant learning* we learn to behave certain ways because we are rewarded for doing so. The most common reward is conditional positive strokes from other people. When people are stroked for behaving in certain ways they will increase that behavior. If people behave in certain ways and do not get strokes for that behavior, they will decrease such behavior. For instance, if Lucy is ignored for playing happily and getting along with others, and instead gets a great deal of attention by having temper tantrums, then she will more frequently have temper tantrums because that is a way for her to get strokes.

If you want to increase the frequency of pleasant conversations in the family, then see to it that everyone gets stroked for being pleasant and does not get stroked for being unpleasant. Giving strokes for the behavior that we want, and seeing to it that we get strokes for ourselves for the behavior that we want, maintains that behavior and increases its frequency. We can arrange to stop behaving in ways we dislike by arranging to not get strokes for that behavior. For example, if we are getting tired of playing "Ain't It Awful" with the neighbors, we can change the situation by seeking out neighbors who are more interested in playing "Ain't It Wonderful." People who pastime Ain't It Wonderful do not stroke Ain't It Awful.

We all have a long history of learning to do things that we couldn't do at all initially. One form of operant learning is called "shaping." In shaping behaviors, we should stroke or otherwise reward a behavior that is approximately like the behavior wanted. For example, if you want Linus to learn how to set the table for a meal, don't wait for him to do it exactly right. Initially, show Linus tools for eating. Tell Linus which tools each person needs—plate, knife, fork, spoon, and so forth. Obviously the first attempts at setting the table will not be "right" by our usual standards. However, Linus needs to get strokes for putting out plates, silverware, etc., even though they aren't in the right positions and of the right quantity. Stroke him as soon as possible after he has done what you want. After Linus is consistently putting out eating tools, only then is it time to expect more. Now Linus will not get stroked merely for setting the utensils on the table, he will have to follow additional instructions. These instructions will include things like, "The spoon goes here, the knife goes here, and the fork goes here." We learn to do the many highly complex things that we have to do in our life by learning simple behaviors first and building on them by combining and adding other things we have learned.

"Grandma's Rule" (from Wesley Becker's *Parents Are Teachers*) is also useful in teaching children. Grandma was fond of saying, "You do what I want you to do *before* you get to do what you want to do." Here are some examples of Grandma's Rule in action: "Eat your vegetables and then you can have some pie." "You can go out and play after you take out the trash." "Take your bath and then you can have some cookies and milk." Grandma's Rule is an important way to help children to learn to follow through on the responsibilities they need to learn.

We all need stroking or some other form of reward for doing the things that we have to do. Some people maintain the fiction that we can do things without getting strokes for it, and they may say things like, "Eloise should want to do her homework just because it's good for her," or, "Kids shouldn't have to be bribed to learn things, they should do it just for the love of learning." When people say such things, they ignore the rewards and stroking that they themselves get for doing things. "Bribery" is misused in this case. *Webster's Unabridged Dictionary, Second Edition*, defines "bribe" in this way: "1. A price, reward, gift, or favor bestowed or promised to induce one to commit a wrong or illegal act. 2. Anything given or promised to induce a person to do something against his wishes." Thus, bribes are not rewards, they are seductions and manipulations that imply not-O.K.-ness.

When things go wrong in a family, the person who misbehaves, disregards other people, makes messes, or whatever, is least uncomfortable about what's going wrong. Therefore, we need to figure out ways to hand the discomfort back to the person who is creating the problem.

A frequent instance of this is in bedwetting. Chuck is

well beyond the age of toilet training and has a history of keeping dry at night. He has no urinary tract infections or physical problem. There is a good possibility that Chuck wets his bed to manipulate the family. If Chuck stays asleep until morning and then promptly arises, dons fresh clothes, and does not have to do anything about the mess, he experiences little discomfort. On the other hand, his parents are forced to cope with wet and smelly clothes, bedsheets, and blankets, all of which require much unpleasant work. To solve the problem, Chuck should be made responsible for all his own dirty linen, thus relieving Mom and Pop of their discomfort and extra work. Children who wet the bed may also be using this problem as a way of expressing anger at their parents, and the source of the anger must be tracked down and dealt with. In cases of persistent bedwetting, professional assistance is needed.

PUNISHMENT

Punishing people for behaviors that you do not like is frequently not a very satisfactory way of dealing with the behavior, although at times it is important to stop someone from doing something that is dangerous by imposing some kind of punishment. If punishment is used alone the person will probably go underground and hide the unwanted behavior from the punishing person. Eventually the troublesome behavior will come up again. To change behavior it is crucial that you follow punishment with clear expectations about the behavior you do want, and stroke that behavior positively when it occurs.

Some children are allowed to play in unrestricted areas before they have adequate control over their own behavior. Punishment before a child is able to exercise some control will only serve to define the child as not-O.K. When Andy is old enough to be allowed some freedom to roam in the neighborhood (the age will depend on the neighborhood) he may need a swat on the behind for going out into the street. If this is all that the parents do, however, Andy will probably learn to go out into the street whenever there aren't any grownups around. Andy also needs to be stroked for following the rules that have been set up about the boundaries for playing in the neighborhood.

Learning also accounts for bad habits. We keep bad habits because we get rewards for their occurrence. To change a bad habit, some positive behavior needs to be rewarded more, and the reward for the bad habit needs to be discontinued.

Teasing amongst children in the family is a common bad habit. Teasing entails a large number of negative strokes, and is usually perpetuated by children's need for stroking from each other.

Amy and Andrew teased each other regularly. Their parents finally decided to stop trying to find out whose fault it was, and asked the children what they could do so there would be less teasing. Amy and Andrew both identified that they wanted to have strokes from each other, and the family together identified the kind of positive strokes that Amy and Andrew would like to exhange. In addition, the family established penalties for negative strokes, and the parents started stroking Amy and Andrew for playing together cooperatively.

Sometimes parents attempt to teach their children mainly by scolding rather than praising. Andrew misbehaves, gets caught, is scolded, and then stops misbehaving. The parents get some reward from this because scolding and criticizing seem to work, since Andy has stopped misbehaving for a while. Wesley Becker tells the story of Peter:

Peter got most of his attention from his mother by misbehaving. If Peter did behave, Mother probably took that time to get some of her chores done and to take care of her other three children. Very likely Peter's mother taught Peter to misbehave. She was caught in the "criticism trap." Peter got more and more attention from his mother for bad behavior, and less and less attention for good behavior. The more mother criticized, scolded, and punished, the worse Peter got. Only when she clearly rewarded Peter for good behavior did he get better.

Three outstanding books on the application of theories of learning to childrearing are: *Parents Are Teachers*, by Wesley C. Becker; *Living With Children*, by Gerald R. Patterson and M. Elizabeth Gullion; and *Families*, by Gerald R. Patterson.

EMOTIONAL LEARNING

We learn to feel certain ways and have certain bodily responses which are learned elaborations of the basic emotions of mad, glad, and scared. (Sad is learned early in life. See Chapter 3 on Emotions.) This form of learning is called respondent (*emotional*) learning. Several decades ago a psychologist performed an experiment that illustrates how emotional learning works.* The psychologist took a young child and showed the child a soft, fuzzy white bunny. Every time the bunny was shown to the child, the psychologist made a very loud, scary noise and the child burst into tears. Soon the child was afraid of the bunny even when the noise was not made. The child also started showing fear about other soft white things, such as cotton balls. The fear had generalized. It moved from being a specific fear to include a host of things which were similar. Over a period of time this fear went away because the experimenter stopped pairing the loud noise and the bunny.

If something bad happens we associate the surrounding events with that bad thing. When something similar happens, we will show a similar response. If similar events occur often enough without something bad happening, then we eventually give up the fear.

One way to get over learned bad feelings such as fear is to re-experience similar situations without the bad event occurring. Pam Levin's Think Structure is helpful in figuring out how to get rid of learned emotions that you don't want. If Ron fills out the sentence to read, "I am afraid that if I make demands I will be punished instead of taken care of, and so I suffer and get scared," he writes his own prescription for getting rid of the bad feelings. Ron needs to experience making demands and not being punished. After he has had some practice making demands without getting punished, he can give up his old scare about making demands.

* Since that era psychologists have re-examined their ethical commitments to experimental subjects. Today other means would be used to learn this information.

Joey and his Daddy were visiting some friends. While they were there, the friends' dog came in. Fido bit Joey slightly and frightened him severely. After this visit Joey was apprehensive whenever he was around dogs and frightened whenever one got within several feet of him. Joey's father dealt with this fear in several ways: 1) He talked with Joey about dogs and what dogs are like, and told Joey some ways to tell which dogs were friendly and which dogs were not. 2) He saw to it that when Joey was around dogs, Joey felt adequately protected, and also arranged it so that any dogs Joey was near did not come any closer to him than was comfortable for him. Joey's dad also arranged for them to visit homes with small friendly puppies, and gradually allowed the puppies to come closer to Joey, but no closer than Joey was comfortable with. Eventually Joey's natural curiosity over lively young puppies outweighed his fear, and he was willing to approach the young dogs and pet them and play with them. After this new learning experience Joey was no longer inappropriately afraid of dogs and had Adult information on what kinds of dogs to avoid.

MODELING

Modeling is imitative learning. We learn to do certain things because we find pleasure in imitating some valued person. Most parents eventually hear themselves in their children who do such things as scold the cat using exactly the same mannerisms, gestures, and tones of voice that the parents themselves use when they scold the children. Our children learn to imitate our posture, speech, and beliefs, and the way we think. In some instances, when kids are being rebellious, they will turn the imitation inside out and backward, and very conscientiously behave the opposite of their parents. For example, Luanne was sad and depressed a lot of the time. When she was young she decided she didn't like the way her mother acted, because her mother was irresponsible, frequently angry, and quite punitive. Luanne learned to be quite responsible and never punished, even when it was appropriate. Her mother knew how to enjoy herself and have fun. Luanne carried her rebellion too far; she decided that she was going to be unlike her mother in *all* respects, so she made the decision that "if Mother knows how to have fun, then I will never let myself have any fun." When Luanne acknowledged her rebellion she decided to give some of it up and enjoy herself more.

In the next chapter we will discuss some of the specific problems that children and families face, and discuss some ways of dealing with these particular problems.

SUMMARY

We are continuously solving problems whether or not we think about the process itself. Dealing with problems regularly is part of being human. Problems are often not identified as problems unless our usual repertoire of coping techniques does not work.

When our usual methods fail, we need more concentrated means of analyzing the problem. Information that needs to be gathered and analyzed includes the following: "What, precisely, is the problem? Whose problem is it?" These questions need to be answered because we often get sidetracked by secondary issues and misidentify the problem.

Other questions to be asked are: What kinds of strokes are we getting? Are these the kinds of strokes we want? Are family members defining each other as not-O.K.? Is this a script problem? Are we in "the Drama Triangle"? Who is being passive? Is the problem typical for a certain developmental stage? How does the problem look using the "Think Structure"?

What can be done about the problem? How can the thinking, feelings, and behavior in myself and others be changed? Does the situation need to be changed? What specific techniques can we use?

EXERCISES

1. Have each member of the family list the kinds of strokes they get from each other member of the family, and list the kinds of strokes they would like to get.
2. What manipulations does each member of the family use (e.g., whining, yelling, not thinking, taking things)?
3. Andrew, who is twelve, and Lucy, who is eight, want to have a new bedtime. Think of ways that they would ask for a new bedtime from:
   a. I'm O.K.—You're O.K.
   b. I'm not-O.K.—You're O.K.
   c. I'm O.K.—You're not-O.K.
   d. I'm not-O.K.—You're not-O.K.
   How would you be inclined to respond to each of these requests? List responses from parents to such a request from each of the four basic positions.
4. What do you do in your family about teasing, and how does this fit into the Drama Triangle diagram?
5. Think of a problem that is important in your family and fill out the Ego State Inventory (Figure 38, p. 259) about this problem.
6. Think of a bad feeling that you regularly have over and over and fill out the Think Structure on this problem. (A hint: that regular bad feeling is probably a problem-justifying behavior and goes on the last line, *not* the first line.)
7. Do you use Grandma's Rule in your house? List some ways that you do. If you do not use Grandma's Rule, how could you use it?
8. Are there things that you say that children should not do that you do yourself? In what ways are you modeling behavior that you do want your children to show?

READINGS

Becker, Wesley C. *Parents Are Teachers*. Champaign, Illinois: Research Press, 1971.

Ernst, Franklin H. Jr. *Who's Listening?* Vallejo, California: Addressoset, 1968 (reprinted 1973).

James, Muriel, *Transactional Analysis for Moms & Dads*. Reading, Massachusetts: Addison-Wesley, 1975.

Levin, Pamela. "A Think Structure for Feeling Fine Faster." *Transactional Analysis Journal* III, 2 (1973).

Patterson, Gerald R., and Gullion, M. Elizabeth. *Living With Children*. Champaign, Illinois: Research Press, 1968 (revised 1971).

Patterson, Gerald R. *Families*. Champaign, Illinois: Research Press, 1971.

Wyckoff, Hogie. "Between Women and Men." *Issues in Radical Therapy* I, 2 (1973).

Zechnich, Robert. "Games in Childhood." *Transactional Analysis Journal* IV, 2 (1974).

16

Problems and Action Plans

Few lives are lived out without crises and other tribulations. In the midst of crisis we are inclined to think that we are the only persons who have ever faced such burdens. Our awareness that others have faced similar situations is an important consolation in dealing with many problems. When times of trouble arise, an awareness of our need and caring relationships with others can afford important resources in dealing with our own specific problems.

In this chapter we review some of the major problems that can beset us and describe some ways of dealing with them.

Physical Disabilities and Illness

BIRTH DEFECTS

One of the first events following the birth of the baby is to count all of his or her extremities. In many cultures there is a stigma attached to having a less than "perfect" baby. Birth defects range from those that are mildly disfiguring to major defects which will not permit the infant to live for very long. Children who are born with severe defects such as extreme retardation or extensive cerebral palsy can be a profound drain on the resources of the family. While there are strong pressures for the family to continue to keep such a child at home, caring for such a child in our typical family structure usually requires that the other members of the family discount their own needs. In some instances, placing the child in an institution which specializes in care of the retarded, for example, may be the most real and loving thing to do for *all* the members of the family. Such a decision is not to be made lightly or hastily. A decision by a parent that someone else can better care for a child is almost always a painful one, accompanied by guilt at not being able to meet Parental standards of being a good parent, and grief over the loss of someone important.

When a child has some major physical disability, parents can often receive a good deal of assistance and moral support from others who have banded together to deal with that particular problem. There are numerous such groups. One simple way of finding them is to look in the telephone directory of your nearest large city. A cursory review of the telephone listings under "Associations" in one such metropolitan directory revealed associations designed to give information and help about the following disabilities: cerebral palsy, diabetes, epilepsy, heart disorder, hemophilia, kidney disorders, learning disabilities, leukemia, mental illness, multiple sclerosis, muscular distrophy, retardation, and sickle cell anemia. In other areas where there are no established associations, such parents can profitably band together for moral support and also to bring more influence to bear in getting additional help from government organizations, etc.

Children whose birth defects are partially limiting or disfiguring will need to deal with being identified as "different"—that is, they must learn to cope with others who express their fear of "differentness" by teasing—and still go on to be productive and happy members of society. One of the critical factors in a child's ability to cope with the stigma attached to his or her defect depends on the response of the parents and their attitude about having a "less than perfect" child.

As we mentioned earlier, parents engage in many fantasies about an unborn infant. We often attach our hopes and dreams to this unborn person, as well as some of our fears. Some degree of birth defect is not uncommon; one child in ten is born with a defect of some sort. When the baby is born and the defect is immediately obvious, the parents must deal with their own emotional response to that event. The most common response—and the most healthy—is grief.

Grief is an important healing experience. Whenever we are faced with an important loss, a death in the family, say, or discover that we have a less than physically perfect child, the normal response is grief. Grief is a combination of anger and sadness; anger that the event has occurred, and sadness over the loss. Healthy grief allows us to give up our wishes for what cannot be and frees up energy for the Adult problem-solving that needs to be done. If such grief is held back and not expressed at the time that the loss occurs the person will experience an ongoing blockage of energy until the griefwork is done. Some people are inclined to feel not-O.K. about their anger and sadness; it is very important to understand that these feelings are normal and natural, indeed necessary. This same experience of loss and mourning occurs also when a defect is discovered later on during the child's life. While it is now possible to assess deafness in newborns, in the past many parents did not recognize that their child was deaf until normal speech patterns did not develop as they should.

ILLNESS

When dealing with sick infants, our ingenuity is often taxed because the usual ways of comforting a child do not work, and we have to try different ways to make the child comfortable without any clear method of predicting what will succeed. The result may be a fussy, cranky infant no matter what we do. Parents who resolve to be perfect parents feel not-O.K. about themselves because there is nothing effective that they can do. The result is that they are even less effective about caring for the child because of their own not-O.K. feelings.

While many people accept concern and fear as O.K. feelings when their child is sick, they may think that anger is not-O.K. We can expect that we will be angry when all our conscientious efforts are thwarted. Each of our feelings about the illness of an infant must be dealt with, even the ones we don't like.

Where there is chronic illness parents have to deal with issues similar to those of parents of children possessing physical disabilities. It often requires some ingenuity for parents of chronically ill or physically disabled children to help them meet the needs of each of their particular developmental stages. They must walk a line between overprotection, making allowances for the child's disability, and the temptation to press the child into activities that are beyond the child's realistic capabilities. With children who are physically disabled or chronically ill it is particularly important to have a clear assessment of the capabilitise of the child in order to avoid being too lenient or too pushy.

Sick and Disabled Parents

Parents who are sick or disabled also place a stress on the family. It is often tempting (and occasionally even necessary) to force the child to take a more grown-up position, so that he or she can help take care of the parent. It is crucial, though, that children not be encouraged to think that they have major responsibility for the parent and the parent's problems. Parents are for taking care of children, and not the other way around. Children also should be furnished clear, direct, and straightforward information concerning the parent's affliction. While such need not be expressed in gory clinical detail, children nevertheless require a clear and accurate explanation. When children do not possess adequate information they invent their own explanations that are inaccurate and often later became self-blaming. For example, if the parents do not provide accurate information and Father is confined to bed for a heart condition the child may decide that "Daddy got sick because I was mad at him." Once children have latched onto magical explanations a good deal of effort is often required to help them give up those fantasies. Many parents do not give children adequate credit for their ability to deal with tribulations, and withold information about what is going on and what can be done about it. Withholding information is likely to foster a feeling of helpless panic in a child, since it discounts his or her ability to think and to cope.

Problems in Meeting the World

In the course of our growth from infancy to adulthood we face increasingly complex interactions with other people. As young children one of the first complications in our social order is the birth or adoption of another child into the family. When new children come into the family it is important to plan for ways in which the extra demands will not seriously infringe upon the need for strokes of the children already there. So-called "sibling rivalry" means that the older child is perceiving the younger child from a competitive position. If the cooperative position is taken (i.e., everyone's needs can be met, and everyone is supposed to ask for their needs to be met), there will probably be little rivalry between siblings. The arrival of a new child in the family is a long-anticipated event. The children in the family as well as the parents will be engaging in fantasies about what the new infant will be like. One of the most common naive fantasies of young children is that the new baby will be a playmate. If Joey has entertained this fantasy he will inevitably resent the new infant who, instead of being a new companion, reduces some of Joey's freedom.

If the parents have not had to deal with conflicts between their child and other children before the child is old enough to attend nursery school, it is inevitable that some conflicts will come up then. Common problems to be dealt with in the nursery-school years are centered around getting along with others. Such issues as sharing things, making demands, and settling disagreements need to be taught. Often we are tempted to move in and Rescue the children by taking over and settling differences rather than providing them information on what to do. To deal with such squabbles, the first important step is to see that the uproar is calmed down. This may require isolating the two children from each other briefly. Useful questions to ask kids who are squabbling are, "How could you do it differently without turning out mad?" "What's a way that both of you could play with that toy?" "People get angry when you grab things, so what could you do to get to play with that toy without all the other kids getting mad at you?" All of these questions are designed to get the child to use his or her Adult ego state to think about the problem and to give the kids programming about dealing with interpersonal problems. When we talk with children about interpersonal difficulties (or about them in their presence) it is important to define the problem around specific behavior. "Ralph is shy," or, "a bully," for example, are attributions that say, "Well, that's just the way he is." Such attributions discount that the person can change the behaviors. If the problem is identified as "Ralph gets scared about talking to other kids" then problem-solving can center around what to do about the scare, and in developing some ways for him to talk with other kids.

Later on during the grade-school years, children will have to deal with teasing. Children, particularly those in third to fifth grades, are very prone to make other kids not-O.K. when those others possess attributes that the children see as "different." At these ages the boys make the girls not-O.K., and the girls make the boys not-O.K., and some kids get made not-O.K., for wearing glasses, having buck teeth, limping, or innumerable other things.

According to Pamela Levin* part of the function of making other-kids-not-O.K. is to avoid incorporating behaviors that would be undesirable. Thus, if a young boy of this age does not invest some energy into making girls not-O.K. he may incorporate some effeminate behavior into his behavior patterns. Teasing and getting teased also are practice and refinement of the NIGYSOB and Kick Me games that the child has learned at home and is now practicing on the rest of the world. The teaser (Persecutor) and the teasee (Victim) frequently manage to get into scraps in a way that invites a response from a grownup. The invitation is for the grownup to Rescue so that they can all play a three-handed game, which makes the whole game sequence much more interesting and dramatic. The techniques for staying out of the Drama Triangle which were discussed in Chapter 15, Troubleshooting, are useful in dealing with these problems.

---

* In a personal communication to the authors.

During adolescence kids reactivate earlier developmental issues, and earlier problems such as shy behavior or overly aggressive behavior may recur, at least briefly. In addition, teenagers are very much inclined to experiment briefly with patterns of behavior which will later be discarded. For example, a previously well-behaved youngster may attempt some minor delinquencies, try out getting drunk, and after a brief escapade settle down into a more stable pattern. Such behaviors can be rather scary for grownups. Serious rebellious behavior which gets a kid into trouble with the law, or which is self-destructive in some other way, seems to occur most frequently in families where the child feels that the parents will not respond to minor acting up. Some kids who get in serious trouble come from rigid and authoritarian families upon which the children have been hitherto quite dependent. Sometimes a kid from this type of family structure sees getting put into an institution as the only safe way of becoming emancipated from the family. Parents need to respond to such experiments by reporting their Parent, Adult, and Child reactions, and reaffirming their expectations that the adolescent behave responsibly and thoughtfully.

Multiple Parents

Divorces are increasingly common in this country. The events leading to a divorce, the manner in which the divorce occurs, and the events following the divorce all have important influences on children. As in other major life events, children need straightforward, truthful, and understandable information about what is going on. Unfortunately, parents who are in the process of divorce, especially if there is a lot of dissension and anger, are not in any position to provide such dispassionate information. In some instances the parents even lose sight of their basic obligation to their children, and make the children pawns in bitter custody battles. It is often useful to have some informed and dispassionate third party discuss what is going on with the child. As with other important events, children who lack information invent it. Younger children frequently do not understand the mechanics of divorce, and do not recognize that each parent remains a parent even though they are no longer living together. Children's preferences about which parent they will live with need to be taken into account, although it is a disservice to a child younger than about fourteen to demand that they assume any responsibility in the final choice. The notion of having to choose between parents is quite frightening to younger children. Whichever parent the child lives with will have to deal with the fact that the child needs to mourn the loss of the other parent. It is unsettling to see a child actively missing and homesick for a former spouse at whom you yourself are extremely angry and bitter. If the divorce occurred when the child was very young, the child often invents magical fantasies about the absent parent. The child often creates a Super Parent with whom everything would be all right and who would be always nice. This fantasy is often a very persistent one. In many instances children in later grade school or high school may become quite insistent on meeting the other parent. If such a meeting is feasible without causing serious damage to the child, it can be very helpful in demystifying the missing parent.

Teenagers who live with a parent of the opposite sex often feel some discomfort about their own sexual feelings toward that parent, and many teenagers report relief when the parent with whom they are living takes a lover, or develops an attachment for another grownup. As one mother put it, "I couldn't really understand it why Joey was so relieved when my friend Tom moved in with us."

Remarriage

When parents remarry children frequently feel some conflict of allegiance, and need to know that they can be attached to and love a new stepparent without having to give up their claim to the original parent. Some parents also are inclined to give preferential treatment to natural children over stepchildren. Or, fearing that they may do this, inadvertently give preferential treatment to the stepchildren. Decisions about adopting stepchildren can be important psychologically to everyone involved and need to be discussed thoroughly before a decision is made. A useful book for single parents is *A Guide for Single Parents: Transactional Analysis of People in Crisis* by Kathryn Hallett.

Children and Death

Children best understand the concept of death when given straightforward and unembroidered information. Children usually begin thinking about death as a concept at around ages four or five.

A typical conversation about death might go this way:

"Will I die someday, Daddy?"

"Yes, everybody who is born dies someday."

"Will you die someday, Daddy?"

"Yes."

"When?"

"I don't know that. Nobody knows for sure when they will die. I expect to be around for a long time and live to be very old."

"What happens when people die, Daddy?"

"When people die, their bodies stop working. Their heart stops beating and they stop breathing and their brain doesn't work anymore, and then they are dead."

"What does it mean when people are dead, Daddy?"

"It means that they can't give or get strokes anymore, and that the people who are left can't give or get strokes anymore from the person who died."

"That sounds sad."

"Yes, it is sad, and when somebody dies that we love we need lots of strokes from the other people around us, and holding and talking to about being sad."

"What happens to people's bodies after they die?"

"They are usually put in a box called a coffin and put in the ground in a place called a cemetery."

"Does it hurt to be buried in the ground?"

"No, because only people who are alive and can think and breathe can hurt."

"When I die, will I go to heaven?"

"Well, I don't think anybody knows for sure about that. Some people think so and some people don't."

While the details of such a conversation may vary according to our religious convictions, it is important to convey to children the concrete fact that persons who die are no longer a source of stroking. For many children, introduction of such ideas as heaven can encourage magical thinking, with the result that a child may spend hours looking out the window up into the skies, thinking about "Aunt Emma who's up there in heaven." If children are encouraged to think that a dead parent has merely gone to "another place" they may develop the notion that they can physically rejoin that other person by dying also. Such fantasy can be an encouragement to self-destructive thinking, and some suicides even occur on the basis of such thinking.

Grief

The natural response to the death of someone we love is grief. The process of grieving occurs whenever we lose any important source of stroking, and it is just as legitimate to grieve over the loss of a family pet as over a parent, though the depth of the response will be far greater over a parent. The process of grieving appears to have three phases. The initial phase is a period of shock and disbelief. During that time we may feel numb emotionally and find it difficult to accept the fact that a loved one is gone. Following this period of shock, active mourning begins and we experience an upwelling of sadness over the loss. Stroking and comforting from others is an important consolation. In addition to sadness, anger is a normal response to death. More frequently we have mixed feelings about this anger, even though it is normal for us to be angry when an important source of strokes is removed. Many of us fear that our anger at someone's death has somehow magically caused that person to die. While this kind of thinking is often apparent in children, it is not just limited to children, and many grownups also must come to grips with their own magical thinking about death. Finally, we enter a recovery period where the up-welling of grief occurs less and less frequently.

Contrary to what many parents think, it is not necessary or even helpful to protect the child from seeing our own grief responses. Hiding our emotions from children can give them the idea that grownups don't have feelings, or that feelings aren't O.K. Children can stand to see their parents grieving, and all members of an aggrieved family can provide some consolation to the others. We need to let our children know, however, that we can have such strong emotions and still be capable of being responsible for their care.

The Dying Child

All persons are entitled to a dignified and fully human death. This is no less true for children, and if, for instance, the child has a disease which will be inevitably fatal, the child needs to know that, to know the facts about death, and to have an opportunity to say good-by to family and close friends who are important. Over the last several generations a myth has developed that, some-how, death is a topic that should not be talked about. Only by talking about this "unspeakable" topic can we demystify it and return the fact of death to a proper perspective in our lives.

How to Know When You Need an Expert

An expert is somebody who has special knowledge and information that can be useful. Often the neighbor next door, or parents, or close friends are consulted as experts in childrearing. When problems are severe they can out-strip the skills and knowledge of our informal experts, so that we need to consult someone who makes their living by being an expert.

Sometimes the need for special help becomes apparent around a particular crisis; for example, failing grades or expulsion from school are crises which move us to consult such experts as tutors, speech and reading specialists, and psychotherapists. Part of the job of such experts is to establish a clear definition of what the problem is and to propose a course of action.

In other instances we are moved to look for an expert because of a prolonged, gnawing feeling that something is "not quite right," or that "life can be better than this." We are becoming increasingly aware that we are entitled to more in life than mere survival, and that calling on people whose resources can help us increase the quality of our lives is no disgrace.

HOW TO FIND AN EXPERT

Finding the particular kind of competent expert that you need can be complicated:

1. It may be hard to know what kind of expert you need initially.

2. Dealing with some problems may require the co-ordination of several experts; for example, a tutor, pediatrician, and psychotherapist.

3. Experts don't always agree on who the experts are. Membership in certain licensing organizations may increase the likelihood that the person you consult is competent, but it is no guarantee.

4. Many experts are not permitted ethically to demonstrate their competence in a way that is readily accessible to the public.

While searching for the persons who can be most helpful to you, notice those whom your Child trusts, and who have been useful to you. You can use these persons as important resources in finding other competent experts. If, for instance, you trust your pediatrician and have found her services to be useful, it is likely that she will know competent tutors, competent speech therapists, competent psychotherapists, and so forth. If you are seeking help for problems that require the services of several persons, it is often useful to have one of these persons coordinate the joint efforts. Because of a surgical problem, Andrew, age twelve, requires the specialized services of a plastic surgeon, ear, nose, and throat specialist, cardiologist, and pedodontist. After careful inquiry the parents selected a pediatrician who now coordinates the efforts of all of these other specialists. The family will not act on the recommendation of any one of them without first checking it out through the pediatrician. Until the family hit upon this solution they were faced with many difficult decisions because of disagreement amongst the experts.

Ultimately, we parents have the final say about what expert we will use and which recommendations will be followed.

HOW TO GET WHAT YOU NEED

When looking for an expert we need to keep in mind our parental rights and responsibilities. While financial limitations or a scarcity of a particular type of expert in your area may require some compromise, parents have, ideally, the following rights:

1. We are entitled to shop for an expert, and to be clear in our demands on that person. We need to make our own determination on how well we can work with that person, and not make that decision solely on the basis of credentials or lack of them.

2. Parents are entitled to make clear demands. We are entitled to a definition of the problem, to know the alternative solutions to it, and approximately how long each will take.

3. Parents are entitled to get other opinions.

The most effective relationships with experts are those in which Adult-to-Adult information is freely given. If the person you are consulting prefers to take an overly nurturing "I'll take care of everything, don't worry about it" attitude, you may find yourself being treated like an incompetent Child, rather than a grownup with a fully functioning Adult and Parent ego state. Such Parental experts are inclined to discount the parents' own responsibilities in making judgments and decisions about their children's welfare.

CONTRACTUAL OBLIGATIONS

In agreeing to work with an expert you are engaging in a contract in which each of you has rights and obligations. Claude Steiner lists four parts to a contract:

1. *Mutual consent.* Mutual consent means that the expert makes an offer about what can be provided and the parent accepts the offer. In order to make an intelligent offer the therapist must know the nature of the problem and be competent to deal with that particular problem. As parents we need to be as explicit as possible about what we want to have changed. Ideally this offer contains a description of proposed services and a definition of the completed job.

2. *Valid consideration* means that both the parents and the expert are entitled to some benefit from the agreement. The benefit for the parents is amelioration of the problem. The benefit conferred to the expert is usually monetary.

3. *Competency.* Legally certain individuals are not considered competent to enter into contracts. Minors, for instance, need to have the consent and at least partial cooperation of their parents in seeking the help of experts. It is not possible to enter into a contract with persons who are unable to understand the consequences of entering into the contract, or who for some reason do not have a functional Adult ego state. In these instances the contract for care of that person needs to be taken over by someone who is in a position to be responsible.

4. *Lawful object.* Parents seldom seek illegal help for their children. Ethical conflicts occur more frequently. For example, some psychotherapists or physicians may decline on their own moral grounds to consult with someone who is considering an abortion.

When a clearly defined contract is established, both the parents and the expert are in agreement on how to proceed in the speediest possible achievement toward a clearly understood goal, thus ensuring maximum use of the expert's ability and maximum benefit for the family.

SUMMARY

In addition to the usual problems, some families face special crises or chronic problems. Dealing with these problems requires extra resources and, often, help of others outside the family.

The psychological reaction of parents to children with physical disabilities or chronic illness has a crucial effect on the ways the children learn to deal with their disability.

Families split up, merge, are dissolved; parents and children need to solve problems of new allegiances and of old grievances. They need to find ways of establishing an adequate new life.

School and neighborhood stresses may arise, requiring concerted efforts by all the family as well as outsiders to deal with the crisis.

Parents or other loved ones may die. Coping with death is never easy, and parents who are grieving over a loss need extra support to help their children deal with their own grief.

The decision to consult an expert may occur during or after a crisis, or it may arise out of a gnawing feeling that something is not right. Finding the kind of expert needed may require some ingenuity and effort. Parents are entitled to shop for an expert, and to be clear in their demands on that person. We are entitled to know what can be done and approximately how long it will take. Parents are entitled to get other opinions. When consulting with an expert, we do not give up our rights and responsibilities. Helping families and children is a collaborative effort, and needs to be understood that way by everyone involved.

People who keep themselves informed, who feel O.K. about themselves and others, and who are in touch with their feelings are in the best position to be successful parents. Such persons are also likely to be happy and productive in the rest of their lives. It is our commitment to the ideal that we are all entitled to a life of dignity and happiness that has led us to write this book.

READINGS

Arnstein, Helene S. *What to Tell Your Child About Birth, Illness, Death, Divorce, and Other Family Crises.* New York: Bobbs-Merrill Co., Inc., 1962.

Cruickshank, W. M. *Psychology of Exceptional Children and Youth.* Englewood Cliffs, New Jersey: Prentice-Hall, 1963.

Goffman, Irving. *Stigma: Notes on the Management of Spoiled Identity.* Englewood Cliffs, New Jersey: Prentice-Hall, Inc., 1963.

Farberow, N. L. *Taboo Topics.* New York: Atherton Press, 1963.

Glaser, B. G., and Strauss, A. L. *Awareness of Dying.* Chicago: Aldine Publishing Co., 1965.

Hallett, Kathryn. *A Guide for Single Parents.* Millbrae, California: Celestial Arts, 1974.

Kessler, Jane W. *Psychopathology of Childhood.* Englewood Cliffs, New Jersey: Prentice-Hall, 1966.

Kubler-Ross, Elizabeth. *On Dying and Death.* New York: The Macmillan Company, 1969.

Steiner, Claude M., and Cassidy, William. "Therapeutic Contracts in Group Treatment." *Transactional Analysis Bulletin* VIII, 30 (1969).

The International Transactional Analysis Association (ITAA)

The ITAA is an international organization devoted to the advancement of Transactional Analysis (TA) as a science and profession in the public interest.

A world-wide membership is comprised of professionals and nonprofessionals from a variety of specialties. The ITAA is responsible for setting professional standards for training, and for the ethical practice of TA.

It provides an annual directory of membership and affiliated study groups, seminars, and institutes. It publishes the quarterly *Transactional Analysis Journal,* to inform the membership of current studies, issues, and actions of the organization.

ITAA can also refer you to accredited TA professionals in your community.

For further information contact:

The International Transactional Analysis Association (ITAA)
1772 Vallejo Street
San Francisco, California 94123

APPENDICES

APPENDIX I

Glossary

adult a grownup.

Adult ego state an ego state which processes objective facts and estimates probabilities, using the principles of logic.

Adult in the Child (A_1) a primitive data processor within the Child ego state, which gathers and uses information on an intuitive, non-logical, and often non-verbal basis.

attribution a definition of a child by a parent, e.g., "You are stupid."

cathect to direct energy into one ego state. The ego state cathected is the active ego state; the others are observing ego states.

Child the original ego state from which Parent and Adult are elaborated. The Adapted Child follows (or rebels against) Parental directives. The Natural Child is autonomous.

Child in the Child (C_1) the original and most primitive ego state, which is most in touch with bodily functions and needs.

competitive structure a definition of reality which sees nearly all situations as win–lose.

corrective parenting substitutions of earlier Parental programming by cathecting young Child ego states and getting new adaptive messages from a Parental figure (i.e., a therapist).

(to) deal with to negotiate with or otherwise transact with others to a successful resolution of a problem.

Decision a childhood commitment to a certain form of

behavior, which later forms the basis of character; e.g., He made a childhood decision that "nice guys finish last."

discount to deny, disbelieve, or downgrade information which is relevant to the solution of a problem.

Drama Triangle a diagram showing the possible switches of roles in a game or a script. The three major roles are Persecutor, Rescuer, and Victim.

ego state consistent pattern of feeling and experience directly related to a corresponding consistent pattern of behavior.

escalate to increase the amount of emotional energy put into a situation. To escalate a problem—i.e., increase the amount of energy put into maintaining the problem. To escalate over (someone). To put energy into getting someone uncomfortable about their problem behavior.

game a series of ulterior transactions which occurs repeatedly and leads to a bad feeling payoff. Games are unstraight ways of getting strokes and occur when a need is discounted.

griefwork the normal process by which an important loss is resolved. It involves active expression of anger and sadness accompanied by stroking and psychological support from other persons.

injunction a prohibition or negative command from a parent.

internal dialogue transactions between an individual's Parent ego state and his or her Child ego state.

Little Professor see Adult in the Child (A_1).

parent a grownup who has the ongoing responsibility for the rearing of a child.

Parent ego state the ego state which we use to take care of ourselves and others. It is developed through an introjection of actual parental figures.

passive behavior behavior with which someone attempts to get another person to do their thinking for them. The passive behaviors are: do nothing, overadaptation, agitation, and incapacitation and violence.

passive thinking discounting, disregarding important aspects of problem situations. We can discount the problem, the importance of the problem, the solvability of the problem, or our own ability to solve the problem.

permission 1) a Parental license for autonomous behavior; 2) an intervention which gives someone a license to disobey a Parental injunction.

Primitive Parent (P₁) the Parent in the Child ego state, the part of it which scares us into minding, and which adapts to the injunctions and attributions given by parents.

program noun; a plan for living out a certain aspect of one's life. verb; to take in new information in a usable way.

racket seeking unpleasant and familiar bad feelings according to a learned program.

recycling re-experiencing and reworking younger developmental issues during an older developmental stage.

reparenting cutting off early Parental programming and substituting a new and more adaptive program through regression.

resolution 1) a promise made in Adapted Child to follow or discontinue some course of action, e.g., a New Year's resolution to stop drinking 2) the termination of one developmental stage which leads to the onset of the next stage.

script 1) a life plan based on a decision made in childhood, reinforced by the parents, justified by subsequent events, and ending according to plan; 2) any revisions of the early script which form a new life plan.

stimulus hunger a biological need for the organism to receive ongoing stimulation from outside itself.

stroke any unit of recognition. Strokes may be positive or negative, conditional or unconditional.

structure noun; an organized pattern of thinking and behaving and feeling about specific events and problems. verb; to develop structures by learning them from other people, or developing them oneself.

structure hunger the need to organize our time and to fit our experiences into organized patterns.

time structure the distinct methods by which we can organize our time. They are withdrawal, ritual, activity, pastime, games, and intimacy.

transaction a single stroke exchange between two people. A transaction is the basic unit of social relationships.

complementary transaction the ego state addressed is the one which responds.

crossed transaction the ego state responding is different from the one addressed.

ulterior transaction there is a covert transaction conveyed by tone of voice and non-verbal cues which is different from the overt content of the transaction.

Transactional Analysis 1) a system of psychotherapy based on the analysis of transactions which occur during treatment sessions; 2) a theory of personality and human development based on the study of ego states.

APPENDIX II

Ages and Stages

Attachment Stage (Birth to 8-10 mos) The first developmental stage, in which the infant develops an emotional attachment to nurturing grownups, thus insuring survival and developing basic trust.

Exploration Stage (8-10 mos to 2-2½ yrs) The child is actively exploring and is learning the basic physical and psychological laws by which the world runs.

Separation Stage (2-2½ yrs—2½-3½ yrs) "The Terrible Two's," during which the child tests separateness from significant grownups, makes a decision to use Adult ego state (A_2), and agrees to accede to social demands.

Socialization Stage (2½-3½ yrs—5-6 yrs) The preschool and kindergarten ages. The stage during which children learn about social roles, sex roles, and expectations.

Construction Stage (5-6 yrs—11-13 yrs) The developmental stage that occurs roughly during the grade school years. During this stage the child is constructing, but not actively using, a functional Parent ego state (P_2).

Expansion/Consolidation Stage (11-13 yrs—16-18 yrs) Adolescence. The period during which children practice using their Parent ego state to take care of themselves, expand horizons, and try out new Parent information based on wider experience.

Emancipation Stage (16-18 yrs—25-30 yrs) Young adulthood. The years during which a person is independent from the family and experimenting with different life styles without having made a firm commitment to any particular life style.

Creation Stage (25-30 yrs—40-45 yrs) Having committed themselves to a life style, persons in this stage are immersed in childrearing, careers, and community commitments. Productivity and creativity in some form are important needs during this stage.

Evaluation Stage (40-45 yrs—60-70 yrs) The stage which occurs after the children are raised, during which persons are reassessing the script they have been living. They may make decisions to change script and/or try out previously missed experiences.

Resolution Stage (60-70 yrs—death) The final life stage in which the person comes to grips with decreased productivity and the inevitability of death.

INDEX

Games, Scripts
and Archetypes

Note: Page numbers in italics refer to figures.

A

Adapted Child, 87, 93, 96, 123, 124, 126, 192, 221
    See also Child
Adult, 30, *30*, 37, 42, 51, 63, 65, 69-70, 72, 77, 97, 101, 102, 108, 112, 117, 118, 119, 123, 124, 128, 131, 135, 154, 157, 163, 173, 174, 175, 176-77, 179, 184, 187, 198, 200, 203, 204, 205, 209, 210, 221, 250, 251, 256, 257, 258, 277, 278, 284
    behavior of, 37
    history of, 38
    primitive, 72, 87, 88, 98
    on sex, 173
    social response of, 37
    vocabulary of, 37
    voice of, 37
    See also Little Professor
Ain't It Awful, 263
Ain't It Wonderful, 263
Ain't School Awful, 24
American Dream, 144, 162
April Fool!, 138

B

Baby, 127
Baby-Tender, 95
bedtime rituals, 23-24
Boys Are Better Than Girls, 24
Bugs Are Interesting, 24

C

Child, 29-30, *30*, 31-32, *32*, 39, *40*, 42, 51, 57, 69-70, 77, 82, 87, 93, 94, 97, 105-106, 131-132, 137, 138, 156, 171, 177, 184, 187, 188, 199, 200, 202, 205, 207, 209, 213, 221, 250, 251, 258, 278, 283, 284
    behavior of, 35
    function of emotions in, 35-36
    history of, 34-35
    needs of, 63, 65
    primitive, 77
    on sex, 173

Child (*continued*)
  social response of, 34
  vocabulary of, 34, 261
  voice of, 34
  See also Adapted Child;
    Natural Child
chopping, 21-22
Cinderella, 189-90
Cold Pricklies, 17-18, 27
  See also Strokes (subject
    index)
Competent, 256
  See also Incompetent
Critical Parent, 34, 93, 123,
    126, 154, 168, 209
  See also Parent; Pig Parent

D

Don't!, 104-105
Don't Ask, 128
Don't Be, 33, 128
Don't Be a Child, 33, 128
Don't Be Close, 128
Don't Grow Up, 33, 58, 111,
    127
Don't Leave, 127
Don't Pay Attention to Your
    Needs, 176
Don't Think, 111
Drama Triangle, 43-44, *46*,
    107, 250, 253, 255, 258,
    269, 277

E

Electrode, 33
Empty Nest, 208

F

Family Rock, 111
Finicky Eater, 126
Followers, 148-49

G

Grandma's Rule, 264, 270

H

High and Proud, 228
Homemaker, 95, 122, 225,
    230

I

I'm a More Conscientious
    Parent Than You, 255
I'm Not O.K.—You're Not
    O.K., 44, 45, 51, 116,
    238, 252, *252*
I'm Not O.K.—You're O.K.,
    44, 45, 51, 116, 164, 167,
    235, 237-38, 252, *253*,
    274
I'm O.K.—You're Not O.K.,
    44-45, 51, 107, 140, 143,
    149-50, 155, 169, *252*,
    253, 259, 277
I'm O.K.—You're O.K., 44,
    45, 51, 108, 115, 132,
    143, 144, 146-47, 152,
    155, 162, 167, 222, 240,
    252, *252*
I'm Only Trying To Help
    You, 253
Incompetent, 255
Indispensable, 255
It Makes a Difference, 254-55

K

Kick Me, 14, 253, 277

L

Leaders, 148-49
Let Me Show You, 253-54

Little Lawyer, 143-44, 158
Little Professor, 31, 32-33, 86, 93, 98, 104, 123, 124, 144, 166, 179
Losers, 135, 227

M

Mama, 95-96, 111, 112, 178, 224, 225
Marriage and Family, 205-6
menopause scripts, 223
Miracle Worker, 111
Mommy, Don't Leave Me, 255
Mother Hubbard, 224
    See also Mama
My Baby Is More Demanding Than Your Baby, 255
My Daddy Is Better Than Your Daddy, 24

N

Natural Child, 32, 111, 112, 118, 124, 127, 150, 154, 175, 182, 192, 194, 207, 212, 221
    See also Child
Now I've Got You—You SOB, 253, 256, 277
Nurturing Parent, 34, 80, 97, 123, 130, 142, 163, 176, 199, 208, 209
    See also Parent

O

old age scripts, 238-40
Only Competent Person, 254

P

Parent, 29-30, *31*, 38-41, *42*, 51, 56-57, 63, 64, 65, 70, 72, 77, 118, 119, 123, 126, 136, 141-42, 143, 148, 152, 153-54, 156, 162, 175, 176-77, 184, 187-88, 191, 192, 203, 205, 221, 250, 258, 273, 278, 284
    behavior of, 40
    history of, 41
    on sex, 173
    social response of, 41
    vocabulary of, 40
    voice of, 40
        See also Critical Parent; Nurturing Parent; Pig Parent; Supernatural Child
Payoff, 205, 254
Persecutor, 44, *46*, 107, 250, 253, 254, 255-56, 257-58, 277
Pig Parent, 33
    See also Parent; Primitive Parent
Plastic Fuzzies, 18
    See also Strokes (subject index)
Poor Me, 163
Primitive Parent, 32, 33, 57, 75, 94, 131-32
    See also Parent; Pig Parent
Prince Valiant, 189
Proper Eating, 119

R

Rapo, 173
Rebellious Child, 126, 143, 193
Rescue(r), 44, *46*, 107, 169, 250, 253-54, 255-56, 257-58, 276, 277

S

Sarah Heartburn, *164*
School Phobia, 255-56

See What You Made Me Do,
    119
Sissy, 149, 176
Supernatural Child, 33
    See also Parent
Super Parent, 279

T

Teenage Family, 208
Think Structure, 260-61, 268,
    269, 270
Tomboy, 149

U

Uproar, 157, 181-82

V

Victim, 44, *46*, 107, 163, 169,
176, 250, 253-54, 255-
56, 258, 277

W

Warm Fuzzies, 15-19, 27, 127
    See also Strokes (subject
    index)
Why Don't You—Yes, But,
    253
Why Should I?, 158
Winners, 135, 177, 226-27
Workaholic, 191, 262

Y

Young Family, 208
Young Physicist, 90-92, 112,
    118, 131, 138-39

Subject Index

Note: Page numbers in italics refer to figures.

A

adolescence. See Emancipation; Expansion/Consolidation

Attachment stage, 68-75
  exercises relating to, 83-84
  needs of new parents in, 80-81
  neglect in, 73-75
  overprotection in, 73-75
  parenting in, 72-75, 77-80, 82
  strokes in, 72, 75-76, 81
  symbiosis in, 68-72

B

banal scripts, 123-26
bedwetting, 264-65
birth control and family planning, 56-58, 203, 206, 221
birth defects, 163, 165, 209, 272-74
birth order, 126-28

C

child. *See* Attachment; Construction; Emancipation; Expansion/Consolidation; Exploration stages

childrearing:
  cultural values in, 3-4, 6
  exercises relating to, 66
  history of, 2-3
  Italian attitude toward, 209
  Jewish attitude toward, 21-22
  O.K. Parent, 2-10
  programs for, 54-67
  Russian attitude toward, 76
colic, 254
communes, 191-92, 194, 195
conception, attitudes toward, 59-60
Construction stage, 135-60
  ambivalence during, 141-42
  concrete thinking in, 139-40
  contract making in, 146-48
  critical thinking in, 136-37
  exercises relating to, 159
  friendships during, 148-49, 152-53
  group experiences in, 141-42, 147, 148-49
  interpersonal problems in, 140-41
  parenting during, 141-42, 150-59
  peer relationships in, 136
  perceptual skill development in, 140, 146

Construction stage (*cont.*)
  psychological tasks of, 135-36, 148, 157
  racial differentiation in, 136
  rule testing in, 143-45, 157-58
  sex differentiation during, 149
  strokes during, 142
contracts, 146-47, 285
Creation stage, 198-218
  communication in, 203-5
  exercises relating to, 217-18
  family planning in, 203, 205-6
  psychological tasks of, 216-17
  strokes in, 198-201, 202
  See also Marriage; Pregnancy

D

deafness, 274
death, 243, 244, 280-82, 286
divorce and remarriage, 278-80
dogs, 268

E

ego states, 29-30, 34, 36-37, 42, 51, 69-70, 86, 93, 94, 101, 102
  behavior in, 34, 37, 40
  history of, 34-35, 38, 41
  inventory of, 258-59
  social response in, 34, 37, 41
  vocabulary of, 34, 37, 40
  voice of, 34, 37, 40
  See also Adult; Child; Parent
Emancipation stage, 187-97
  careers during, 190-91, 215-16

emotional maturity in, 194
exercises relating to, 195-96
experimental life styles in, 191-92, 193, 194, 195, 202
fighting effectively in, 192-93
as new phase, 187-88, 195
resolution of, 188, 194
scripts for, 188-89
Evaluation stage, 219-33
  careers during, 226-27, 230
  exercises relating to, 231-32
  parenting during, 219-22, 224-25
  physical changes in, 219-20, 222-23, 229-30
  recycling behavior during, 219, 230
  script evaluation in, 227-29, 230
  sexual identity during, 220
exercises:
  in basic position, 52
  on childrearing, 66
  for Construction stage, 159
  for Creation stage, 217-18
  on ego states, 51-52
  on emotions, 52
  for Expansion/Consolidation stage, 184-85
  for Exploration stage, 99-100
  for Evaluation stage, 231-32
  on family patterns, 9-10, 84
  on family stroking, 26-28
  on infant-parent relationship, 83-84
  for life scripts, 52-53
  on maturity and mate selection, 195-96
  on passive thinking and passive behavior, 53
  for Resolution stage, 244-45

exercises (*continued*)
  for Separation stage, 113
  for Socialization stage, 132-33
  for transactions, 52
  for troubleshooting, 270
Expansion/Consolidation stage, 161-86
  attachment during, 165-67
  construction during, 174-75, 184
  exercises relating to, 184-85
  exploration during, 167-68, 184
  parenting during, 162-63, 167, 172-73, 178-82
  peer groups in, 162-63, 166, 170-71
  physical changes in, 154, 162-63, 168, 170-73, 184, 219, 220
  problem behavior during, 278
  psychological tasks of, 162, 168
  recycling behavior in, 165-75, 183-84
  script revision and modification in, 161-63, 176-77
  separation during, 168-70, 183
  sexual identity during, 170-74, 181-82, 184, 220-21, 279
  socialization during, 170-74, 183-84
  strokes during, 165, 173, 177, 178, 182, 183
  trust during, 166-67
experts, 282-85
Exploration stage, 23, 86-100
  change in stroke economy in, 92-95
  exercises relating to, 99-100
  parental energy crisis during, 95-98
  safety during, 91-92

  stimulation in, 98
  stimulus hunger in, 86-90
  strokes in, 84, 91, 94, 97-98

F

fears, 267-68
"flashbacks", 77

G

games, 253-58
  See also individual listings
Gray Panthers, 232, 239, 244
grief, 274, 281-82

I

illness, 274-75, 286
imaginary friends, 128

L

La Leche League, 80
learning:
  emotional, 267-68
  modeling, 268-69
  operant, 263-66
  and punishment, 265-66
  shaping, 263-64

M

magical thinking, 128-30, 131-32, 136-37, 146, 281
marijuana, 175
marriage:
  alternatives to, 191-92, 193-94, 195
  egalitarian, 202, *202*
  scripts, 54-55, 201-3, 213-16

marriage (*continued*)
strokes during, 201-2
teenage, 188-89
See also Creation stage;
Pregnancy; Sex roles
and stereotypes

N

names, significance of, 61-62
nightmares, 130-31
nursery school, 117

P

parenting:
during Attachment stage,
72-75, 77-80, 82
during Construction stage,
141-42, 150-59
during Evaluation stage,
219-22, 224-25
during Expansion/Consoli-
dation stage, 162-63, 167,
172-73, 178-82
learning from children, 212
needs of new parents, 80-
81
problems of, 209-10
as psychological phase, 208-
9
during Separation stage,
104-8, 109-11, 112
during Socialization stage,
131-32
and societal demands, 248-
50
Parents Anonymous, 79-80
passive behavior, 49-51
passive thinking, 48-49
peer groups:
during Construction stage,
136, 141-42, 147, 148-49,
152-53
during Expansion/Consoli-
dation stage, 162-63, 166,
170-71

during Socialization stage,
117, 128-29
pregnancy, 60-61
expectations and feelings in,
206-8
recycling behavior during,
207
problem solving:
analysis, 251-53, 256, 258,
260-61
changing behavior, 261-62
exercises relating to, 270
and stroke economy, 251-
53
See also specific problems

R

recyling behavior:
in Evaluation stage, 219,
230
in Expansion/Consolida-
tion stage, 165-75, 183-
84
in new parents, 77
in pregnancy, 207
in Resolution stage, 236
religion, 176, 242
Resolution stage, 234-45
death preparation in, 243,
244
exercises relating to, 244-
45
life scripts during, 236-38,
244
myths of, 238-40
physical changes in, 241-
42, 244
psychological tasks of,
234-40, 241-44
recycling behavior in, 236
retirement, 234-35, 243
sexual behavior during,
240
stroke deprivation in, 240-
43, 244

S

school problems, 276-77, 286
script(s):
  banal, 123-26
  during Emancipation stage,
    188-89
  evaluation of, 227-29, 230
  exercises relating to, 51-53
  during Expansion/Consoli-
    dation stage, 161-63,
    176-77
  foundations, 59-61
  marriage, 54-55, 201-3,
    213-16
  during Resolution stage,
    236-38, 244
  during Socialization stage,
    116, 129
Separation stage, 101-14
  anger during, 107-8
  exercises relating to, 113
  learning development in,
    108-9
  motor development in,
    101-2
  parenting during, 104-8,
    109-11, 112
  psychological tasks of,
    101, 104
  positive commands during,
    104-5
  resolution of symbiosis in,
    105, 107-8, 111
sex roles and stereotyping,
  121-26, 130, 132, 139,
  149, 176-77, 179, 190,
  193, 199, 201-2, 206-8,
  209, 211, 215-16, 225,
  262
sexuality:
  during Expansion/Consoli-
    dation stage, 170-74
  during Socialization stage,
    121-23, 127, 130, 132
shoplifting, 168-69
sibling rivalry, 276-77

Socialization stage, 115-34
  exercises relating to, 132-
    33
  family position during,
    126-28
  jealousy during, 116
  language use in, 116-18
  magical thinking in, 128-
    30, 131-32
  motor developmeent, 119
  parenting in, 131-32
  peer groups in, 117, 128-
    29
  psychological tasks of, 115-
    16
  rituals in, 119
  scripts, 116-17, 129
  sexuality during, 121-23,
    127, 130, 132
  strokes during, 127
stroke deprivation and hunger, 213, 215-16, 225,
  240-43, 244
stroke economy, 15-19, 26,
  92-95, 251-52
strokes:
  during Attachment stage,
    72, 75-76, 81
  conditional, 12, 15, 26, 91
  and conditioning, 262,
    263, 264, 265-66
  during Construction stage,
    142
  during Creation stage, 198-
    201, 202
  discounting of, 21-22
  double-level, 21-22
  during Expansion/Consoli-
    dation stage, 165, 173,
    177, 178, 182, 183
  exchanging, 21-25, 41
  exercise relating to, 26-28
  during Exploration stage,
    84, 91, 94, 97-98
  during marriage, 201-2
  negative, 12, 13-15, 26,
    124
  positive, 12, 26

during Resolution stage, 240-43, 244
during Socialization, 127
unconditional, 12, 15, 26, 81
symbiosis, 69-72, 105, 107-8, 111-12

time structure, 23-26
tobacco, 175
toilet training, 102-4, 258, 264-65
transactions, 41-43, 51
  complementary, 42
  crossed, 42
  ulterior, 42

T

teachers, 135
teasing, 138, 200, 266, 277

Z

Zero Population Growth, 206

Authors and Therapists

E

Becker, Wesley, 15; *Parents Are Teachers*, 264, 266
Benedek, Therese, 69
Berne, Eric, 4, 11-12, 23, 25, 54-55; *Games People Play*, 30
Binet, Alfred, 3

C

Campos, Leonard, *Introduce Yourself to TA*, 8
Close, Henry T., "On Parenting," 248-50
Colton, Helen, 21-22

E

Erikson, Erik, 3
Ernst, Frank, *Who's Listening?*, 34

F

Freud, Sigmund, 124

G

Gesell, Arnold, *Child From Five to Ten, The*, 3

Gullíon, M. Elizabeth, *Living With Children*, 266

H

Hallett, Kathryn, *Guide for Single Parents: Transactional Analysis of People in Crisis, A*, 280

J

James, Muriel, *Born to Win*, 8, 260
Johnson, William, 172
Jongeward, Dorothy, *Born to Win*, 8, 260

K

Kinsey, Alfred C., 172

L

Levin, Pamela, 73n, 260, 277

M

McCormick, Paul, *Introduce Yourself to TA*, 8
Maslow, Abraham, 11

Masters, Virginia, 172
Mead, Margaret, 3

P

Patterson, Gerald R., *Families*, 266; *Living With Children*, 266
Piaget, Jean, 3

S

Samuels, Solon, 21
Schiff, Aaron, 25, 48
Schiff, Jacqui Lee, 48, 56, 68
Spitz, René, 11-12
Spock, Benjamin, *Baby and Child Care*, 3, 79

Steiner, Claude, 15-19, 285

V

Vance, Jennie Lou, 261

W

Weiss, Jon, 74n
Weiss, Laurie, 74n
Wilder, Laura Ingalls, *Little House on the Prairie*, 38-39
Wyckoff, Hogie, 224

Z

Zechnich, Robert, 253-55